Digital Forensics Basics

A Practical Guide Using Windows OS

Nihad A. Hassan

Apress®

Digital Forensics Basics: A Practical Guide Using Windows OS

Nihad A. Hassan
New York, New York, USA

ISBN-13 (pbk): 978-1-4842-3837-0   ISBN-13 (electronic): 978-1-4842-3838-7
https://doi.org/10.1007/978-1-4842-3838-7

Library of Congress Control Number: 2019933884

Managing Director, Apress Media LLC: Welmoed Spahr
Acquisitions Editor: Susan McDermott
Development Editor: Laura Berendson
Coordinating Editor: Rita Fernando

Cover designed by eStudioCalamar

Cover image designed by Freepik (www.freepik.com)

Distributed to the book trade worldwide by Springer Science+Business Media New York, 233 Spring Street, 6th Floor, New York, NY 10013. Phone 1-800-SPRINGER, fax (201) 348-4505, e-mail orders-ny@springer-sbm.com, or visit www.springeronline.com. Apress Media, LLC is a California LLC and the sole member (owner) is Springer Science + Business Media Finance Inc (SSBM Finance Inc). SSBM Finance Inc is a **Delaware** corporation.

For information on translations, please e-mail rights@apress.com, or visit http://www.apress.com/rights-permissions.

Apress titles may be purchased in bulk for academic, corporate, or promotional use. eBook versions and licenses are also available for most titles. For more information, reference our Print and eBook Bulk Sales web page at http://www.apress.com/bulk-sales.

Any source code or other supplementary material referenced by the author in this book is available to readers onGitHub via the book's product page, located at www.apress.com/9781484238370. For more detailed information, please visit http://www.apress.com/source-code.

Printed on acid-free paper

To my mom, Samiha. Thank you for everything.
Without you, I'm nothing.

—Nihad A. Hassan

Table of Contents

About the Author

 **Nihad A. Hassan** is an independent information security consultant, digital forensics and cybersecurity expert, online blogger, and book author. He has been actively conducting research on different areas of information security for more than a decade and has developed numerous cybersecurity education courses and technical guides. He has completed several technical security consulting engagements involving security architectures, penetration testing, computer crime investigation, and cyber open source intelligence (OSINT). Nihad has authored five books and scores of information security articles for various global publications. He also enjoys being involved in security training, education, and motivation. His current work focuses on digital forensics, antiforensics techniques, digital privacy, and cyber-OSINT. He covers different information security topics and related matters on his security blog at `www.DarknessGate.com` and recently launched a dedicated site for open source intelligence resources at `www.OSINT.link`. Nihad has a bachelor's of science honors degree in computer science from the University of Greenwich in the United Kingdom. Nihad can be followed on Twitter (@DarknessGate), and you can connect to him via LinkedIn at `https://www.linkedin.com/in/darknessgate`.

About the Technical Reviewer

Rami Hijazi has a master's degree in information technology (information security) from the University of Liverpool. He currently works at MERICLER Inc., an education and corporate training firm in Toronto, Canada. Rami is an experienced IT professional who lectures on a wide array of topics, including object-oriented programming, Java, e-commerce, agile development, database design, and data handling analysis. Rami also works as an information security consultant, where he is involved in designing encryption systems and wireless networks, detecting intrusions and tracking data breaches, and giving planning and development advice for IT departments concerning contingency planning.

Acknowledgments

I start by thanking God for giving me the gift to write and convert my ideas into something useful. Without God's blessing, I would not be able to achieve anything.

I want to thank the ladies at Apress: Susan, Rita, and Laura. I was pleased to work with you again and very much appreciate your valuable feedback and encouragement.

Specifically, to book acquisitions editor Susan McDermott, thank you for believing in my book's idea and for your honest encouragement before and during the writing process. To book project editor Rita Fernando, you were very supportive during the writing process. You made authoring this book a joyful journey. To book development editor Laura Berendson, thank you very much for your diligent and professional work in producing this book.

I also want to thank all the Apress staff who worked behind the scenes to make this book possible and ready for launch. I hope you will continue your excellent work in creating highly valued computing books. Your work is greatly appreciated.

Naturally, I'm saving the best for last. In Chapter 9, I use a photo for a child to describe a digital steganographic technique in images. This photo is of my brother's son Omran. I want to thank this beautiful child for adding a pleasant touch to the technical script!

Introduction

If you are a newcomer to the digital forensic field and you do not know where to start, this is your book! *Digital Forensics Basics* is your introductory guide to understanding and implementing digital forensics to investigate computer crime using Windows, the most widely used operating system. This book will provide readers with the necessary skills to identify an intruder's footprints and to gather the necessary digital evidence in a forensically sound manner to prosecute in a court of law.

Geared toward users with no experience in the field, this book will teach the readers the basic elements, concepts, tools, techniques, and common activities of digital forensics, so they will become well prepared to participate in investigations and understand the process of finding, collecting, and analyzing digital evidence.

Digital Forensics Basics is written as a series of tutorials, with each task demonstrating how to use a specific computer forensics tool or technique. Information presented in this book is suitable for users with varying IT skills, so both professional computer users and beginners will gain the necessary knowledge to uncover and use digital evidence effectively in any kind of investigation. In addition to its up-to-date contents, a dedicated section is reserved for Open Source Intelligence (OSINT) gathering, a topic missed in most digital forensics books.

As the number of people who are entering the digital age continually increases, experienced computer forensics investigators will remain in high demand in the future to investigate cybercrimes. This book is all you need to start your journey in this field with confidence.

Target Audience

1. Police and other law enforcement personnel

2. Defense and military personnel

3. E-business security professionals

4. Systems administrators

5. Computer security professionals

6. Judges and lawyers (with no technical background)

7. Banking, insurance, and other professionals

8. IT students

Summary of Contents

Here is a brief description of each chapter's contents:

- Chapter 1, "Introduction: Understanding Digital Forensics": In this chapter, we introduce the term "digital forensics" and differentiate between it and other kinds of cybersecurity domains. We briefly cover the concept of digital evidence, its various types, and where we can find it in electronic devices. There is no formal process for applying digital forensics investigations across the globe; however, we introduce the general phases of any digital investigation process and what tasks are required as a part of each phase.

- Chapter 2, "Essential Technical Concepts": In this chapter, we cover important technical concepts about computers that must be well understood by any digital forensic examiner. We describe how computers store and represent data digitally, the concept of operating system file structure and its types, and hash algorithms and how we can use them to verify the authenticity of any piece of digital data. We also discuss types of computer storage and the file system types supported by Windows OS.

- Chapter 3, "Computer Forensics Lab Requirements": In this chapter, we cover the essential tools needed to assemble a digital forensic lab. We talk about the characteristics of the physical facility that are going to house the lab, needed electrical equipment, and lab furniture and hardware devices related to digital investigation work; we also cover the minimum technical requirements for the forensic workstation(s) we are going to use for analyzing digital evidence. We discuss the design and security requirements of the lab network, then we move to talk about forensic software and the importance of validating computer forensic tools by a credible body before using it officially in the investigation.

- Chapter 4, "Initial Response and First Responder Tasks": In this chapter, we talk about the mission and services provided by the first responder for any investigation that involves digital evidence. We cover the first responder's toolkit, the first responder's tasks upon arriving at the crime scene, and the practical aspects of identification, seizure, and transport of gathered evidence stored on electronic media to the forensic lab for detailed examination.

- Chapter 5, "Acquiring Digital Evidence": In this chapter, we cover the main task conducted during any digital forensics investigation, which is capturing computer memory images. We discuss how to capture volatile memory (live acquisition), such as RAM memory and other volatile data like network information, and nonvolatile memory (static acquisition), such as HDD, tape, SSD, flash thumb, and any similar digital storage medium. We also list possible challenges that a digital forensic examiner may face during the acquisition process.

- Chapter 6, "Analyzing Digital Evidence": In this chapter, we demonstrate how to analyze acquired forensics images from both volatile and nonvolatile memory. The focus was on using free and open source software to do the analysis job.

- Chapter 7, "Windows Forensics Analysis": In this chapter, we cover the main areas where forensics artifacts can be found in Windows operating systems. A dedicated section for Windows 10–specific forensic features is also included.

- Chapter 8, "Web Browser and E-mail Forensics": In this chapter, we thoroughly cover how to investigate the most used web browsers—Google Chrome, Firefox, and IE/Edge—for forensic artifacts. The work described in this chapter depends on manual analysis, but some simple, free tools that can aid investigators in automating their forensics work are also mentioned.

- Chapter 9, "Antiforensics Techniques": In this chapter, we describe the nature of digital antiforensics techniques and explain how these techniques may be used to mislead the forensic investigation process, thereby making it very difficult to carry out a digital investigation or even gather enough evidence to debate during a trial.

- Chapter 10, "Gathering Intelligence from OSINT Sources": Open source intelligence (OSINT) refers to all information that is publicly available. In this chapter, we define the various types of OSINT, describe its main users and the legal implications of its use, and learn how it can be used in different scenarios by different parties to acquire valuable intelligence from publicly available resources.

- Chapter 11, "Digital Forensics Report": In this chapter, we cover the main elements of the final digital forensics investigative report, where an investigator presents his/her findings from the digital forensics examination to the entity impacted by the cyberattack or to a court of law, if it is a public investigation.

Comments and Questions

To comment on or ask technical questions about this book, send an e-mail to the book author at nihad@protonmail.com. For additional references about the subject, computer security tools, tutorials, and other related matters, check out the author's blog at www.DarknessGate.com and the author's dedicated portal for OSINT resources at www.OSINT.link.

CHAPTER 1

Introduction: Understanding Digital Forensics

As the world goes digital, the use of computerized systems to provide services and store information becomes prevalent in both the public and private sectors. Individuals also use computing devices heavily in their daily lives; it is rare to see a person who is not dependent on some form of computing device to organize his or her digital data or to communicate with others.

The threat of cybersecurity is unquestionably growing more serious over time. A recent estimate shows that by 2021, cybercrime damages will cost the world $6 trillion annually,[1] while the spending on information security products and services will grow to $93 billion in 2018, according to the latest forecast from Gartner, Inc.[2] Cybersecurity Ventures expects the damage caused by ransomware attacks will increase to $11.5 billion in 2019[3]; at that time, a ransomware attack will target businesses every 14 seconds. This dollar amount does not include the costs of attacks against individuals, which are expected to exceed even this number!

---

[1]CSO, "Top 5 Cybersecurity Facts, Figures and Statistics for 2018," June 1, 2018. www.csoonline.com/article/3153707/security/top-5-cybersecurity-facts-figures-and-statistics.html

[2]Gartner, "Gartner Says Worldwide Information Security Spending Will Grow 7 Percent to Reach $86.4 Billion in 2017," June 1, 2018. www.gartner.com/newsroom/id/3784965

[3]Cyber Security Ventures, "Global Ransomware Damage Costs Predicted To Hit $11.5 Billion By 2019," June 1, 2018. https://cybersecurityventures.com/ransomware-damage-report-2017-part-2/

© Nihad A. Hassan 2019
N. A. Hassan, *Digital Forensics Basics*, https://doi.org/10.1007/978-1-4842-3838-7_1

The increase in cybercrimes, terrorist threats, and security concerns in addition to the increased awareness of the importance of data on the part of authorities and business corporations has encouraged them to act and develop different digital forensics tools and methodologies to counter such threats. Nowadays, anything related to the examination, interpretation, or reconstruction of digital artifacts in a computing environment is considered within the discipline of digital forensics.

Digital forensics can be used in different contexts like government, the private sector, financial institutions, and legal; many organizations already use it as a part of their disaster recovery planning. In this introductory chapter, we will define the term "digital forensics"; describe its objectives, usage, main users, and professional certifications; look at the governmental and institutional organizations that promote its methodologies and best practices; learn about its different types; and describe its core element, which is the digital evidence.

Note!   During this book we will use the term "computing device" to refer to a digital device in the form of a smartphone, laptop, personal digital assistant (PDA), tablet, thumb drive, or any other electronic device that can store digital information.

What Is Digital Forensics?

Digital forensics is a branch of forensic science that uses scientific knowledge for collecting, analyzing, documenting, and presenting digital evidence related to computer crime for using it in a court of law. The ultimate goal is knowing what was done, when it was done, and who did it.

The term "digital forensics" is widely used as a synonym for computer forensics (also known as cyberforensics) but has expanded to cover investigating all devices that are capable of storing digital data, like networking devices, mobile phones, tablets, digital cameras, Internet of Things (IoT) devices, digital home appliances, and other digital storage media like CD/DVD, USB drives, SD cards, external drives, and backup tapes.

Under this wider definition, digital forensics is also responsible for investigating nearly all cyberattacks against computerized systems like ransomware, phishing, SQL injunction attacks, distributed denial-of-service (DDoS) attacks, data breach, cyberespionage, compromised accounts, unauthorized access to network infrastructure, and other related cyberattacks that can cause commercial or reputation loss.

Conducting computer forensic investigation requires implementing rigorous standards to stand up to cross-examination in court. This includes acquiring data (both static and volatile) in a forensically sound manner, analyzing data using court-accepted forensics tools, searching in the collected data to find evidence, and finally presenting findings to court in an official report. If these procedures are incorrectly implemented, we risk damaging or destroying digital evidence, making it inadmissible in a court of law.

Digital forensics is considered a relatively new branch in the cybersecurity domain that is becoming increasingly important with the proliferation of crimes and illegal activities in cyberspace. Compared with traditional forensic science (DNA profiling, blood tests, and fingerprinting), digital forensics is not a mature science; the fact that this science deals with fast-paced changes in the computing environment, in addition to its span over many disciplines (like the legal system, law enforcement, business management, information technology, and the borderless nature of the Internet) makes it a very challenging field that requires continual development of its methodologies, tools, and laws to counter the ever newly emerging variations of cybercrime.

Note!   "Forensically sound" is a term used in the digital forensics community to describe the process of acquiring digital evidence while preserving its integrity to be admissible in a court of law.

Digital Forensics Goals

From a technical standpoint, the main goal of digital forensics is investigating crimes committed using computing devices like computers, tablets, cell phones, or any other device that can store/process digital data and extracting digital evidence from it in a forensically sound manner to be presented in a court of law. Digital forensics achieves this in the following ways:

1. Finding legal evidence in computing devices and preserving its integrity in a way that is deemed admissible in a court of law.

2. Preserving and recovering evidence following court-accepted technical procedures.

3. Attributing an action to its initiator.

4. Identifying data leaks within an organization.

5. Accessing possible damage occurring during a data breach.

6. Presenting the results in a formal report suitable to be presented in court.

7. Providing a guide for expert testimony in court.

Cybercrime

In a nutshell, cybercrime includes any illegal activity committed using a type of computing device or computer networks such as the Internet. The US Department of Justice (DOJ) defines cybercrime as "any criminal offense committed against or with the use of a computer or computer network." The major motivation behind cybercrime is financial gain (example: spreading malware to steal access codes to bank accounts). However, a good portion of cybercrime has different motivations, like interrupting service (for example, DDoS attacks to stop services offered by the target organization), stealing confidential data (example: consumer data, medical information), exchanging copyrighted materials in an unlawful way, and cyberespionage (corporate trade and military secrets).

Cybercrime Attack Mode

Cybercrime can be originated from two main sources: insider attacks and external attacks.

- Insider attacks: This is the most dangerous cyberrisk facing organizations today, as it can last for a long time without them knowing about it; such attacks come when there is a breach of trust from employees—or other people like former employees, third-party contractors, or business associates—working within the target organization who have legitimate access to its computing systems and/or information about its cybersecurity practices and defenses. Economic espionage falls under this category.

- External attacks: This kind of attack originates from outside the target organization, usually coming from skilled hackers. Such attacks constitute the largest attacks against organizations around the world. A black hat hacker can try to penetrate the target organization's computing networks from another country to gain unauthorized access. Sometimes external attackers gain intelligence from an insider (disgruntled employee) in the target company who has information about its security systems to facilitate their illegal access.

How Are Computers Used in Cybercrimes?

Cybercrime can be divided into three main categories with regard to how the computing device was used to commit a crime.

1. A computing device is used as a weapon to commit a crime. Example: Launching denial-of-service (DoS) attacks or sending ransomware.

2. A computing device is the target of a crime. Example: Gaining unauthorized access to a target computer.

3. A computing device is used as a facilitator of a crime. Example: Using a computer to store incriminating data or to make online communications with other criminals.

Example of Cybercrime

Different types of computer threats are associated with varied types of damaging effects. For example, some threats may damage or corrupt your installed operating system and force you to reinstall it. Another type may steal your credentials and saved passwords. Still other threats may not bring any harm to your PC; instead, they will track your online activities and invade your privacy.

Today, criminals are smarter than ever before, and malicious programs are more sophisticated. Modern malware can infect a target computing device and remain undetected for a long time. The motive behind the majority of cyberattacks nowadays is not to damage your machine, but instead to steal your money, to access your private information, or to acquire your logon credentials.

Similar to traditional crime, cybercrime can be grouped into various categories according to the malicious actor's objective for applying it. The following are the most common forms of cybercrime.

Malware Distribution

Malware is short for "malicious software" and is any software employed to bring damage to computing devices (computers, smartphones, etc.) or the stored content (data or applications). Malware corruption can manifest in different ways, such as formatting your hard disk, deleting or corrupting files, stealing saved login information, gathering

5

sensitive information (your files and private photos), or simply displaying unwanted advertisements on your screen. Many malware variants are stealthy and operate silently without the user's knowledge or awareness. Malware is a term used to refer to many types of malicious software such as computer viruses, worms, Trojan horses, spyware, ransomware, rootkit, scareware, and adware.

Ransomware Distribution

Ransomware is computer malware that installs silently on the user's machine. Its objective is to deny access to user files, sometimes encrypting the entire hard drive (HD) and even all the attached external drives and connected cloud storage accounts. It then demands that the user pay a ransom to get the malware creator to remove the restriction so the user can regain access to the system and stored assets.

CryptoJacking

This is a piece of code, usually written in JavaScript, that infects your computer silently via web browser to mine cryptocurrencies. As the cryptocurrency wave is on the rise, more cybercriminals are using such techniques for commercial gain using other peoples' computers without their knowledge. This attack consumes much of the target computer's CPU speed.

Hacking

Hacking is the process of invading your privacy by gaining unauthorized access to your computing device or internal network. Hackers usually scan your machines for vulnerabilities (such as unpatched Windows updates) and gain access through them. After gaining access, they may install a keylogger or a Trojan horse to maintain their access, to begin stealing information, or to spy on user activities.

SQL Injections

This is a hacking technique that allows hackers to attack the security vulnerabilities of the database that runs a web site. An attacker enters SQL code into target web site web forms and executes it to force the back-end database of the web site to release confidential information to the attacker.

Note!   Modifying computer program code to steal money in small amounts is also a crime committed by evil programmers or anyone who has access to the financial software source code.

Pharming

This is a cyberattack intended to redirect users from a legitimate web site to a fraudulent site without their knowledge. The end goal is usually to infect the target computer with a malware.

Phishing

Phishing messages come in different shapes, such as SMS messages, e-mails, and web site links (URLs), all of which are designed to look genuine and use the same format as the legitimate company they pretend to be. Phishing aims to collect user-sensitive details (such as banking information, login credentials, and credit card info) by tricking the end user into handing the information to the attacker.

Note!   The United States Computer Emergency Readiness Team (US-CERT) defines phishing as follows: "…an attempt by an individual or group to solicit personal information from unsuspecting users by employing social engineering techniques. Phishing e-mails are crafted to appear as if they have been sent from a legitimate organization or known individual. These e-mails often attempt to entice users to click a link that will take the user to a fraudulent web site that appears legitimate. The user then may be asked to provide personal information, such as account usernames and passwords, that can further expose them to future compromises. Additionally, these fraudulent web sites may contain malicious code."[4]

---

[4]US-CERT, "Report Phishing Sites," June 1, 2018. www.us-cert.gov/report-phishing

E-mail Bombing and Spamming

E-mail bombing occurs when an intruder, or a group of intruders, sends a large volume of e-mails to a target server or target e-mail account, making it crash. Spam is unsolicited e-mail that usually sent to a large number of users for commercial purposes (showing ads or promotions); however, many spam e-mails contain disguised links that can lead the victim to phishing web sites or to malicious web sites hosting malware to further infect the user's machine.

Identity Theft

Identity theft is stealing personal information about people and using it in an illegal context.

Cyberstalking

This is an invasion of the user's privacy; it works when an intruder follows a target person's online activity and tries to harass/threaten him or her using verbal intimidation via e-mail, chat services, and social media. The wide reach of social media sites and the vast amount of personal details available publicly make cyberstalking a major problem in today's digital age.

Using Internet Network Illegally

Spreading illegal contents and selling illegal services and products. Example include spreading hate and inciting terrorism, distributing child pornography online, and selling drugs and weapons (especially in the darknet market).

DDoS Attacks

A DDoS attack is an attempt to make an online service unavailable by overwhelming it with traffic from multiple sources. Attackers build networks of infected computers, which could be millions of machines, known as botnets, by spreading malicious software through e-mails, web sites, and social media. Once infected, these machines can be controlled remotely by a bot master, without their owners' knowledge, and used like an army to launch an attack against any target.

Social Engineering

Social engineering is a kind of attack that uses psychological tricks (social tricks) over the phone or uses a computing device to convince someone to hand over sensitive information about himself or herself or about an organization and its computer systems.

Software Piracy

This is the unauthorized use, downloading, and distribution of pirated material like movies, games, software, songs, books, and other intellectual property products.

Cybercrimes could be conducted by either one person or a group of organized criminals; the latter is more dangerous as it has the resources to conduct and develop sophisticated attacks against target organizations and individuals.

Digital Forensics Categories

Digital forensics can be grouped according to the source of the acquired digital evidence.

Note!   "Digital evidence" is a term that refers to the sum of digital artifacts found on the target computing device that can be used as evidence in a court of law. Digital evidence is covered thoroughly later on in this chapter.

Computer Forensics

This is the oldest type of digital forensics; it is concerned with investigating digital evidence found on desktop computers, on laptops, on digital storage devices (like external hard drives, thumb drives, and SD cards), and in random access memory (RAM), in addition to operating systems and installed application traces and their associated logs. The main activity of this type is recovering deleted data from the target device's storage and analyzing it for incriminating or exonerating evidence.

Mobile Forensics

Mobile forensics is a type of digital forensics concerned with acquiring digital evidence from mobile devices. Mobile devices include any computing device (such as phones, smartphones, tablets, and wearable devices such as smart watches) able to make phone calls using standard communication networks like GSM, 3G, 4G, and so on. Such a device is usually location aware, meaning that it has a built-in GPS or similar satellite positioning system. The proliferation of mobile technology among users globally will soon make mobile forensics the most used branch among other digital forensics types.

Network Forensics

This type of digital forensics is concerned with monitoring and analyzing traffic flow in computer networks to extract incriminating evidence (e.g., discovering the source of security attacks) or to detect intrusions. Data flow through networks can be captured as a mass in real time and stored for later analysis or analyzed in real time with an option to save only segments of interesting events for further offline analysis (this option require less storage space). Network forensics deals with volatile (live) data only, unlike other digital forensics types.

Database Forensics

Database forensics is concerned with the analysis of data and metadata existing within a database such as Microsoft SQL Server, Oracle, MySQL, and others. Database forensics looks for who accesses a database and what actions are performed to help uncover malicious activities conducted therein.

Forensics Data Analysis

This branch deals with analyzing corporate structured data to prevent and discover fraud activities resulting from financial crime. It looks at meaningful patterns within corporate data assets and compares it with historical results to detect and prevent any misuse of corporate resources.

There are also other specific types of digital forensics like e-mail forensics, cloud storage forensics, forensics for specific application (e.g., Web browser forensics), file system forensics (NTFS, FAT, EXT), hardware device forensics, multimedia forensics (text, audio, video, and images), and memory forensics (RAM [volatile memory]); however, all these are small subbranches that fall within the main types already mentioned.

Digital Forensics Users

Digital forensics can be used in different contexts in virtually all sectors and businesses. The widespread usage of computing technology and Internet communications makes this science integrated across different domains.

Law Enforcement

Digital forensics was originally developed to aid law enforcement agencies in applying the law and to protect society and businesses from crime. Law enforcement officials use digital forensics in different contexts to detect offenses and associate illegal actions with the people responsible for them. Indeed, using digital forensics is not limited to cybercrimes, as most traditional crimes may require collecting digital evidence from the crime scene (e.g., a mobile phone found at a murder scene will certainly require investigation, and the same applies to a laptop and/or thumb drives found in a drug dealer's home).

For the law enforcement computer forensics specialist, a predefined digital forensics methodology should be followed strictly when collecting, preserving, analyzing, and presenting digital evidence. The investigation procedures will largely depend on the jurisdiction responsible for investigating the subject crime. A search warrant is usually needed, where applicable, before the law enforcement officer can seize the hardware (computing device) involved in the crime.

Civil Ligation

Using digital forensics in civil ligation has become big business these days. Business corporations use digital forensics techniques and methodologies as part of their electronic discovery process to find incriminating digital data that can be used as evidence in a civil or criminal legal case. E-discovery is considered an integral part of the justice system, although the implemented digital forensics procedures in civil ligation are somehow different from the one applied in criminal cases in terms of the procedures used to acquire digital evidence, investigatory scope, and the legal consequences of the case.

Most cases in business corporations are motivated by financial gain. Example include violations of the company's policy, financial theft, intellectual property theft, fraud, bribery, tax evasion, misuse of company resources, industrial espionage, embezzlement, and commercial dispute. Other known corporate digital-related crimes includes e-mail harassment, gender and age discrimination, and sabotage. Companies utilize digital forensics techniques as a part of their e-discovery process to discover and retrieve digital evidence in order to know the source, entity, or person responsible for such violations. The outcome of such investigations may lead to terminating the offending employee, giving a warning (if the violation is limited and unimportant), or prosecuting him/her if the case is to be taken to a court of law.

Using digital forensics in civil ligation is not limited to the business world; personal cases like family problems and divorce also fall under this category.

Legal Tip!   You can find the Federal Rules of Evidence that govern the introduction of evidence at civil and criminal trials in US federal trial courts at `www.rulesofevidence.org`.

Intelligence and Counterintelligence

Intelligence agencies use digital forensics techniques and tools to fight terrorist activities, human trafficking, organized crime, and drug dealing, among other dangerous criminal activities. Digital forensics tools can help officers uncover important information about criminal organizations through investigating a criminal's digital devices, monitoring networks, or acquiring information from publicly available sources such as social media sites—known as open source intelligence (OSINT)— about the person/entity of interest.

Note!   OSINT refers to all information that is publicly available. OSINT sources are distinguished from other forms of intelligence in that they must be legally accessible by the public without breaching any copyright or privacy laws. Chapter 10 will discuss OSINT in some detail.

Digital Forensics Investigation Types

Digital forensic investigations can be broadly segmented into two major categories according to who is responsible for initiating the investigation:

1. Public investigations

2. Private (corporate) sector investigations

Public investigations involve law enforcement agencies and are conducted according to country or state law; they involve criminal cases related to computer investigations and are processed according to legal guidelines settled by respected authorities. These investigations usually pass three main stages: complaint, investigation, and prosecution (see Figure 1-1).

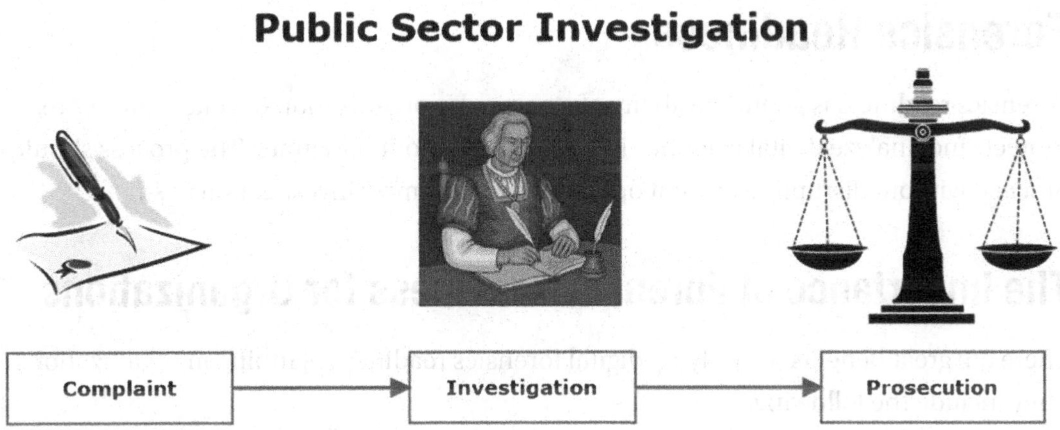

Public Sector Investigation

Complaint ➝ Investigation ➝ Prosecution

Figure 1-1. General public sector criminal investigation flow

Private investigations are usually conducted by enterprises to investigate policy violations, litigation dispute, wrongful termination, or leaking of enterprise secrets (e.g., industrial espionage). There are no specific rules (or laws) for conducting such investigations as it depends on each enterprise's own rule; however, many organizations are now following strict procedures for investigating digital crimes internally. These procedures are similar to public investigations when investigating crime, as some cases can be transferred later to court and becomes official criminal cases.

Enterprises can reduce ligation related to computer crime by setting a clear policy that can be easily read and understood by their employees. Such policy can also make digital forensics investigation (once needed) easier to conduct with minimal downtime of the running business. The most important policy that should be signed by all enterprise employees is computer usage policy. This policy defines how employees can use company IT equipment like computers and networks and promises them that there will be legal consequences if they violate these terms.

Note!   Always treat a private investigation as if it will end up in court. This will force you to follow strict investigatory procedures when building your case and thus protect your organization's private assets if the case ends up in court.

Forensics Readiness

Forensics readiness is about the ability of a particular organization to collect, preserve, protect, and analyze digital evidence in a forensically sound manner. The process should proceed without disrupting current operations to minimize investigation cost.

The Importance of Forensic Readiness for Organizations

There are great benefits to applying digital forensics readiness planning in organizations. They include the following.

- High response to incidents with digital evidence. When an incident (e.g., data breach or information leakage) that requires the collection of digital evidence occurs, the existence of a clear e-discovery process in place will help organizations act promptly and acquire digital evidence in a forensically sound manner.

- Compliance with government-applied regulations. Since 2015, US Federal Rules of Civil Procedure[5] have imposed a set of requirements on parties involved in a legal dispute on how to collect and preserve digital evidence in order to be acceptable in a court of law. Forensic readiness will reduce the cost of acquiring digital evidence and will certainly lead to faster resolution if the case is taken to court.

- Strengthening organizational security defense. Utilizing forensic readiness will make an organization well prepared to handle internal and external security incidents and able to identify an attack quickly before it dives deeply into its IT infrastructure (e.g., monitoring usage on endpoint computers may uncover dangerous malware, such as ransomware, before the infection spreads to the entire organization's network).

- Minimizing internal attacks. As we already said, internal threats (e.g., originating from a disgruntled employee) are more dangerous than external attacks; the existence of a forensic readiness plan in an organization will make malicious insiders fear being caught if they carry out any illegal activities.

- Increasing an organization's security posture. Forensic readiness planning will make an organization stand out as an entity with great defense against cyberthreats. Customers will be more willing to deal with this organization as their confidential transactions will be protected and secure. Investors will also be assured that their investment is protected and there is a limited possibility of launching successful attacks against this organization and consequently damaging their investment.

---

[5]"Federal Rules of Civil Procedure 2018 Edition," June 1, 2018.
www.federalrulesofcivilprocedure.org/frcp/title-v-disclosures-and-discovery/
rule-26-duty-to-disclose-general-provisions-governing-discovery

---

ELECTRONIC DISCOVERY REFERENCE MODEL (EDRM)

EDRM (www.edrm.net) is a popular standard for improving e-discovery and information governance. This is a conceptual standard for the e-discovery process that outlines standards for the recovery and discovery of digital data during an investigation, litigation, or similar proceeding. An investigator can choose to engage some steps in the model or perform the steps in a different order than shown in Figure 1-2.

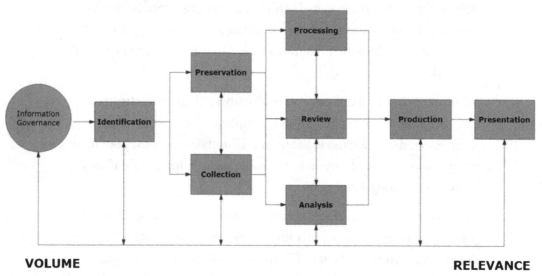

Figure 1-2. *EDRM reference model*

Developing a forensic readiness plan has become a must for any organization or corporation that wants to survive in today's digital age.

Digital Evidence

According to the a Universe study report,[6] the amount of digital data produced by humans and machines (e.g., IoT devices) will exceed 44 zettabytes by the year 2020

---

[6]EMC Corporation, "The Digital Universe of Opportunities," June 1, 2018. www.emc.com/ infographics/digital-universe-2014.htm

(1 zettabyte = 1 billion terabytes). People are increasingly accessing the Internet and using it on a daily basis to socialize, send e-mails, and browse the Internet; most of these activities will produce traces and remain present on users' computing devices for many years to come. Most computer users are not tech savvy; they might think that the deletion of a file erases it completely and forever from their hard drive, but this is quite wrong. Data stored on storage units can be restored even after formatting the drive many times; although certain tools can be used to further wipe hard drive space to make it irrecoverable (this is discussed in Chapter 9), even these advanced tools can still leave traces, allowing computer forensic investigators to obtain essential evidence to help them solve criminal cases and prevent other crimes using computer forensic techniques.

Note!   The ability to restore deleted data from storage units depends on its type and the installed operating system, as we are going to see later in this book.

Computer forensics involves acquiring digital evidence-sometimes known as electronically stored information (ESI)-from a computer hard drive, a mobile phone, a tablet or PDA, or other storage media (like CD/DVD, USB thumb drive) among other places, in a systematic way; this ESI is to be used in court during trials.

Digital Evidence Types

1. We can differentiate between two main types of digital artifacts according to who has created them:

2. User-created data

3. User-created data includes anything created by a user (human) using a digital device. It includes the following and more:

4. Text files (e.g. MS Office documents, IM chat, bookmarks), spreadsheets, database, and any text stored in digital format,

5. Audio and video files,

6. Digital images,

7. Webcam recordings (digital photos and videos),

8. Address book and calendar,

9. Hidden and encrypted files (including zipped folders) created by the computer user,

10. Previous backups (including both cloud storage backups and offline backups like CD/DVDs and tapes),

11. Account details (username, picture, password),

12. E-mail messages and attachments (both online and client e-mails as Outlook),

13. Web pages, social media accounts, cloud storage, and any online accounts created by the user.

Files created by a computer user also contain metadata; the metadata could be either produced on purpose by the computer user (e.g., author name and e-mail) or generated automatically by the software used to create it (e.g., GPS coordination of a specific photo, captured camera type, and resolution). As we insist in Chapter 2, metadata should also be investigated thoroughly during any investigation, as it may contain substantial evidence about the case in hand.

Warning!   In Windows OS, you can view any file metadata be right-clicking over it and selecting "Properties." However, keep in mind that whenever you access a file under Windows, you are changing some system-created metadata (last access date) about it, which should be taken into account during investigation.

Machine/Network-Created Data

Machine/network-created data includes any data which is autogenerated by a digital device. It includes the following and more:

1. Computer logs. These include the following logs under Windows OS: Application, Security, Setup, System, Forward Events, Applications, and Services Logs,

2. Router logs, including third-party service provider (e.g., Internet service providers (ISPs) commonly store users' account web browsing history logs),

3. Configuration files and audit trails,

4. Browser data (browser history, cookies, download history),

5. Instant messenger history and buddy list (Skype, WhatsApp),

6. GPS tracking info history (from devices with GPS capability),

7. Device Internet protocol (IP) and MAC addresses in addition to the IP addresses associated with a LAN network and the broadcast settings,

8. Applications history (e.g., recently opened file on MS Office) and Windows history,

9. Restore points under Windows machines,

10. Temporary files,

11. E-mail header information,

12. Registry files in Windows OS,

13. System files (both hidden and ordinary),

14. Printer spooler files,

15. Hidden partition and slack space (can also contain hidden user information),

16. Bad cluster,

17. Paging and hibernation files,

18. Memory dump files,

19. Virtual machines,

20. Surveillance video recordings.

We can summarize "digital evidence" as any kind of file or data/metadata that is presented in digital format (binary format) and could be used during a trial.

Locations of Electronic Evidence

Digital evidence is commonly found on hard drives; however, with the continual advance of computing technology, digital evidence becomes present in almost all digital-aware devices. The following list shows most of the different devices that must be investigated for digital evidence:

1. Desktops

2. Laptops

3. Tablets

4. Servers and RAIDs

5. Network devices like hubs, switches, modems, routers, and wireless access points

6. Internet-enabled devices used in home automation (e.g., AC and smart refrigerator)

7. IoT devices

8. DVRs and surveillance systems

9. MP3 players

10. GPS devices

11. Smartphones

12. PDA

13. Game stations (Xbox, PlayStation, etc.)

14. Digital cameras

15. Smart cards

16. Pagers

17. Digital voice recorders

18. External hard drives

19. Flash/thumb drives

20. Printers

21. Scanners

22. Fax machines (e.g., incoming and outgoing fax numbers)

23. Copiers (e.g., recently copied files)

24. Fixed telephony and cordless phones (e.g., calls made, received, and answered, voice messages and favorite numbers)

25. Answering machines

26. Backup tapes

Note!   There are different sources of digital evidence, and each one requires a different method/tool to acquire it. The focus of this book will be on acquiring digital evidence from computers running Windows OS in addition to thumb drives and external hard drives.

Tip!   Digital devices can contain other sources of evidence like fingerprints, DNA, and other identifiers that should not overlooked during investigation.

Challenge of Acquiring Digital Evidence

Criminals use different ways to frustrate digital forensic examiners by destroying and hiding their incriminating activities; also, seizing digital devices is subject to different laws across states and countries. The following lists the main obstacles facing examiners when obtaining digital evidence:

1. Locked computer with a password, access card, or dongle.

2. Digital steganography techniques to conceal incriminating data in images, videos, audio files, file systems, and in plain sight (e.g., within MS Word document).

3. Encryption techniques to obscure data, making it unreadable without the password.

4. Full disk encryption (FDE) including system partition (e.g., BitLocker drive encryption).

5. Strong passwords to protect system/volume; cracking them is very time consuming and expensive.

6. File renaming and changing their extensions (e.g., changing DOCX into DLL, which is a known Windows system file type).

7. Attempts to destroy evidence through wiping the hard drive securely using various software tools and techniques.

8. Removing history from the web browser upon exit and disabling system/application logging where available.

9. Physically damaged digital media; for example, we cannot retrieve deleted files from a failed HDD before repairing it.

10. Sensitivity of digital evidence; if not handled carefully it might be destroyed. Heat, cold, moisture, magnetic fields, and even just dropping the media device can destroy it.

11. Easy alteration of digital evidence; for instance, if a computer is ON, you must leave it ON and acquire its volatile memory (if possible), but if the computer is OFF, leave it OFF to avoid changing any data.

12. Laws governing the collection of digital evidence and device seizure, which differ from one state to another (and between one country and another). Cybercrimes can cross boarders easily through the Internet, making the lack of cyberlaw standardization a major issue in this domain.

13. The issue of data ownership; for example, if investigators captured a USB thumb drive that belongs to a suspect, but the data inside it is fully encrypted and protected with a password, the suspect can deny its ownership of this thumb, making the decryption process very difficult to achieve without the correct password/key file.

Note!   You might think physical damage to media devices will render them useless and prevent any recovery of data from it. This is completely wrong. Advanced digital forensics labs have the ability to restore data from heavily damaged devices like burned, smashed, and sunken devices. So always take the device to an expert digital forensic examiner to analyze it.

The techniques mentioned briefly herein to frustrate computer investigators will be described in some detail in Chapter 9; however, keep in mind that the majority of criminals are not tech savvy. Those people will not employ advanced methods to cover their tracks. Even though some of them may use different privacy techniques to cover their files and activities on the computer, the majority will not implement them 100% correctly, and this will leave a door open for examiners to do their job and break in to acquire valuable information from the suspect computing device.

Who Should Collect Digital Evidence?

Digital evidence should be examined only by trained professionals who have the expertise and knowledge to handle sensitive data without destroying it during the investigation. Those investigators should have the following general skills.

- Analytical thinking: This includes the ability to make correlations between different events/facts when investigating a crime.

- Solid background in IT knowledge: This includes wide knowledge about different IT technologies, hardware devices, operating systems, and applications. This does not mean that an investigator should know how each technology works in detail, but he should have a general understanding of how each technology operates.

- Hacking skills: To solve a crime, you should think like a hacker. Knowing attack techniques and cybersecurity concepts is essential for a successful investigation.

- Communication and organizational skills: An investigator should have documentation skills to organize his/her findings and present them to other members of the team and to attorneys and judges.

- Understanding of legal issues concerning digital crime investigations.

- Excellent knowledge of technical skills related to digital forensics like data recovery and acquisition and writing technical reports.

- Online searching skills and ability to gather information from publicly available sources (i.e., OSINT).

THE ROLE OF EXPERT WITNESS

Sometimes, a digital forensics professional will play the role of expert witness in a court of law, but what differentiates an expert witness from a nonexpert witness or conventional witness?

The typical witness will testify on what he saw or heard, while the expert witness will have the opportunity to give his/her opinion to the court. Judges and jury are not always familiar with the technical details associated with digital crimes, so an expert witness should help them to assimilate and understand these technical details.

An expert witness does not have to hold an advanced academic degree to testify, however. He needs to show a proven technical ability that clearly demonstrates he fully understands the subject he is going to testify about. To make expert witness testimony effective in court, it is recommended that this expert have the ability to convey complicated technical details for something easy to assimilate by nontechnical people like judges and jury members. Often, such people work in the teaching field and authors can play this role very well.

Chain of Custody

Chain of custody is an integral part of any digital forensic investigation process. Proper chain of custody must declare clearly how digital evidence was discovered, acquired, transported, investigated (analyzed), preserved, and handled between different parties involved in the investigation. The ultimate goal is to ensure the integrity of digital evidence through knowing all persons who were in contact with this evidence from its acquisition to its presentation in a court. If we fail to understand who was in contact with the evidence during any phase of investigation, the chain of custody will be jeopardized and the acquired evidence will become useless in a court of law.

To maintain a correct chain of custody that is acceptable in a court, an audit log must be maintained for all acquired digital evidence that tracks the movements and possessors of digital evidence at all times. A correct chain of custody will enable investigators to answer the following questions in a court of law:

1. What is the digital evidence? (E.g., describe the acquired digital evidence.)

2. Where was the digital evidence found? (E.g., computer, tablet, cell phone, etc.; also to be included is the state of the computing device upon acquiring the digital evidence–ON or OFF?)

3. How was the digital evidence acquired? (E.g., tools used; you also need to mention the steps taken to preserve the integrity of evidence during the acquisition phase.)

4. How was the digital evidence transported, preserved, and handled?

5. How was the digital evidence examined? (E.g., any tools and techniques used.)

6. When was the digital evidence accessed, by whom and for what reason?

7. How was the digital evidence used during the investigation?

Chain of custody is all about documentation; every movement of digital evidence must be documented (see Figure 1-3), so an investigator can prove that the subject evidence has not been altered during investigation and that no external evidence has been planted to mislead the investigation.

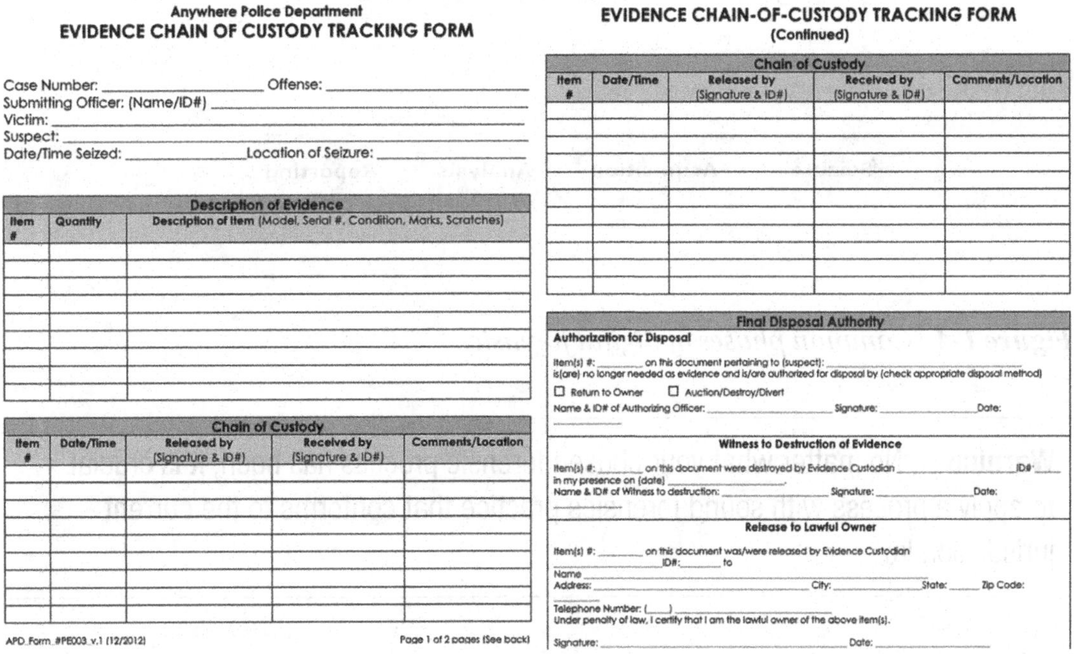
Anywhere Police Department
EVIDENCE CHAIN OF CUSTODY TRACKING FORM

Case Number: ______ Offense: ______
Submitting Officer: (Name/ID#) ______
Victim: ______
Suspect: ______
Date/Time Seized: ______ Location of Seizure: ______

Description of Evidence		
Item #	Quantity	Description of Item (Model, Serial #, Condition, Marks, Scratches)

Chain of Custody				
Item #	Date/Time	Released by (Signature & ID#)	Received by (Signature & ID#)	Comments/Location

APD_Form_#PE003_v.1 (12/2012) Page 1 of 2 pages (See back)

EVIDENCE CHAIN-OF-CUSTODY TRACKING FORM
(Continued)

Chain of Custody				
Item #	Date/Time	Released by (Signature & ID#)	Received by (Signature & ID#)	Comments/Location

Final Disposal Authority
Authorization for Disposal
Item(s) #: ______ on this document pertaining to (suspect): ______
is(are) no longer needed as evidence and is/are authorized for disposal by (check appropriate disposal method)
☐ Return to Owner ☐ Auction/Destroy/Divert
Name & ID# of Authorizing Officer: ______ Signature: ______ Date: ______

Witness to Destruction of Evidence
Item(s) #: ______ on this document were destroyed by Evidence Custodian ______ ID#: ______
in my presence on (date) ______.
Name & ID# of Witness to destruction: ______ Signature: ______ Date: ______

Release to Lawful Owner
Item(s) #: ______ on this document was/were released by Evidence Custodian ______ ID#: ______ to
Name ______
Address: ______ City: ______ State: ______ Zip Code: ______
Telephone Number: (___) ______
Under penalty of law, I certify that I am the lawful owner of the above item(s).
Signature: ______ Date: ______

Figure 1-3. *Sample chain of custody form (template) suggested by the National Institute of Standards and Technology (NIST) to track digital evidence during legal investigations. Source:* `www.nist.gov/document/sample-chain-custody-formdocx`.

A predefined investigation methodology should be followed when acquiring, preserving, and analyzing digital evidence, and this what we are going to cover next.

Digital Forensics Examination Process

There is no standard form or methodology that outlines the steps to conducting digital forensic investigations across the globe. For instance, different approaches are already in place with various numbers of steps or phases. However, all approaches divide the work into the four main phases shown in Figure 1-4:

1. Seizure

2. Acquisition

3. Analysis

4. Reporting

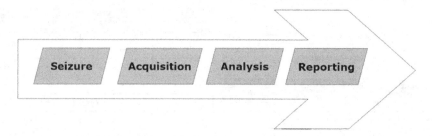

Figure 1-4. *Common phases of digital forensics*

Warning!   No matter what your chosen forensic process has been, it is crucial to apply a process with sound forensics practice that conforms to the current jurisdiction laws.

Seizure

In this phase, the physical evidence (digital device) will be seized and transferred safely to the forensic lab. This evidence can be any computing device type such as laptop, tablet, mobile phone, external hard drive, USB flash drive, wearable device (e.g., digital watch), or even a desktop PC. Remember, you need to have a permission from the proper authority (e.g., court warrant) to seize the suspect's machine.

Upon arriving to the crime scene, the suspect digital device should be examined by a well-trained technician to ensure the digital evidence is acquired/preserved in a forensically sound manner. If the suspect computer was still running, then we should consider acquiring its volatile memory (RAM) if possible. The old-school practice was to unplug the computer and then seize it in a special antistatic case. However, modern forensic practices appreciate the great importance of acquiring volatile memory while the PC is still running. RAM memory can contain a wealth of information like cryptographic keys, IM chat logs, unencrypted contents, clipboard contents, and process information, among other things. Acquiring RAM memory should be documented along with the tool used in the final investigative report, as the tool used to extract RAM content will bring minor changes to the target operating system files, RAM memory, and hard drive.

Acquisition

This phase deals with the computing secondary storage device (e.g., HDD, solid state drive [SSD], thumb drive, tape drive) and with the volatile memory (RAM) if the computer was still running. In this phase, a computer forensic examiner will conduct a duplication of the suspect hard drive (this is also known as a bit-to-bit image) to create a complete image of the seized hard drive. Analysis will be performed on the digital copy later. Examiners usually use hardware duplicators or software imaging tools like the DD command in Linux to duplicate drives. Remember that the suspect hard drive should be write-protected when conducting the duplication process to avoid tampering with the original evidence. If the suspect machine was still running, RAM memory should be acquired considering the different scenarios, as we are going to see in Chapter 4.

Note!   It is very important to have more than one copy (image) of the acquired suspect hard drive. The forensics analysis will be conducted on a copy of the digital evidence, so that original media will remain intact and can be verified at a later stage for accuracy.

Analysis

In this phase, the contents of the acquired forensic image file are investigated using a set of tools to search for interesting leads within the acquired image. Hidden, deleted, and encrypted files in addition to IM chat logs, Internet browsing history, and deleted e-mails can all be recovered using specialized tools like EnCase, Sleuth Kit, Volatility, and Forensic Toolkit (FTK) from AccessData, to name a few.

During this phase, hash signature analysis is used (as we are going to see in the next chapter) by the forensic tool to identify notable files or to exclude known ones. Acquired image file contents are hashed and compared to precompiled lists such as the Reference Data Set (RDS) from the National Software Reference Library, which tries to collect software from various sources and incorporate file profiles computed from this software into an RDS of information. The RDS can be used to review files on the seized computers by matching file profiles in the RDS. This will help alleviate much of the effort involved in determining which files are important as evidence on computers or system files that have been seized as part of criminal investigations. You can download a single 7GB ISO image containing all data from www.nsrl.nist.gov/Downloads.htm.

Forensic tools can also perform searches within the acquired image file using keyword search terms or phrases. This will effectively speed up the investigation and help investigators to find relevant information quickly.

Incriminating evidence will be recovered and analyzed to reach conclusions related to the case at hand. All these facts will be presented later in a formal report, as we will see in the next stage.

Note!   If you do not know what is meant by hash, check the "Hash Analysis" section in the next chapter. For now, consider hashing as a digital fingerprint (a set of unique strings) of any digital data. It is used to compare the original evidence (e.g., the sum of data existing on a hard drive) to the acquired forensic image of the same hard drive. When the two hash values match, this means that the two files are 100% identical.

Reporting

In this phase, the examiner produces a structured report about his/her findings. Such a report is usually prepared for nontechnical people (like attorneys, judges, and juries). Writing style, terminology, and the way facts are presented should be taken into consideration when writing the report. Evidence should be presented along with the report, mostly in digital format.

The general content of forensic report should contain the following:

- Summary of key findings.

- Description of tools (both hardware and software) used during the investigation process and the function of each in addition to the version of the software tools.

- Method used to acquire the digital evidence.

- Description of the digital evidence (image content) and the interesting artifacts found within it (e.g., Internet browsing history, e-mail history, USB registry analysis, deleted files found). It is preferable to use screen captures where applicable to describe to the reader steps undertaken to analyze digital evidence.

- Explanation of technical terms used like "unallocated disk space," "Host Protected Area," and the like so nontechnical people can understand the technical terms mentioned in the report.

- Conclusion of the investigation.

The original suspect hard drive and digital copies of it (images) should be presented along with the report to the court.

Digital Forensics Process Official Guides

Digital forensics is considered an emerging discipline in the cybersecurity domain; there are many official and organizational attempts to standardize and address digital investigation procedures. The following are the most reputable organizations that have tried to standardize the process of digital forensic investigations through published guides:

- NIST published a guide titled "Guide to Integrating Forensic Techniques into Incident Response" (`http://csrc.nist.gov/publications/nistpubs/800-86/SP800-86.pdf`) that addresses most issues related to handling computer security incidents in addition to making general recommendations for performing a digital forensic process and how to conduct it on four different groups of data sources: files, operating system, network traffic, and applications.

- US DOJ published a guide titled "Forensic Examination of Digital Evidence: A Guide for Law Enforcement" (`www.ncjrs.gov/pdffiles1/nij/199408.pdf`) that describes procedures and best practices for the examination of digital evidence. Other guides from the same source are "Electronic Crime Scene Investigation: A Guide for First Responders," which can be found at `www.ncjrs.gov/pdffiles1/nij/187736.pdf`, AND "Digital Evidence in the Courtroom: A Guide for Law Enforcement and Prosecutors," which can be found at `www.ncjrs.gov/pdffiles1/nij/211314.pdf`.

- The Association of Chief Police Officers, which leads the development of policing practices in the United Kingdom, has also published a guidance called "ACPO Good Practice Guide for Digital Evidence" to ensure the authenticity and integrity of evidence during computer forensic investigations. Currently, the last updated version of the guide is version 5, you can find it at `www.acpo.police.uk/documents/crime/2011/201110-cba-digital-evidence-v5.pdf`.

There are many bodies interested in developing digital forensics standards in collaboration with different actors like government bodies, digital forensics investigators, and academia; one of these is the Digital Forensic Research Workshop (`www.dfrws.org`).

Digital Forensics Certifications

Acquiring a digital forensics certificate will prove your ability to follow specific processes to handle security incidents, and some certifications will demonstrate your ability to use a specific forensic tool from a specific vendor. Certification also helps you to stay competitive and up to date in your field and show your commitment to the digital forensics profession. The following are the most popular digital forensics certifications currently available. This list is not inclusive and shows prices as of this writing.

1. Computer Hacking Forensic Investigator (CHFI) (`www.eccouncil.`
    `org/programs/computer-hacking-forensic-investigator-`
    `chfi/`) offered by EC-Council. The exam covers forensics
    tools, analytical techniques, and steps involved in acquiring,
    maintaining, and presenting digital forensic evidence in a court
    of law. You can attempt the CHFI exam without attending an
    official training; however, you need to pay a nonrefundable $100
    eligibility application fee. You must renew this certification every
    three years (various options are available to renew EC-Council
    certifications).

2. Certified Forensic Computer Examiner (CFCE) (`www.iacis.com/`
    `certifications/cfce`) offered by the International Association
    of Computer Investigative Specialists (IACIS). This certificate
    requires candidates to register for an official course to be eligible
    to register for its exam. Without the official training, candidates
    need to pay for registration fee and pass a background check to
    enroll in the CFCE program and sit for the exam. This certification
    has high value and excellent recognition among other digital
    forensics certificates.

3. GIAC Certified Forensic Examiner (GCFE) and GIAC Certified
    Forensic Analyst (GCFA) (`www.giac.org`). Both certifications are
    offered by GIAC, focus on computer forensics investigation and
    incident response, and cover collecting digital evidence from both
    Windows and/or Linux computer systems. Certification is valid for
    four years and a maintenance fee of $429 must be paid every four
    years. You need to take official training before attempting these
    exams.

4. Certified Computer Crime Investigator (types: basic and
    advanced) (`www.htcn.org/site/certification-requirements.`
    `html`) offered by the High Tech Crime Network. To sit for this
    exam you need to have three or five years' experience (three
    for basic and five for the Advanced level) directly related to the
    investigation of technical incidents or technical crimes in either
    law enforcement or corporate. You also need to have followed

a training related to cybercrime offered by an approved center or organization, and finally you have to write a narrative report describing some criminal cases you have already solved.

5. AccessData Certified Examiner (ACE) (`http://accessdata.com/training/computer-forensics-certification`) offered by AccessData the vendor of FTK. Obviously, this certification measures a candidate's ability to use the latest version of this tool in investigations. There is no formal training required before attempting this exam. Exam recertification is required every two years. Current exam fees $100.

6. EnCase Certified Examiner (EnCe) (`www2.guidancesoftware.com/training/Pages/ence-certification-program.aspx`) offered by OpenText. This certification measures a candidate's ability to use Guidance Software's EnCase computer forensic software. No formal training is required in order to attempt this exam. EnCe certifications are valid for three years from the date obtained and the cost of renewal is $75.

Digital Forensics vs. Other Computing Domain

Digital forensics is considered a standalone domain, although it has some overlap with other computing domains such as computer security (also known as cybersecurity), data recovery, and disaster recovery. The ultimate aim of digital forensics is to acquire, preserve, and analyze digital artifacts in a forensically sound manner to be used in a court of law.

Computer security aims to protect systems and data according to specific security policy set by individuals or organizations, whereas digital forensics tries to explain how a security policy came to be violated. One of the aims of computer security is to protect user data and ensure his/her privacy by using encryption, access controls, and steganographic techniques, while digital forensic tries to recover passwords, access encrypted files, discover hidden data, investigate violation of access controls, and recover deleted files and wiped disks for evidence.

Computer data recovery involves recovering data from computers that was deleted by a mistake or lost because of power failure or hardware crash. Many data recovery cases involve fixing hardware damage to hard drives or other digital storage units.

In data recovery, the user usually knows what he is looking for; however, in digital forensics, an investigator is searching for hidden data and intentionally deleted files to use as evidence during a trial.

Disaster recovery has many things in common with digital forensics, as it uses many of its techniques to restore data that has been lost; the main difference between these two is the final outcome of the process and the way to achieve it. The ultimate goal of digital forensics is still acquiring data following strict procedures so that it can be admissible in a court of law.

Finally, e-discovery is concerned with searching within a large volume of digital data sets (e.g., backup tapes, storage servers) for interesting evidence that can be presented in a court of law as a part of corporate private investigations. E-discovery does not deal with damaged hardware as is the case with data recovery. When used in US courts, e-discovery processes are usually conducted under the Federal Rules of Civil Procedure ("FRCP") guidelines.

Chapter Summary

In this chapter, we introduced the term "digital forensics" and differentiated between it and other kind of cybersecurity domains. We briefly covered the concept of digital evidence, its types, and where we can find it in electronic devices. There is no formal global process for conducting digital forensics investigations; however, we introduced the general phases of any digital investigation process and what tasks are required as a part of each phase.

There have been many attempts made to standardize digital forensics standards and process through published guides by some recognized official bodies; the most important ones are those published in the United States and the United Kingdom.

Digital forensics experts are needed in virtually all industries and sectors, from nonprofit organizations to government entities to private corporations and enterprises. As more companies are shifting most of their work digitally, we can expect to see a tremendous growth in demand for digital forensics experts in coming years.

In the next chapter, we will cover the main technical concepts that any digital forensics-or cybersecurity-expert needs to understand before beginning his/her investigation.

CHAPTER 2

Essential Technical Concepts

What you should already know before starting your investigation

Conducting a digital forensics investigation requires a thorough understanding of some of the main technical concepts of computing. Knowing how data is stored in computers, number theory, how digital files are structured, and the types of storage units and the difference between them are essential areas to know how to locate and handle digital evidence. While this book is intended for those with working knowledge of using computers in general (especially Windows OS), there are some technical theories that first must be discussed because of their importance in conducting digital forensics examinations. This chapter will cover those basic concepts.

Data Representation

Obviously, computers store, process, and represent digital data in a specific way. In this section, we will briefly discuss how a computer represents data, discussing common numbering systems, and introduce the major encoding scheme used by computers to produce text that is readable for humans. Let us begin with the common numbering system.

Decimal (Base-10)

Decimal is the most widely used numbering system that we use every day when performing math calculations (e.g., 10 + 11 = 21); it is referred to as the base-10 system because it uses 10 digits or symbols (0, 1, 2, 3, 4, 5, 6, 7, 8, 9) to represent its values.

© Nihad A. Hassan 2019
N. A. Hassan, *Digital Forensics Basics*, https://doi.org/10.1007/978-1-4842-3838-7_2

In decimal, the position of the number gives meaning to the value it represents, where each digit is multiplied by the power of 10 associated with that digit's position.

For example, consider the decimal number 5437. This number is interpreted as follows:

$$5437 = 5000 + 400 + 30 + 7$$

Or more precisely:

$$5437 = 5 \times 10^3 + 4 \times 10^2 + 3 \times 10^1 + 7 \times 10^0$$

An understanding of the decimal numbering system is essential, as the other numbering systems follow similar rules.

Binary

Computers store data in binary format, which is the base-2 numeral system represented by 1's and 0's. Binary, the language of the computer, follows the same rules as decimal. However, unlike decimal, which has 10 symbols and multiplies by the power of 10, binary has two symbols (0 and 1) and multiplies by the power of two.

In computers, each 1 OR 0 is called a bit (or binary digit); the sum of eight bits is called a byte. The highest-order bit is located in the leftmost bit and has the highest value; this bit is called the Most Significant Bit (MSB). On the opposite side, the lowest bit value is located in the rightmost bit and is called the Least Significant Bit (LSB). Table 2-1 helps you to identity bit value from its position when working with binary numbers.

Table 2-1. *Representation of a Binary Number*

MSB	Binary Digit							LSB
2^8	2^7	2^6	2^5	2^4	2^3	2^2	2^1	2^0
256	128	64	32	16	8	4	2	1

For example, consider the binary number 110011010. To translate it into decimal, see Table 2-2.

Table 2-2. *Convert Binary to Decimal*

Binary	Decimal
1×2^8	256
1×2^7	128
0×2^6	0
0×2^5	0
1×2^4	16
1×2^3	8
0×2^2	0
1×2^1	2
0×2^0	0

$$2 + 8 + 16 + 128 + 256 = 410$$

Please note that all data is stored in computers in binary: your digital pictures, YouTube videos, posts and tweets to social media, e-mails, and anything else on a computer is stored in binary format.

Warning!   Sometimes it is unclear whether a written number is binary or decimal; for example, the number 10 can be interpreted as "ten" in decimal OR as "1" and "0" in binary (equivalent to "two" in decimal value). To overcome this, it is advisable to write a subscript that mentions the numbering schema used. For example: 10_2 means that the Base-2 numbering schema is used. Binary numbers are sometimes written using the prefix 0b (e.g., 0b11001), while the decimal does not have any prefix.

Hexadecimal (Base-16)

Also known as Hex, this numbering system uses 16 digits or symbols to represent its values. It contains the following numbers and letters:

0, 1, 2, 3, 4, 5, 6, 7, 8, 9, A, B, C, D, E, F (capital letters are used to represent numbers from 10 to 15).

You will encounter Hex numbers frequently when working with computers and other digital systems, especially when investigating the memory address location. The main motive behind this numbering schema is to represent long binary values in a compact order which is easy to read by humans. Hex achieves this by grouping each bits (binary digit) in one group. For example:

$1100\ 1100\ 1101\ 0101_2$ is easier to read and understand than
1100110011010101_2

Hex also helps us to write shorter lines to represent specific values; for example, to write my name **Nihad Hassan** in binary, I need to write the following:

01001110 01101001 01101000 01100001 01100100 00100000
01001000 01100001 01110011 01110011 01100001 01101110

The same in Hex would be as follows:

4E 69 68 61 64 **20** 48 61 73 73 61 6E (the number 20 in Hex
represents the space between the two words).

Obviously, Hex is shorter and easier to understand by humans.

In Hex, place value is determined by powers of 16, instead of 10. For example, to convert from Hex to decimal:

$19A_{16} = (1 \times 16^2) + (9 \times 16^1) + (10 \times 16^0) = 256 + 144 + 10 = 410_{10}$

A is equal to **10** in decimal. See Table 2-3.

Table 2-3. *Hex, Binary, and Decimal Equivalents*

Decimal	Hexadecimal	Binary
0	0	0000
1	1	0001
2	2	0010
3	3	0011
4	4	0100
5	5	0101
6	6	0110
7	7	0111
8	8	1000
9	9	1001
10	A	1010
11	B	1011
12	C	1100
13	D	1101
14	E	1110
15	F	1111

Hex numbers can be distinguished from other numbering systems by writing the prefix Ox or placing a subscript 16 or suffix H.

TIP! USING THE CALCULATOR TO CONVERT BETWEEN NUMBERING SYSTEMS

You can use the calculator associated with all Windows versions to convert between different numbering systems. To use the Windows calculator, open the Cal application and select "Programmer" as your selected interface (see Figure 2-1).

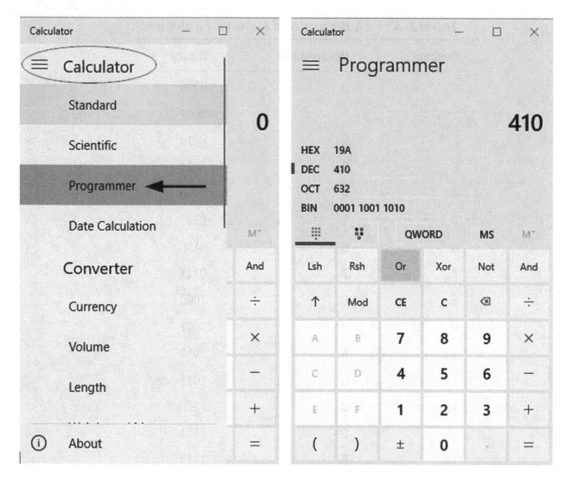

Figure 2-1. *Using the Windows calculator to convert between different numbering systems*

Computer Character Encoding Schema

As we already said, everything in computers is represented by 0 or 1, but maybe you are wondering how the 1 or 0 will eventually end up on our computer screen as letters like A, B, M, C, V, and so on.

Computers use character encoding schema to convert binary numbers into meaningful text that a human can read (e.g., the text you see when reading this book on your computing device). There are two major encoding schemas used by computers to represent text:

ASCII (American Standard Code for Information Interchange) was invented a long time ago and is still supported on nearly all text editors. ASCII has only a limited ability to represent all letters from all languages across the globe, as well as punctuation and other special symbols from other languages, because it uses seven bits or 128 values only. There is another extended version of ASCII, named Extended ASCII, that supports 256 characters, but it still doesn't offer support for all international languages. The ASCII code table can be found at `https://ascii.cl`.

Unicode encoding, created by The Unicode Consortium (`https://unicode.org`), is a widely used character-encoding schema that provides a unique number for every character from any international language. Unicode is supported in major operating systems, software packages, mobile devices, and web applications. Unicode is often defined as UTF-8, UTF-16, UTF-32, or UCS-2.

Understanding how computers store and represent data is essential in digital forensics; for example, an investigator may need to extract and open a file from unallocated disk space of the target hard drive or from a raw dataset without using the program (e.g., MS Word) that originally created this file. This technique is called file carving, and it is used effectively to recover deleted files and fragments of files from wiped or damaged hard drives.

To conduct file carving, it is essential to know how we can distinguish a file from its signature, and this is what we are going to cover in the next section.

File Structure

Digital files are composed of a sequence of bits: each file type has a particular encoding scheme that describes how information is stored within this file. This schema called "file format." The file format can be either free (like Portable Network Graphics [PNG], which is a raster image format standardized by ISO/IEC) or proprietary (like the Windows Media Audio [WMA] file format).

Some file formats have the ability to store more than one content type; this is the case in many popular formats that store multimedia contents. For example, the Ogg format can store video, audio, text, and metadata in one container. AVI, WAV, and 3GP also fall under this category.

As users, we distinguish file type from its extension. For instance, MS Word file has the DOCX or DOC extension, and MS Excel has the XLSX or XLS extension. However, as digital forensic investigators, we cannot depend on the file extension alone to determine file type, as this can be easily changed to whatever you want (e.g., an MS Word file can be changed to a DLL or PNG file to conceal its true identity). To counter for such concealment techniques, we must check the file signature (header) to know its type.

Most digital files have a signature that is located in the first 20 bytes of the file; you can check this signature by opening the subject file using Windows Notepad or any other text editor like Notepad++. For example, we have a file named *sales.docx*; we can change its extension to JPG and then open the JPG file using a Hex editor (I'm using HxD editor, which you can download from www.mh-nexus.de) and investigate its first 20 bytes (see Figure 2-2).

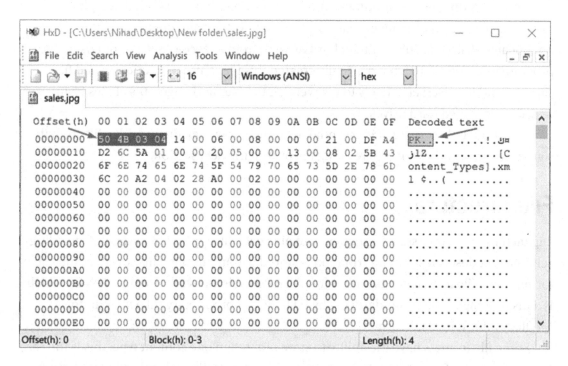

Figure 2-2. *Investigation of the first bytes of a file could reveal its true file format; the first four bytes refer to MS Word file format (Open XML Format Document)*

FREE HEX EDITORS

There are many free Hex editors available out there; if you prefer to use one other than the one we are using, check the following for alternatives:

- Free Hex Editor Neo (www.hhdsoftware.com/free-hex-editor)

- wxHexEditor (www.wxhexeditor.org/home.php)

- PSPad (www.pspad.com/en)

To see a list of 518 file signature, you can go to www.filesignatures.net, where you can use site's search functionality to query the database for a particular file signature.

Tip!   To see a list of common file extensions organized by file format, go to **https://fileinfo.com/filetypes/common**.

Note!   If you come across a file type and you do not know how to open it, you can check www.openwith.org; this site lists most file extensions along with the needed free program to open each one.

Fortunately, most forensic software can match a file signature with its associated extension; some tools even group all files with headers (signature) that do not match their extension.

Digital File Metadata

Metadata is data about data. Most digital file types have metadata associated with them. It usually comes integrated into the same file; however, some file types store their metadata in a separate file. Metadata holds data that describe the file it's associated with. For example, some metadata included in an MS Word file might include author name, organization name, computer name, date/time created, and comments.

From a digital forensics perspective, metadata can be very useful in many cases. For example, we can track different authors of a file (e.g., an MS Office file) through the associated metadata. We can also search within the file's metadata to locate interesting information (major operating systems already support searching within the file metadata information), and most computer forensic suites support searching within acquired forensic image files' metadata.

We can edit the metadata of many types of digital files without using any third-party tools under Windows OS. For example, we can edit the metadata info of an MS Office file by just right-clicking a file ➤ Properties, which should make the file Properties window appear (see Figure 2-3). (You can get the same result by selecting the file and pressing Alt+Enter to view the file's Properties window.)

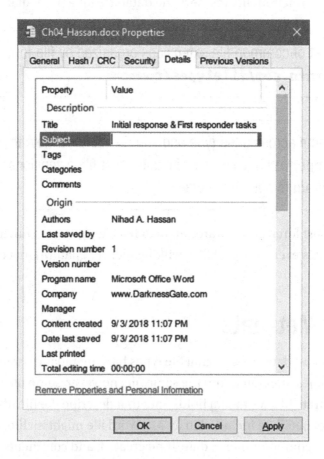

Figure 2-3. *Viewing MS Word file properties*

An image file's metadata holds important forensic information such as the timestamp for when the photo was taken and GPS coordinates of where it was taken (if enabled in the capturing device), in addition to camera details and settings (see Figure 2-4). You can view image metadata info under Windows in a similar way to viewing MS Office files.

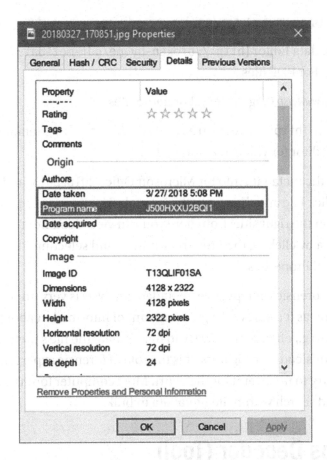

Figure 2-4. *Viewing image metadata info can reveal the capturing device type/ model (in this figure, SAMSUNG J5 Model 500H was used to capture the photo)*

There are many freeware tools that can view and edit a digital file's metadata. Here are some popular ones:

1. Exif Pilot (www.colorpilot.com/exif.html). Image metadata editor/viewer.

2. ExifTool by Phil Harvey (`www.sno.phy.queensu.ca/~phil/ exiftool`). Read, write, and edit metainformation for a wide variety of digital files (most image formats).

3. GIMP (`www.gimp.org`). Image editor; can manipulate/view image file metadata.

4. XnView (`www.xnview.com/en/`). View/edit image metadata.

5. Pdf Metadata Editor (`http://broken-by.me/pdf-metadata- editor`). For PDF files.

6. Mp3tag (`www.mp3tag.de/en`). For audio files.

7. MediaInfo (`https://mediaarea.net/en/MediaInfo`). Metadata viewer/editor for video and audio files.

8. To view the metadata info for Microsoft Office 2010, 2013, and 2016, Click File and then go to the Info tab. The Properties panel will be on the right side; from here you can view document metadata by clicking the Properties button and selecting Advanced Properties.

From a digital forensics perspective, metadata analysis is very important for any type of investigation as it can reveal a great amount of information about the case at hand. Some users (e.g., offenders) may try to manipulate the file's metadata to remove the evidence and mislead investigators. It is the role of forensic experts to discover such tampering and to try to uncover it for the court. Most computer forensics tools allow for easy extraction and search within file metadata in bulk.

Timestamps Decoder (Tool)

As we already saw, digital files contain different metadata within them; the most important is the timestamp metadata, which is used to represent different date/time events associated with the file of interest like last access date/time, last modified date, and creation date. During our investigation, we may encounter date/time that is encoded in a specific way and we need to decode it (e.g., date/time values are in Windows registry written in binary format and need to be translated into ASCII). The Decode tool can perform this job. You can find it at `www.digital-detective.net/ digital-forensic-software/free-tools`.

Hash Analysis

Hashing is an important concept in the digital forensic field; actually, you must calculate any digital evidence hash value (whether it is a hard disk image or a single file) you acquire during your investigation to prove that the acquired data (i.e., the digital evidence) has not been tampered with.

Hash works by implementing a hash function to convert a digital file (input) into a fixed string value (output); the resultant hash value is unique and cannot be generated again using other file or piece of data. You can find the hashing value of any digital file or any piece of data by using a hash generator tool. The most famous cryptographic hash algorithms are MD5 and SHA-256.

In digital forensics investigations, hashing (also known as digital fingerprinting) is used twice: the first time to verify the acquired forensics image before the analysis begins (to make duplicate copies of the acquired forensics image) and the second at the end of the examination to verify the integrity of the data and the forensics processing during investigation.

How to Calculate File Hash

All digital forensics suites offer hashing capabilities; however, you can use a third-party tool or simply use the hashing tool that exists as a built-in feature in Windows OS.

Method One: Using a Third-Party Tool

- Febooti Hash and CRC (`www.febooti.com`). Install this tool on your Windows PC, right-click over the file whose hash you want to calculate, select Properties, and go to the Hash/CRC tab.

- HashMyFile from `www.nirsoft.net/utils/hash_my_files.html`. This is a portable tool that shows hash values of selected folders/files using different hashing algorithms (e.g., md5, SHA 256).

Method Two: Using the Built-In Windows Hashing Feature

To do this, go to the Windows Start menu and select Windows PowerShell. Run the command in Figure 2-5, replacing *C:\Hassan_9781484227985_Online.pdf* with the path to the file whose hash you want to view.

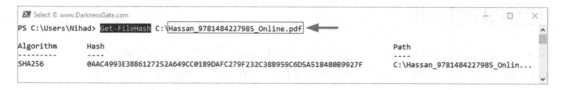

Figure 2-5. *Using Windows PowerShell to calculate a digital file's hash*

When using PowerShell to calculate a file hash, Windows defaults to the SHA256 algorithm; however, you can specify the cryptographic hash function to use by adding the **-Algorithm** parameter after the file path followed by one of the following cryptographic hashes (SHA1, SHA256, SHA384, SHA512, MD5).

Memory Types

In computers, memory refers to the hardware piece responsible for storing information for immediate or later use. We can distinguish between two main types according to how long information remains stored on them.

Volatile Memory

Volatile memory keeps information for a short time; actually, it needs power to retain data, but when power is turned off, it loses its information quickly. An example of volatile memory is RAM.

Nonvolatile Memory

Nonvolatile memory can retain data for long time, even after power is turned off. It is usually used for long-term persistent storage. Examples of such memory are computer hard drives, flash memory, and ROM (read-only memory).

Types of Computer Storage

We can differentiate between two types of computer storage: primary storage and secondary storage (see Figure 2-6).

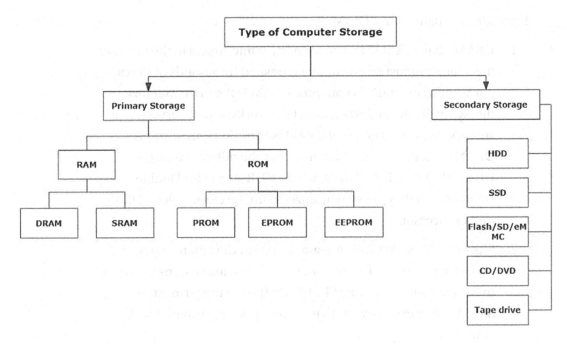

Figure 2-6. *Types of computer storage*

Primary Storage

Also known as main storage and system storage, this type has a volatile memory that loses stored data when power is turned off. Primary storage is used to store data and programs for temporary use, has limited storage capacity and faster read/write operations compared with secondary storage, and is considered more expensive. The main primary storage memory found in computers is RAM and cache (CPU memory).

RAM

This is the most important component of any computing device: it is a volatile memory—with great speed compared to secondary storage media—that is used mainly to store all information that your computer needs to process right now or in the near future. For example, when launching a web browser, it will load into RAM memory. From a digital forensics perspective, a wealth of information can be found in RAM like executable programs, network sessions, web browsing history, IM chat, passwords, photos, decrypted files, and so on. Capturing a RAM image becomes mandatory in any digital forensic investigation that includes a running computer.

There are two main types of RAM:

1. DRAM (dynamic RAM). The term "dynamic" refers to the fact that this memory must be constantly refreshed (thousands of times per second) to retain its contents. DRAM is the main memory that we typically see installed on PCs, workstations, servers, and smartphones. A variation of DRAM is SDRAM (synchronous DRAM), a generic name that describes the different types of DRAM (DDR2, DDR3, DDR4, where DDR stands for Double Data Rate) as they are synchronized with the clock speed of the microprocessor.

2. SRAM (static RAM). This is usually used in CPU memories (CPU, cache); it is very fast (more than DRAM) because it does not need to be refreshed constantly like DRAM (hence the term "static"). SRAM is very expensive and uses more power compared with DRAM.

As we already said, both RAM types are volatile, meaning they will lose contents when the power is turned OFF.

ROM

As its name implies, this memory is used to perform read operations only; it does not have any write access. This memory is nonvolatile, as it retains the information within it, whether or not there is power. This kind of memory is used in computers and in many other digital devices to store firmware programs (software stored on hardware devices—like computer motherboard and graphics card—that provides instructions on how that device should operate). Modifying data in ROM is very difficult and requires special programs to access it.

There are three types of ROM:

1. Programmable ROM (PROM)

2. Erasable programmable ROM (EPROM)

3. Electrically erasable programmable ROM (EEPROM)

We will not discuss the types of ROM memory in detail; however, keep in mind that all types are nonvolatile memory.

Secondary Storage

Secondary storage is also known as external memory or auxiliary memory. This is nonvolatile memory that retains its contents, whether there is power or not. It is used for long-term data retention. Compared with primary storage like RAM, secondary storage has low speed, but costs much less than primary storage.

Common types of secondary storage include the following.

HDD

HDD is the main permanent storage (nonvolatile) location of data in a computer. It uses magnetic storage technology to store data for later usage. HDD uses a mature technology that has been used since 1960, when it become the dominant secondary storage device for different types of computing devices like desktops, servers, and laptops. Any digital forensic investigator has certainly dealt with HDD; this technology is expected to remain in use for many years to come.

The HDD drive comes in two shapes, fixed (internal) and external. The first one (fixed) is located inside the computing device, while the external HDD can be connected to the computing device through a USB or eSATA cable to increase available storage.

HDD devices store data on platters: a platter is a round metal disk made of aluminum, glass, or ceramic covered with a magnetic material that stores data on both sides (top and bottom surface). A hard disk can have a number of platters; consumer hard drives with capacities of less than 500 GB will contain only one platter. For large-capacity consumer hard drives, the number of platters can range from one to five depending on the HDD's physical size, capacity, manufacturer, and model.

A platter is divided into a number of tracks. The tracks form a complete ring on each platter. These tracks are divided in turn into an equal number of sectors. A partition is a section on the disk (logical storage unit). As we know, a hard disk can have multiple partitions. The main purpose of disk partitioning is to treat one physical disk drive as if it were multiple disks. This allows us to use different file system types (FAT, NTFS) on each partition in addition to separating operating system partitions from user file partitions.

There are two types of partitions:

- Primary partition
- Extended partition

Each HDD can be divided into four primary partitions or three primary partitions and one extended partition. A primary partition will hold operating system booting files, while the extended partition, can be subdivided into 24 logical partitions; however, newer file systems can surpass the limit of 24 logical partitions.

Note!   A partition can include tracks from more than one platter. For example, a partition can span over two platters.

How Is Data Stored on the HDD?

As we have already said, each platter contains thousands of tracks, and each track is divided into sectors. Each track on the platter holds the same number of sectors. A hard disk can hold millions of sectors. The common storage capacity of each sector is 512 bytes; however, newer file systems can hold up to 4 KB. All file systems that are used by Windows organize hard disks based on cluster size (a cluster consists of a number of sectors). Cluster size represents the smallest amount of disk space that can be used to hold a file.

Cluster size is dependent on the file system used and the size of a partition, and it ranges from 4 to 64 sectors. This makes a single cluster able to store up to 64 KB of data using the default settings. Each cluster can hold data from only one file at any one time. Subsequently, if we have a text file of 11 KB, it will occupy one cluster (assuming the cluster size is 32 KB); the remaining storage size (21 KB) will stay untouched and is called slack space (see Figure 2-7). Slack space can be used to store incriminating data or it can simply contain previously recycled leftover files that can be restored for possible evidence.

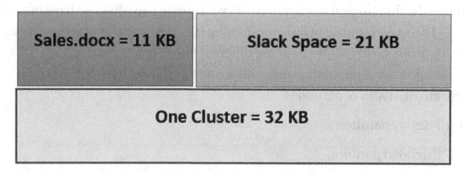

Figure 2-7.   *One cluster can hold only one file at a time*

DISK SLACK CHECKER

There is a tool from Karen Ware called "Disk Slack Checker" (www.karenware.com/
powertools/ptslack), which can calculate available slack space on a hard disk
(see Figure 2-8).

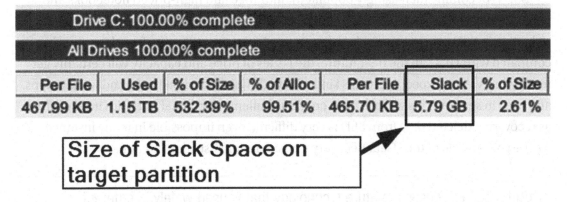

Figure 2-8. *Using "Disk Slack Checker" from Karen Ware to calculate available
slack space on target volume*

The platters inside HDDs spin at high speed in order for the other parts to write/
read information to and from platters; accordingly, this kind of disk is also known as a
mechanical hard drive.

There is a modern type of hard drive called a solid state drive (SSD) that uses NAND
flash memory (nonvolatile) to store information, and this what we are going to talk about
in the next section.

SSD

We can consider SSD as the modern type of the HDD. Similar to flash memory, SSD has
no moving parts (platters); it saves data into a series of NAND flash cells or microchips
(NAND is composed of a set of transistors similar to the one used in RAM; however,
this type of transistor does not need to be continually refreshed so it can retain its data,
making it a type of nonvolatile memory). The SSD uses a kind of controller (which is an
embedded processor) to determine how to store, retrieve, and cache data.

The absence of mechanical moving parts makes SSD consume less power and enjoy high speed compared with a typical HDD (10×). At the beginning of its usage, SSD suffered from a major disadvantage, which was the limited number of write cycles it had; however, as the technology advances, SSD manufacturers are working to resolve this problem by creating more efficient algorithms that spread data equally on all cells, thus making all cells in SSD live longer without any problems.

SSD is becoming increasingly popular in midrange and high-priced notebooks and workstations, and as the technology continues to advance daily, we can expect to see a reduction in SSD price. Capacity is also an issue: SSD units still suffer from low capacity compared with HDD. In the near future, the issues of price and capacity will certainly get resolved, so we can expect to see this kind of hard drive in most notebooks and workstations, and even in servers. This will certainly create a challenge for digital forensics investigators, as recovering deleted data from SSD is very difficult, even impossible in many instances, as we are going to see in the "Data Recovery Considerations" section later on.

Note!   The HDD uses a mature technology that is used widely in different computing environments. Despite the advantages of speed, silence, and less power consumption of the SSD type, HDD will remain in wide use for many years to come.

Embedded MultiMediaCard (eMMC)

This is a cheap replacement for an SSD drive; it is a flash-based nonvolatile storage used in many budget Android smartphones, Windows tablets, and low-end laptops (generally the ones that come with Intel Atom CPU). eMMC has similar architecture to SD cards (both store information in flash memory), and it is designed to be as cost effective as possible. This makes it lack the speed and durability of the SSD drive. eMMC comes soldered onto the device motherboard, and thus you cannot remove it separately from the device. This kind of storage has limited capacity; the most common sizes are 32, 64, and 128 GB.

Optical Data Storage

This type of storage stores data in an optically readable medium. Examples of such media include CD-ROM, DVD, and Blu-ray disks. The acquisition of CD/DVD is similar to acquiring a hard drive; we need to create an image of the target CD/DVD's contents and then investigate it using appropriate digital forensics tools.

DATA MEASUREMENT CHART

Table 2-4 is a useful data measurement chart.

Table 2-4. *Data Measurement Chart*

Data Measurement	Size
Bit	Single Binary Digit (1 or 0)
Byte	8 bits
Kilobyte (KB)	1,024 bytes
Megabyte (MB)	1,024 KB
Gigabyte (GB)	1,024 MB
Terabyte (TB)	1,024 GB
Petabyte (PB)	1,024 TB
Exabyte (EB)	1,024 PB
Zettabyte (ZB)	1 billion TB

HPA and DCO

Host protected area (HPA) is a reserved area created by the HDD manufacturer that is not accessible by the user, the OS, or the BIOS. This area usually contains HDD-supporting utilities (like diagnostic and recovery programs) and sometimes boot sector files of the installed OS.

Note   BIOS (Basic Input Output System) is a software program installed on computer motherboard and used to store the configuration settings of other computer hardware components such as hard drive, CPU and memory.

The device configuration overlay (DCO) is a reserved area on an HDD that is not supported by all HDD manufactures; it is located at the end of the disk after the HPA partition. HPA and DCO can both coexist in the same hard disk, but DCO should be created before HPA.

From a digital forensics perspective, both DCO and HPA areas will survive even after a full disk format is performed, making them an ideal place for possible offenders to conceal incriminating data.

Many computer forensics suites are capable of accessing and imaging these areas on a hard drive; most hardware acquisition tools can image these two areas. Always consult the computer forensic tool you want to use for such capabilities.

Table 2-5 lists popular programs that can be used to view, copy, or edit HPA and DCO areas. Figure 2-9 shows an example of one tool.

Table 2-5. *List of Tools for Viewing/Editing Data in HPA and DCO*

Program Name	URL
Fiesta	http://sourceforge.net/projects/fiesta
TAFT	www.vidstrom.net/stools/taft/
ATATool	www.datasynergy.co.uk/products/misc/atatool.aspx
HDAT2	www.hdat2.com/
DiskCheckup	www.passmark.com/products/diskcheckup.htm

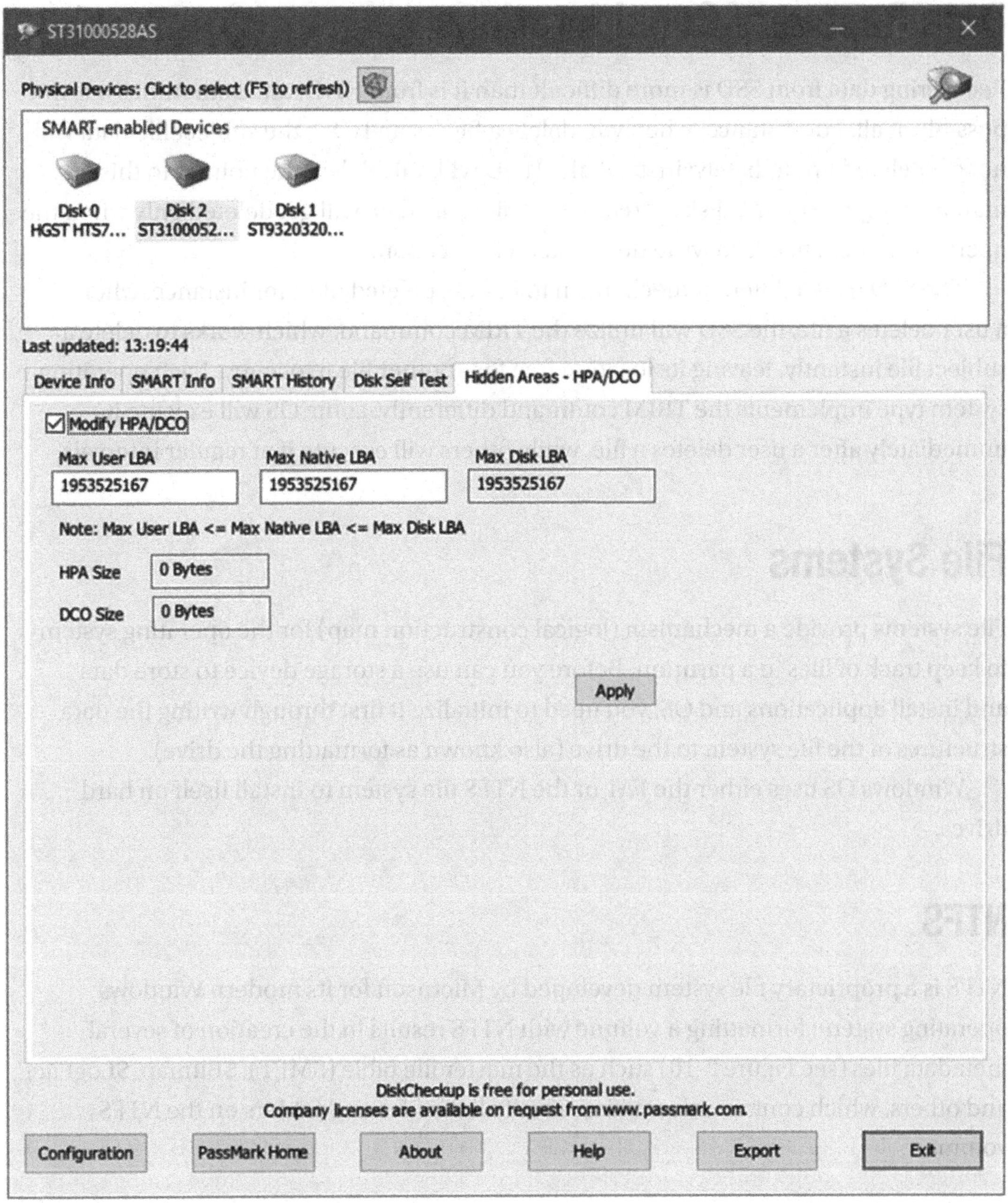

Figure 2-9. Using DiskCheckup from PassMark to edit HPA and DCO size areas

Data Recovery Considerations

Recovering data from SSD is more difficult than it is from HDD, and sometimes it is not possible at all. For instance, when you delete a file on an HDD, the subject file data will not get deleted immediately; instead, the HDD will only delete the pointer to this file, marking its space on the disk as free. The subject file data will get deleted only when the operating system needs to write new data on its location.

The SSD uses a different mechanism to handle deleted files; for instance, when a user deletes a file, the SSD will utilize the TRIM command, which works to delete a subject file instantly, leaving its location free for another file to occupy. Each operating system type implements the TRIM command differently: some OS will execute it immediately after a user deletes a file, while others will execute it at regular intervals.

File Systems

File systems provide a mechanism (logical construction map) for the operating system to keep track of files in a partition. Before you can use a storage device to store data and install applications and OS, you need to initialize it first through writing the data structures of the file system to the drive (also known as formatting the drive).

Windows OS uses either the FAT or the NTFS file system to install itself on hard drives.

NTFS

NTFS is a proprietary file system developed by Microsoft for its modern Windows operating system; formatting a volume with NTFS results in the creation of several metadata files (see Figure 2-10) such as the master file table ($MFT), $Bitmap, $LogFile, and others, which contain information about all the files and folders on the NTFS volume.

Partition boot sector	Master File Table	System Files	File Area

Figure 2-10. *Sample formatted new technology file system volume*

In the NTFS file system, each file stored within it is composed of a set of data streams: the primary stream (has no name) is the one that holds the actual data a user sees when opening a file. The other stream is called the alternative data stream (ADS). Digital forensics examiners should search within data streams of all files stored on an NTFS partition, as they can contain hidden data.

To learn how an offender can create an ADS file and conceal secret data—or even a malware—within it, and also how an investigator can detect such files manually and by using different third-party tools, you can check my articles on the subject on the SECJUICE web site:

1. Hiding in Plain Sight with NTFS Steganography (`www.secjuice.com/ntfs-steganography-hiding-in-plain-sight`)

2. Playing in the Dark Corners of Windows With ADSs (`www.secjuice.com/data-destruction-techniques-in-windows`)

FAT

FAT (file allocation table), one of the oldest file systems still in use, has four variations: FAT12, FAT16, FAT32, and FATX. Microsoft had used FAT as the default file system for all its old Windows versions including Windows NT.

FAT is more portable than the NTFS file system because you can use it on different devices. For example, FAT is commonly used in digital cameras, SD cards, smartphones, USB thumb drives, and many embedded devices. Storage devices formatted with FAT can be read across different platforms easily, unlike the NTFS, which can only be read by Windows OS.

NTFS surpass FAT in many areas; for example, NTFS supports large file sizes and file encryption feature. NTFS is used by Microsoft to install its modern Windows OS versions like Windows 8 and 10 and the new Server editions.

Computing Environment

The computing environment will heavily affect your choice of how to capture digital evidence. As the technology advances and Internet speed increases, we can expect to see a significant transformation from centralized computer architectures to noncentralized or distributed computer architectures in the next few years.

The following are the most common computing environments.

Personal Computing Environment

This might be the most prevalent one these days. In this environment, all programs are installed locally and executed from the same machine. Data is also saved to the machine's local hard drive. Laptops, desktops, printers, tablets, and even smartphones are examples of personal computing environments. This environment is the easiest one to deal with in case a personal device become a part of a criminal investigation, as the location of evidence is tied to the subject device only.

Client Server Computing Environment

In this environment, there are two machines: a client (e.g., personal computer, laptop, or tablet) and a server. The client requests data from the server via an HTTP connection, and the server responds with data. An example of such an environment is the e-mail server you interact with to get your e-mails.

Distributed Computing Environment

In this environment, applications are installed and executed on several computers; this allows one application to split its functions into multiple components, with each component working on a dedicated computer. Data storage is also distributed in this type of environment, and clients and other applications need to communicate with remote servers via networks to access data or to use programs. Capturing digital evidence in such an environment is challenging, as users' private data and logs can be scattered among different remote servers, which in turn can be located in different geographical areas under different jurisdictions. The volume of data (and logs) that need to be investigated is also an issue in such environments, because the volume can be huge in many cases.

Cloud Computing

Cloud computing is a modern technological model, developed as a result of the explosive growth of the Internet and online communications, that allows a service provider to deliver various computing services to users through the Internet.

The range of computing services that can be offered in this way is wide; for example, instead of purchasing an external hard drive to store your backup data, you can store this data on a cloud provider for a small fee. The cloud provider will be responsible for managing user data in the cloud (e.g., making backup copies and protecting this data from malicious software and cyberattacks).

Cloud computing is not only tied to storing user's data; enterprises are using cloud computing to reduce IT infrastructure costs. For instance, a company can use a cloud computing service that provides needed applications (like MS Office suite) for its work, instead of purchasing a software license for each user individually. The cost appears more when using expensive software like SQL Server and Windows Server OS; paying for using such software on a usage basis while at the cloud is more cost effective than installing them on premises. Enterprises apply different cloud computing models, as we are going to see next.

Software as a Service (SaaS)

In this model, a user purchases an account on a cloud computing provider and selects which applications s/he wants to install. In this way, a user will do his/her work on a cloud (remote) server instead of using these applications on the local machine. Examples of such services are Google Apps for Education and Microsoft Office 365.

Platform as a Service (PaaS)

This model is popular among software/web development companies, where a customer—a web development company, for example—pays for an account on a cloud service provider that supplies customized environment according to client need (e.g., to install needed web development tools, prepare the development and testing environment, etc.). This allows a customer to begin its work fast with minimum cost.

Infrastructure as a Service (IaaS)

In this model, a cloud provider provides the hardware (physical server and data center's hardware) needed by the client through the Internet on a rent basis. The client purchases and installs needed applications and OS and configures them according to business needs. Such service is usually used by web hosting providers and enterprises for storage, backup, and recovery of data outside of the company's premises.

What we care about from this discussion is that cloud computing services will add additional difficulty for law enforcement officials when investigating criminal cases. For example, what if a UK citizen who is a suspect in a criminal case uploaded his data to a cloud storage provider who is located in Singapore; can the UK police force the Singaporean provider to hand over a copy of user data?

Windows Version Variations

There are different versions of Windows OS; as a digital forensics investigator, you must know how to collect current Windows OS information so you will be aware about some differences between versions during the acquisitions and analysis phases.

To learn the current Windows version of a computer running Windows 8 and beyond:

1. Press and hold the Windows key along with R;

2. Type winver in the search box and press Enter;

3. The Windows version and build number should appear (see Figure 2-11).

Figure 2-11. *Windows version "About" box*

To check for operating system information in Windows 7, go to Control Panel ➤ System and look under Windows edition for current version information.

IP Address

You will absolutely encounter information that requires understanding the addressing schema used in the Internet and many private networks during your investigations, so understanding IP protocol is a prerequisite for any digital investigator. In this section, we will briefly talk about the concept of IP address and how computing devices get connected to the Internet.

What Is an IP Address?

An IP address is a unique address that distinguishes a computing device when connected to the IP network. An IP address is similar to a fingerprint; hence, no two devices can have the same IP address on the same IP network. IP is commonly combined with another protocol named Transmission Control Protocol (TCP), which allows a computing device to establish a virtual connection between a destination and a source to exchange information.

Currently, there are two IP addressing schema in use: IP version 4 and IP version 6.

IP v4 is the most used one on earth; currently, most online services are using it. IP v4 uses a 32-bit address schema and can hold up to 4.3 billion addresses; however, with the explosive growth of the Internet and the increased number of IoT devices, this number has become limiting and may run out soon. This has led to the development of another standard named IP v6, which can accommodate more than 7.9×1028 times as many addresses as IP v4.

IP addresses come in two types: public and private.

Public IP addresses: This allows direct connection to the Internet and is assigned by your ISP, where each IP is unique. For example, an e-mail server needs to have a public IP address that is unique globally. A public IP address can be either static or dynamic.

- Static IP address. This address is fixed—just like your phone number—and remains the same as long as the ISP is reserving it for you.

- Dynamic IP address. This one changes each time the user connects to the Internet. The ISP uses a protocol called Dynamic Host Configuration Protocol (DHCP) to assign IP addresses automatically to their subscribers.

To determine whether you are using a dynamic or static IP address, use the command-line prompt in Windows and type the following:

ipconfig /all

Find the line containing DHCP Enabled (Figure 2-12) under your current network connection; if DHCP Enabled is set to Yes, then you most likely have a dynamic internal IP address.

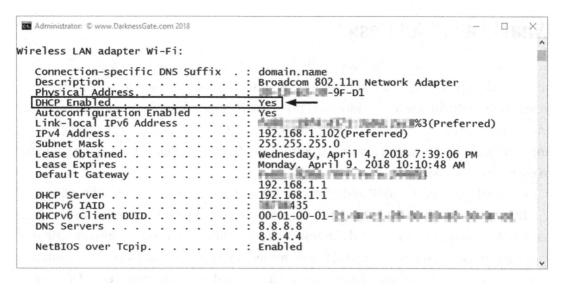

Figure 2-12. *Determine whether your PC is using a dynamic or static IP address. In this case, we're using a dynamic IP address.*

Private IP addresses (a.k.a. local IP address): This is a non-Internet-facing IP address for devices usually sitting behind a routing device. All devices existing in a closed network (e.g. Home or school networks) will use private IP addresses. These addresses are usually assigned automatically using the DHCP of the router.

Note!   DHCP is a network protocol used on IP networks. It works by dynamically allocating IP addresses to a set of connected hosts based on a preconfigured pool of addresses.

Digital Forensics Resources and Study Materials

As the technology continues to advance daily, digital forensics examiners must constantly continue to learn new skills, techniques, and know-how to use different tools to solve cybercrimes. Criminals are becoming ever more clever and are using powerful exploitation tools to commit their crimes and to hide their digital traces. Forensics examiners should continue their educational efforts in the field to stay on top of industry changes. For instance, reading books (such as this one), following training programs, attending industry conferences and other educational events, talking with peers, and reading reputable resources online will help you to stay up to date with this domain.

In this section, we will mention some useful online resources that can help you to stay current with the latest technologies and techniques in the field.

Reference web sites:

1. OSINT: The author's dedicated portal for OSINT resources (www.osint.link)

2. DarknessGate: The author's IT security and digital forensic reference portal (www.darknessgate.com)

3. Cyber Forensicator (www.cyberforensicator.com)

4. DFIR Training: Check the "Resources" section (www.dfir.training)

5. Tools Watch (www.toolswatch.org)

Blogs:

1. Another Forensics Blog (az4n6) (http://az4n6.blogspot.com)

2. Black Bag (www.blackbagtech.com/index.php/blog)

3. Malware Byte Blog (https://blog.malwarebytes.com)

4. Security Score Card (https://securityscorecard.com/blog)

5. Forensic Focus (www.forensicfocus.com)

6. SANS Digital Forensics and Incident Response Blog (https://digital-forensics.sans.org/blog)

7. Digital Forensics Magazine
(http://digitalforensicsmagazine.com/blogs)

8. Heimdalsecurity blog (https://heimdalsecurity.com/blog)

9. Hak5 (https://shop.hak5.org/blogs/news)

IT security news:

1. Dark Reading (www.darkreading.com)

2. CIO (www.cio.com/category/security)

3. PC Mag (http://sea.pcmag.com)

IT security/forensics tutorials:

1. Info security institute (https://resources.infosecinstitute.com)

2. Forensics Wiki (www.forensicswiki.org)

3. Life in Hex (https://lifeinhex.com)

IT security alerts

1. US-CERT (www.us-cert.gov/ncas/alerts)

2. Norse: Global cyberattack map (www.norse-corp.com)

Chapter Summary

In this chapter, we've covered important technical concepts about computers that must be well understood by any digital forensic examiner. We describe how computers store and represent data digitally, the concept of operating system file structure and its types, and hash algorithms and how we can use them to verify the authenticity of any piece of digital data.

Computers have mainly two types of memory:

- Volatile memory: This type needs power to retain its data, and it loses stored data as soon as power is turned off (e.g., RAM).

- Nonvolatile memory: This type retains its data even after the power is turned off, like hard drives and flash memory.

There are different types of computing environments. The simple one is called the personal computing environment (e.g., PC, tablet, and smartphone); this type is relatively easy to investigate as data is usually stored locally on the device hard drive. Other computing environments like cloud and network computing are more complex and require specialized computer forensics tools and expertise to investigate them.

As we insisted before, the technical concepts presented in this chapter should be understood well by any digital forensic examiner; this knowledge is needed not only to investigate security incidents, but also to understand how to present these ideas in simple terms to other casual computer users like judges and juries.

CHAPTER 3

Computer Forensics Lab Requirements

Software and hardware tools you need to begin your investigation

With the increased number of cybercrime attacks that hit both the public and the private sector, the need for computer forensics lab to capture and analyze digital evidence with high accuracy increases. You may think that computer forensics labs are limited to law enforcement agencies. However, this is not true: many corporations in the United States maintain digital forensics labs with advanced investigation capabilities that exceed those of many police labs.

As we talked about in Chapter 1, digital forensic investigations can be broadly segmented into two types, public and private investigation. Obviously, law enforcement agencies and security services are the pioneer in establishing digital forensics labs; however, with the advance of computing technology and the widespread use of smartphones and wearable devices, most typical crimes have now become associated with a type of digital evidence. This crowds police labs with long waiting lists of digital evidence from various legal cases that need to be investigated. The long waiting lists—which may sometimes last for months or years—encourage large and even mid-sized corporations to have their own in-house lab to investigate cybercrime issues related to their work and property.

Today's banks, tech companies, retailers (such as Amazon and Walmart), and utility providers are using their own digital forensics labs to speed the investigation process and to reduce the various costs associated with digital investigations. Compared with police labs, private corporations have more flexibility in terms of procuring the latest software (including upgrades) and hardware needed for supplying their labs, while some police labs may still use old software versions because of budget limitations and the lack of trained professionals.

© Nihad A. Hassan 2019
N. A. Hassan, *Digital Forensics Basics*, https://doi.org/10.1007/978-1-4842-3838-7_3

In-house digital forensics analysts usually work closely with law enforcement agencies to solve cases related to their businesses. For instance, once someone finds evidence of or witnesses an illegal activity (e.g., violation of polices, industrial sabotage, leaking secrets, or other related crimes), the reporting company's digital forensic investigators or the e-discovery team will contact law enforcement and work with them hand in hand to capture and analyze acquired evidence and to move the case to a court of law.

Having an in-house digital forensics lab in today's digital age is a great investment for any company which values its data assets; however, this comes with a cost. For instance, assuming that just one forensic analyst is hired and one forensic workstation is supplied with the main necessary tools to do the job (both hardware and software), even the smallest lab will have an annual expenditure of no less than $150,000! Small companies may not be willing to pay for this extra expense if they face few incidents. Many small and medium-sized corporations outsource their digital forensics work to an accredited third-party digital forensics laboratory to save costs.

Accrediting digital forensics lab is a key issue to consider, whether you are planning to establish an in-house lab for your organization or you think to outsource your digital forensics work to a third-party provider. Accreditation ensures that your laboratory— or the one whose services you want to use—meets the established standards of the authoritative body in terms of using reliable methods, appropriate tools (in terms of hardware and software), and competent personnel to perform its duties.

Digital forensics labs can come in different sizes: of course, the budget plays a crucial role when planning for the lab, but the expected tasks (work scope) required for this lab will be the cornerstone in determining the needed equipment and software tools. For instance, large corporations are investing in creating advanced labs that handle all types of computing devices and cases like malware, external breaches, network, GPS, and mobile forensics. These labs have well-trained professionals and contain the latest versions of forensic software in addition to different specialized hardware tools. No matter the size of your forensics lab, it must contain the minimum tools to capture, preserve, analyze, and present digital evidence in a forensically sound manner.

A small digital forensics lab is the most prevalent: only a small budget is needed and it can initiate quickly. Such labs are usually run by one to five people and focus on handling one type of device (e.g., mobile forensic or Windows OS forensic). It does not need pricey equipment like the networking infrastructure and security solutions needed by the big labs; however, it still needs to have the appropriate digital forensic software to analyze evidence in addition to essential hardware like a hardware write blocker (some are incorporated into the forensic workstation itself), cables, appropriate storage solutions, and other electrical devices like UPS and digital cameras, in addition to a dedicated forensic computer to do the analysis.

Before listing the software and hardware equipment necessary for the forensic lab, it is essential to discuss the physical facility requirements of this lab. Maintaining the security and integrity of the digital evidence in addition to that of the lab's equipment should be a top priority, especially since these labs might become a target of cybercriminals in order to stop or interrupt investigations.

Lab Physical Facility Requirements

The following basic physical requirements are highly preferable to have in any digital forensic lab:

1. Must have one entrance door.

2. Preferable to have no windows in the lab.

3. Lab must be soundproof, meaning no one can eavesdrop on the conversations happening within the lab. This can be achieved by using soundproofing material on the ceiling and walls, and using carpet on the floor.

4. Must have an alarm system at the entrance in addition to a biometric system to handle access to the lab. The access biometric system must record each visit to the lab; this log must remain backed up for many years to come for auditing purposes.

5. Surveillance cameras should cover the entire lab, especially the main entrance and digital evidence room. The video recorder of the surveillance system (where video recording files are stored) should be stored in the most secure room in the lab, which is the "evidence storage room."

6. Must have fire suppression systems.

Note!   For high-risk investigations like cases related to national security, basic
lab requirements are not enough. An advanced lab with high security measures
must be used; such a lab must be provided with special coating materials to
cover floors and walls to prevent electromagnetic radiation (EMR) emitted from
the lab's electronic devices to prevent electronic eavesdropping. More information
on this issue can be found at `www.sans.org/reading-room/whitepapers/`
`privacy/introduction-tempest-981`.

The floor plan in Figure 3-1 is a suggested design for a digital forensic lab suitable for
large private and government organizations. In Figure 3-2, you will find a suggested floor
plan for a small company or house lab.

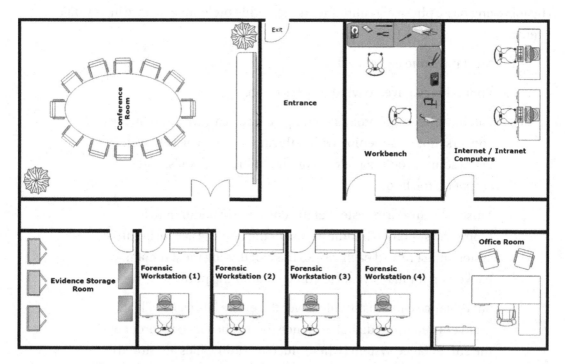

Figure 3-1. *Floor plan for large digital forensic lab: license server and internal lab
network equipment in addition to Internet networking devices (router, firewall,
and IDS) can be placed in the Internet/intranet room*

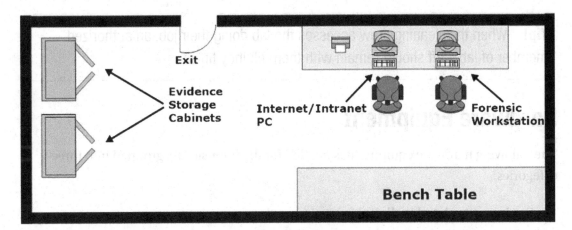

Figure 3-2. *Small digital forensics lab suitable for home or small companies*

Note!   It is advisable to have extra unoccupied space, for the lab's future expansion if possible.

Environment Controls

The lab environment must be strictly controlled to avoid damaging forensic equipment and seized digital devices. The following environment controls must be in place.

1. Air cooling system to absorb heat generated from workstations. This is very important, as forensic workstations can remain operational for a number of days during evidence analysis (e.g., cracking a password) and this will produce heat, especially in small spaces.

2. The lab must be well organized and clean. It must have healthy climate in terms of temperature, low humidity, and pure air.

3. Good lighting in the entire lab and in each individual forensic workstation room.

4. Electricity organizer equipment to avoid a sudden drop in power, and UPS units for the complete lab and especially for forensic workstations, storage server, and surveillance cameras.

Tip!   When the cleaning crew accesses the lab doing their job, an authorized member of lab staff should remain with them till they finish.

Hardware Equipment

The following hardware equipment is needed for the forensic lab, grouped into three categories:

Equipment related to digital forensics work

1. Licensing server (this is required by some digital forensics suites).

2. Storage server configured for the standard removable hard drives (used to store digital evidence images and data processed and extracted from those images); this server must never get connected to the Internet.

3. Forensic workstation(s) (covered in the section "Forensic Workstation").

4. Portable forensic laptop (used outside lab to capture evidence and for doing some analysis).

5. Dedicated computer(s) for accessing the Internet/intranet.

6. Administrative computer for log management and other issues.

7. Hardware write blocker. This is a hardware piece that connects the media that contains digital evidence (like HDD) to a forensic workstation; the purpose of this device is to prevent any modifications to the data on the evidence drive during the acquisition process.

8. Portable CD/DVD drive.

9. USB reader.

10. HDD and SSD enclosure with USB 3.0 interface.

11. SD card reader.

12. External hard drives and USB thumbs (USB 2.0 and USB 3.0) of different sizes.

13. Tape drives for long-term data archiving.

14. Data cables and connectors: Ethernet cables, RJ-45, BNC, modular adapters, ribbon cables, DIN split cables, VGA split cable, USB cables, audio cables, cable extenders, HDMI cables, FireWire (IEEE 1394), DVI cables, S video cables, DVI-to-DVI cables, serial cables, custom serial cables, SATA cables (mSATA and SATA Express), optical fiber cable, serial attached SCSI.

15. Other tools like screwdrivers, multimeter, flashlight.

Office electrical equipment

1. Uninterrupted power supply (UPS) for each workstation/server and networking device.

2. Projection device (in conference room).

3. Printer.

4. Scanner.

5. Photocopier.

6. Paper shredder.

7. Digital cameras, including video cameras, and accessories.

8. Telephone (preferably wireless).

9. Wi-Fi access point.

10. Headset.

11. Symmetrical power supply.

Networking devices

1. Router and switch device to connect forensic workstations with the storage server within the lab.

2. Internet network; should be separated from the lab's internal network. You need a firewall, a switch, and a router (the three components can be combined in one device).

3. Networking cables.

Please note, there should be an isolated network within the lab that connects forensic workstations and the storage server used to store digital evidence image copies. The server must be placed in the evidence room to restrict access to it. No Internet access is allowed for this lab-specific network.

Forensic examiners may need to research online for more information about their findings or to collaborate with peers, so an Internet connection should be available within the lab through a direct line to the intended computer(s) only.

Furniture and Consumable Materials

Forensics examiners will spend hours sitting at their workstations when investigating a digital evidence, so they must feel comfortable in their seat to remain productive. Use ergonomic chairs (which must be adjustable according to user needs) for forensic workstations; computer screens must also be of good quality as examiners will be staring at them for a long time. Computer monitor must be adjusted to be facing the examiner's head at least 20 inches away, and the top line of the screen should be at or below eye level to avoid possible health effects on the examiner such as neck and head pain, excessive fatigue, and eye strain.

Aside from the furniture, the digital forensic lab has administrative work, so the following general office consumables are also required in the lab:

Paper, pens and pencils, staples, toner cartridge, labels, envelopes, envelope sealer, folders, sheet protectors, suspension files, binders, clipboards and files, markers and highlighters, punches, staplers and staples (including electric), plastic static bags, nonelectronic whiteboards, notice boards and accessories, packaging material (e.g., cardboard boxes).

Evidence Container

Collected storage media that contain original digital evidence (like HDD, SSD, flash drive, SD cards, smartphone, tablets, CD/DVD) must be stored in a secure locked room within a safe closed cabinet. The cabinets in the evidence storage room must protect against fire and flood, and must withstand if the lab collapses as a result of an earthquake; the cabinet must also protect the contents from electromagnetic emanations to avoid damaging seized equipment. The entire room must be secured from general access using proper security methods that can be automatically recorded, like digital lock and keycard access. The evidence room must contain a log that must be signed by each one visiting the room detailing the visit's purpose and the date/time when the visit took place. This helps to maintain the chain of custody of seized evidence.

Forensic Workstation

The latest version of Windows OS (64-bit version) is recommended for the forensic workstations. The following Windows 10 editions are recommended because of their support for high-end hardware and intensive computing tasks:

- Pro for Workstations—very recommended.

- Windows 10 Enterprise.

Both editions support up to 6 TB RAM and four processors; however, compared with modern Windows Server editions (Windows Server 2016 Standard edition supports 24 TB of RAM memory), those two editions are less expensive in terms of the license, as they belong to the Windows desktop product line.

Now, let us discuss needed hardware for the forensic workstations. Obviously, when working with digital evidence, a powerful computer is needed to process and search within image files. Forensic computers require high levels of processing power and large amounts of RAM memory; they also need a lot of storage and many expansion slots to attach different types of devices. Building a forensic workstation is expensive; however, it is still considered a cost-effective solution for small companies compared to purchasing a ready-made computer forensic workstation, which costs much more.

The following are the recommended hardware specifications when building a basic forensic workstation from the ground up:

1. RAM memory: At least 24 GB (DDR4). More is great!

2. CPU: At least two physical CPUs (Intel i9 8th-generation processor has 10 cores and 20 threads) for each workstation.

3. Motherboard: One that can accommodate the required number of processors and amounts of RAM, along with the video controller card.

4. Hard drives: A combination of SSD and HDD—at least 512 GB of SSD and 4 TB of HDD.

5. Video controller: Nvidia Geforce, latest version is recommended with at least 8 GB of GDDR5X memory.

6. Triple burner (Blu-ray, DVD, CD).

7. External hard drive enclosure with USB 3.0 interface.

8. Write-protection: You can purchase this piece individually or you can purchase one that can be integrated into your workstation. The hardware write blocker must support data acquisitions from SATA, SAS, IDE, USB, FireWire, and PCIe storage devices. Some manufacturers include UltraBlock (https://digitalintelligence.com/products/ultrablock) and Tableau Forensic Universal Bridge, which can be integrated into your machine (www.guidancesoftware.com/tableau/hardware//t356789iu).

9. Advanced cooling system: It is preferred to use liquid CPU cooling system with—at least—dual fans.

10. LCD panel with high resolution (full HD IPS display), at least 22 inches for better display.

11. Ports

   • USB 3.0 ports

   • Thunderbolt 3

   • Microphone and headphone jack.

   • Integrated LAN controller to access the lab's LAN network.

These are the preferred hardware pieces for building a forensic workstation; please keep in mind that your lab needs to have at least one portable digital forensic laptop workstation for acquiring and performing some analysis on data outside the lab. For instance, it is preferable to purchase one forensic laptop from a vendor which specializes in offering such ready solutions.

Commercial Ready-Made Digital Forensic Workstation

There are many vendors who specialize in building ready-made forensic workstations; these workstations tend to be powerful in terms of processing power and storage and have integrated hardware equipment for digital forensic work like a hardware write blocker and a hard drive duplicator. The following are two vendors offering ready-made workstations:

1. Tri-Tech Forensics (`www.tritechforensics.com/Digital-Forensics/DF-workstations`). Prices begin from $5800 for the workstation and $2300 for the digital forensic laptop workstation.

2. Digital Intelligence (`https://digitalintelligence.com/store`).

Forensic Software

The type of forensic software needed for your lab will depend on your work scope; for instance, the type of operating system (Windows, Linux, or Mac) and the file system you are going to examine will determine your required forensic tools.

Most popular computer forensic suites are built for Windows OS; the open source counterpart is mainly geared toward Linux with some being also ported into Windows OS. Let us begin with the commercial tools.

Commercial Forensics Tools

Digital forensic software tends to be costly, so it is advisable to research well before purchasing a forensic suite. Ask other forensic examiners and try to install a trial copy of the software you are intending to purchase. The following are the most popular commercial computer forensic suites: check each web site for tool price/license.

1. EnCase (`www.guidancesoftware.com`)

2. Belkasoft Evidence Center (`https://belkasoft.com`)

3. FTK (`https://accessdata.com/products-services/forensic-toolkit-ftk`)

4. X-Ways Forensics (`www.x-ways.net/forensics`)

Free and Open Source Forensic Tools

There are many free and open source code digital forensics tools; a few come with rich features similar to the commercial suites, while the majority are small tools built to perform a specific function (e.g., retrieve browser history or extract e-mail header information). In this section, we will list the most popular free and open source digital forensic tools.

1. The Sleuth Kit (`www.sleuthkit.org`): Supports both Linux and Windows.

2. Autopsy: A graphical interface to The Sleuth Kit and other digital forensics tools (`www.sleuthkit.org/autopsy`).

3. dd for Windows (`www.chrysocome.net/dd`): A forensic imaging tool for Windows systems.

4. Magnet RAM Capture: Capture RAM memory (`www.magnetforensics.com/free-tool-magnet-ram-capture`).

5. Belkasoft Live RAM Capturer (`https://belkasoft.com/ram-capturer`).

6. Volatility: Analyzes RAM (volatile memory) images (`www.volatilityfoundation.org`).

7. Memoryze: Captures and analyzes memory images and on live systems. Can include the Windows Paging file in its analysis (`www.fireeye.com/services/freeware/memoryze.html`).

8. Mandiant Redline: Live memory analysis; includes Memoryze tool within it (`www.fireeye.com/services/freeware/redline.html`)

9. Bulk Extractor: Scan an acquired hard drive digital image and extract useful information from it such as e-mail addresses, credit card numbers, URLs, and other types of information (`http://downloads.digitalcorpora.org/downloads/bulk_extractor`).

10. Encrypted Disk Detector: Check for encrypted volumes on a computer system during incident response (`www.magnetforensics.com/free-tool-encrypted-disk-detector`).

Linux Distribution for Digital Forensics

These are specialized Linux distributions preconfigured for digital forensic works. They contain a live operating system—usually Linux based—which is bootable from a CD/DVD or a USB thumb drive and contains a plethora of tools for digital forensics.

1. CAINE (www.caine-live.net).

2. DEFT (www.deftlinux.net).

3. Helix3 Free version (https://e-fenseinc.sharefile.com/d/sda4309a624d48b88).

4. SANS Investigative Forensics Toolkit (SIFT) (http://digital-forensics.sans.org/community/downloads); Vmware appliance.

5. Santoku Linux for Mobile Forensics (https://santoku-linux.com).

6. Kali Linux Forensics Mode (www.kali.org/downloads).

Virtualization Technology

Virtualization technology allows examiners to install more than one operating system on the same workstation; this proves useful when conducting malware analysis (to avoid infecting the forensic workstation) or when testing forensic tools before using them officially. The virtual machine will run in a sandbox isolated entirely from its host machine's operating system. Popular virtual machines include VirtualBox (www.virtualbox.org) and Vmware Workstation Player (www.vmware.com/products/player/playerpro-evaluation.html).

Laboratory Information Management System (LIMS)

A content management system is needed in the lab to organize the reception, tracking, handling, and return of evidence in the digital forensic laboratory. You can use an open source content management system for this task: Drupal (www.drupal.org/home) and Moodle (https://moodle.org) are examples.

Other Software

During your analysis of the digital evidence, additional software will be needed like digital file metadata viewers, MS Office suite or the free alternative Open Office, compressed file (ZIP, RAR) extractor, data recovery tools, antivirus software for the Internet/intranet PCs, different operating systems including legacy OS like Windows XP and 2000, different file type viewers, and different programming languages (in order for some tools to work).

Tip!   During a digital forensic analysis, a lot of different tools will be used; your selection of tools will depend on how effective each tool for the task in hand. Sometimes, it is preferred to use two different tools to analyze the same piece of data if you are in doubt.

Validation and Verification of Forensics Hardware and Software

It is the responsibility of the digital forensic laboratory to determine whether a new technique, method, or hardware or software tool is suitable to use during the investigation process.

Forensics software/hardware is considered valid for use during an official trial if it has been used previously by a reputable scientific lab, law enforcement agency, educational institute/university, or the like. However, if a specific tool or methodology is new and not approved/used previously by such bodies, it is the responsibility of the lab to test it, validate its results, and finally document the finding before using it in evidence testing. A specific procedure must be in place to perform internal validation and verification of new tools and methodologies (including the in-house-developed tools and methods); each lab has its own rules to conduct this process.

Tip!   For small labs, it is advisable to reduce the hassle and opt to use externally ready validated tools.

To check the reliability of computer forensic tools, NIST has launched the Computer Forensic Tool Testing (CFTT) project (`www.nist.gov/itl/ssd/software-quality-group/computer-forensics-tool-testing-program-cftt`) to establish a methodology for testing computer forensic software tools. This project will effectively help examiners to select the best tools (both hardware and software) to conduct examination in addition to understanding the tools' capabilities based on the testing report published by NIST.

Lab Manager

The digital forensic lab must have a manager (also known as the technical supervisor) to ensure a smooth flow of work in the digital forensic lab and that the work done meets established quality standards. The following are the main duties of the lab manager:

1. Suggest work process for managing cases.

2. Support the most complex forensic analysis cases handled by the lab.

3. Ensure that lab staff are trained according to implemented quality standards.

4. Conduct annual check on lab personnel performance.

5. Support the technical development of junior digital forensics staff.

6. Enforce ethical standards among lab staff.

7. Create, monitor, and enforce lab policies and procedures for staff.

8. Oversee facility maintenance.

9. Oversee court testimony before presenting it officially.

10. Check lab software and hardware equipment and ensure that everything is functioning properly.

11. Procure lab consumable material needs.

12. Approve validation studies conducted on different forensics tools (both hardware and software) and give final approval to use them in the lab.

13. Research new methodologies and recommend new software and hardware tools to be used in the lab.

14. Handle—or supervise—the disposition of sensitive materials.

15. Suggest future expansion for the lab.

16. Represent the lab to clients and at specialized events such as conferences, seminars, and so on.

Secrecy Requirements

The identity of people working in the digital forensic lab must keep secret. The role of the forensic team is to find who is behind a criminal activity, and some crimes could be committed by terrorist groups or criminal organizations who will be willing to stop investigations of their activities in any way.

Lab Data Backup

Backing up is a way to protect your sensitive data when a failure happens to your computing device. It is essential to have at least three copies of your data (one offsite and one at lab) in a secure, safe location, and these must be protected with a strong password so you can retrieve your important data in the case of system failure, virus attack, or natural disaster. The backup should include the data on the forensic workstations and in main storage server – if you have one.

Windows offers a free backup feature (suitable for the forensic workstations) that can be accessed from Control Panel ➤ Backup and Restore (Windows 7). This utility will allow you to back up your Windows drive onto an external drive. The feature is available in Windows 7, 8, and 10. However, Windows versions 8 and 10 have another backup utility called File History, which can also be configured to back up your personal/work files to an external drive or network location.

Note!   File history backup-specific folders relate to the current Windows user account by default (e.g., desktop, contacts, OneDrive, and so on). To configure it to back up other folders or drives, you should use the File History app. Go to Settings ➤ Update and Security ➤ Backup and then click "More options" in the "Back up using File History" panel to include more locations in your backup.

If you prefer to use third-party backup software, here are two free options:

1. Comodo Backup (www.comodo.com/home/backup-online-storage/comodo-backup.php): This is a free backup solution that is easy for ordinary computer users; it walks you through a wizard and asks you exactly what you want to do. It can back up data to a local drive, optical media like a CD/DVD/BD disc, network folder, external drive, or FTP server; it can also be sent to a recipient over e-mail. The backup can be divided into pieces and protected with a password. Recovering data is easy and needs only a few clicks.

2. Cobian Backup (www.cobiansoft.com/cobianbackup.htm): This is a multithreaded program that can be used to schedule and back up your files and directories from their original locations to other directories/drives on the same computer or another computer in your network. FTP backup is also supported in both directions (download and upload). Cobian works silently in the background to check your backup schedule and perform the required tasks.

For the forensic storage server, which tends to be a high-end RAID server, a specialized program should be used to perform backup and restore from it.

Training Requirements

Lab staff must have adequate training to do their job. The following are the minimum training requirements for lab staff:

1. Computer hardware

2. Networking basics

3. General computer forensic knowledge (this book is adequate for this task!)

4. Forensic software specific training (e.g., FTK, EnCase)

5. Legal training covering digital crime laws implemented in different countries, search warrants, testifying in courts, and determining the effective jurisdiction law when investigating a case.

The field of digital forensics requires continual learning, research, and communicating with others in the field. As a digital forensic professional, you should have a general understanding about the latest technologies.

Lab Policies and Procedures

Lab polices and procedures define the internal rules that must be followed by lab workers during their work in the lab. The lab policy includes rules for the following work areas, and more may be needed:

1. Lab physical security policy (e.g., security measures that need to be followed to access the lab area).

2. Accessing top restricted area policy: Who is authorized to access the evidence storage room?

3. Handling digital evidence (e.g., a write blocker should be attached to the suspect hard drive when acquiring it).

4. Evidence seized at response scene.

5. Evidence analysis (e.g., steps and tools to handle each piece of evidence).

6. Evidence chain of custody (e.g., documenting who has accessed digital evidence since its arrival to the lab, and also when and why).

7. Evidence disposition (e.g., how sensitive materials should be disposed of securely: a paper shredder for paper files, destruction equipment to safely destroy [physically] hard drives and other storage media).

8. Digital forensic report writing (e.g., the standard layout for reporting case analysis results).

9. Expert testimony evaluation.

10. Backup policy.

11. Training polices.

12. Quality standards.

The lab has specific preprinted forms for each type of work conducted within it or in the field; for instance, the evidence acquisition form (which record descriptions of evidence) and the chain of custody form are the most two important forms used in labs. Other work stages will also have their own form that detail what happened during this stage.

Documentation

Adhering to policies and procedures mentioned in the previous section is important for smooth and accurate work in the digital forensic lab. Each piece of work during the investigation process needs to be supplemented by paper/electronic forms, and examiner notes are also very important and need to be documented in detail during the investigation process. This allows another examiner to continue working on the specified case and allows the lab's quality assurance staff to repeat the process again to ensure that the exact same results are produced every time.

Documentation is an integral part of digital forensic investigations; it begins in the field before obtaining the seized computing device and continues in the lab till reaching testimony. Litigation processes in the courts may span for months and years, and without this documentation, an examiner—who may be required to testify in court—may forget key facts from his/her case investigation, and this may result in weakening his/her testimony to the judge and jury.

Lab Accreditation Requirements

Accreditation ensures that your digital forensic lab is following a set of recognized standards imposed by the authoritative body. The accredited body will check your lab to see whether it is using reliable investigation methods, court-accepted hardware and software, and trained personnel, and if your lab's physical layout meets established standards.

The accreditation is very important for any digital forensics lab, and we are going to briefly discuss the steps needed for any organization to start the accreditation process.

There are five steps in the accreditation process.

Step 1: Self-Assessment

Conduct a self-assessment of your current or planned digital forensic lab by answering the following questions:

1. Why you want to get accredited? What are the advantages for obtaining an accreditation? Is the accreditation required to improve services offered? Or to gain new customers?

2. What is the appropriate standard to be accredited to (e.g., ISO 17025 or 17020)?

3. What accreditation body do you want to conduct your accreditation process through? The most popular accreditation body for digital forensic laboratories is the American Society of Crime Laboratory Directors (ASCLD). The ASCLD (`www.ascld.org`) offers guidance on managing a forensic lab and auditing lab functions and procedures.

Note!   Other accreditation bodies include the United Kingdom Accreditation Service (`www.ukas.com/sectors/forensic-science`) and the ANSI-ASQ National Accreditation Board (`www.anab.org/forensic-accreditation/iso-iec-17025-forensic-labs`).

---

4. What is your lab's work scope? For example, do you want to focus on mobile forensics, GPS forensics, or computer forensics? You need to decide which specific services you want to get accreditation for.

5. What are the current best industry practices that fall within your accreditation scope? Determine these in order to define the best investigation methodologies, software tools, and hardware equipment to propose for your lab's work.

6. Do you have support for accreditation from the organization's top management?

Step 2: Identifying the Current Level of Conformance to the Target Accreditation Standards

After answering the previous questions, conduct a self-assessment of your current organization's work to see how much it will cost to get accredited to the intended standard. You need to check the following:

1. Your current lab practices—if you already have them—and the methodologies and tools used within it. For example, list how you capture digital evidence, what tools you use to investigate it, and how you write the case's final report.

2. List people working in the lab along with their professional certifications in addition to any training programs they follow in the digital forensic domain.

3. Create a checklist of all quality requirements imposed by the accrediting body to achieve the accreditation.

Step 3: Closing the Gap

Bridge the gap between your lab's current practices and practices required by the accreditation standard. Identify weak areas that need to be improved. Prioritize your needs by fixing the most nonconforming services first. You can also achieve incremental accreditation by accrediting one service each year (e.g., accredit computer forensics in the first year and mobile forensics in the second year). You can also seek help from other accredited private labs and government organizations.

Step 4: Implementation

In this step, you need to train your lab staff to update their work to meet standards required by the accredited body.

Step 5: Conformance to Standards Documentation

Document conformance to the accreditation standard by updating the following practices:

1. Policies and procedures (e.g., the method used to capture digital evidence must be implemented according to the subject accredited standard).

2. Resources (e.g., software and hardware needed, certifications or training programs that must be followed by lab workers).

3. Performance.

Accreditation costs money and it is not mandatory for each digital forensic lab; however, acquiring accreditation will prove that your lab is following the quality standards issued by the accreditation body and will give additional credibility to your work.

Chapter Summary

A computer forensic laboratory is where you conduct your investigations, store your acquired digital evidence, and do much of your forensics work. Labs contain different sets of hardware and software tools that help examiners to acquire and analyze digital evidence and finally present their findings in a formal report.

In this chapter, we covered the essential equipment needed to create a digital forensic lab. We talked about the characteristics of the physical facility that is going to house the lab; we listed needed electrical equipment, lab furniture, and hardware devices related to digital investigation work; and we covered the minimum technical requirements of the forensic workstation responsible for analyzing digital evidence. We discussed the design and security requirements of the lab network, and then we talked about forensic software. There are different types of this: some are commercial while others are either closed source and free or open source.

It is recommended for the forensic software to be validated by a credible body before using it in investigation; in-house developed tools or ones that are not externally validated must undergo a verification process internally before being used officially in investigations.

Not only is the lab composed of hardware and software tools; the human aspect is the cornerstone of its work. Lab employees must have adequate skills to do their specified jobs, a set of policies and procedures that govern lab work must be strictly followed, and quality tests should be continually preformed to ensure the lab's conformance to predefined quality standards set by an official accredited body (e.g., the ASCLD) or its parent organization.

This chapter is the last one to discuss the prerequisites for initiating a digital crime investigation. In the next chapter, we will begin to talk about the investigation process to solve cybercrime, starting with the procedures that must be followed to obtain the digital evidence and secure the crime scene.

CHAPTER 4

Initial Response and First Responder Tasks

What you should do upon arriving to the crime scene

When an incident that involves digital evidence is reported, the entity (public agency or private laboratory) responsible for conducting the investigation will send one or more individuals to investigate the case; this person is called the "first responder," and he/she is responsible for conducting the initial investigation of the incident to determine its root cause.

The first responder can come from different backgrounds: he/she might be a network administrator, system administrator, law enforcement officer, or investigating officer. First responders have usually followed some form of official training in the digital forensic field.

The main role of the first responder is to identify, collect, preserve, and transport digital evidence to the forensic lab in addition to identifying the root cause of an incident. To do this correctly and legally, the first responder must be fully aware of the relevant legislation within the jurisdiction where he is going to investigate the incident.

From a technical perspective, the first responder must have a thorough understanding of digital forensics procedures; he/she should know how to acquire digital evidence in a forensically sound manner, so acquired evidence can be used in a court of law. A first responder needs to have appropriate IT knowledge covering different computing domains, and s/he should also understand how to deal with different IT equipment, so s/he can know where to look for digital evidence.

Before the first responder arrives at the crime scene, he/she needs to identify their work scope clearly to avoid missing any detail related to the subject case. The first responder's toolkit should be ready to be taken with him/her upon request: this toolkit—as we are going to see later—should contain the appropriate software and hardware tools

© Nihad A. Hassan 2019
N. A. Hassan, *Digital Forensics Basics*, https://doi.org/10.1007/978-1-4842-3838-7_4

to manage different scenarios that the first responder will face. For instance, the digital crime scene can be very complicated because it can contain different types of computing devices with different OS, servers, and network devices, and it can also span different geographical areas, even to cloud storage servers located in other jurisdictions.

The first thing a first responder needs to consider is how to understand exactly what is required from him/her in relation to the reported incident. The first responder needs to ask the reporting person/company some questions to determine the scope of work. The main questions include the following: Does the reporting body need to investigate the case officially so they can move it to court later? Or do they just want to confirm that an attack was made against their computerized systems and ensure that no further damage can happen? In many cases, the required task from the first responder is to investigate the root cause and type of attack and then work to return the systems to work as quickly as possible to avoid any business interruption.

Note!   The volume of digital data found at crime scene can become enormous these days, so the scope of investigation should be defined very well to avoid getting lost in the overload of data.

Before we begin talking about first responder tasks and challenges, we need to cover a key point in digital forensics investigations, which is the legal issue. Obtaining a search warrant or a consent to seize and investigate digital devices is a must for any type of investigation, as without such legal paper, the investigation can be considered unlawful and evidence acquired will not be admissible in a court of law.

Search and Seizure

Law enforcement officers need a search warrant to search and seize digital devices. In the United States, the Fourth Amendment limits the ability of government agents to search for and seize evidence without a warrant. Any evidence obtained in violation of the Fourth Amendment is inadmissible in a court of law.

The Fourth Amendment states:

The right of the people to be secure in their persons, houses, papers, and effects, against unreasonable searches and seizures, shall not be violated, and no Warrants shall issue, but upon probable cause, supported by Oath or affirmation, and particularly describing the place to be searched, and the persons or things to be seized.

The Fourth Amendment was created to limit US law enforcement's ability to search private premises without a proper search warrant. The search warrant should be very specific in terms of what areas can be searched and what items or persons can be seized from the crime scene.

This principle applies to digital crimes also; hence, any computing device which is capable of storing user data is considered private property that needs a search warrant in order to be searched and seized by law enforcement officials.

We will not delve deeply into the legal area; however, keep in mind that before collecting any digital evidence you need a form of legal consent to search or seize the evidence in question. In this section, we will list choices available for digital forensic examiners to search and seize digital evidence.

Consent to Search

In this type, the owner of the computing device cooperates with investigators and allows them to search and acquire digital evidence without an official search warrant. This usually happens when the owner of the device is not the suspect or when an employee has previously signed a search and seizure form as a condition for employment. In this case, you can acquire digital evidence without asking for any consent from him/her.

See Figure 4-1 for a sample "consent to search" digital device form created by Regional Computer Forensics laboratory (`www.rcfl.gov/san-diego/documents-forms/consent-to-search/view`).

CONSENT TO SEARCH MOBILE DEVICE/ COMPUTER
EQUIPMENT / ELECTRONIC DATA

I, _____, hereby authorize _____, who has identified him/herself as a law enforcement official, and any other person(s), including but not limited to a computer forensic examiner he/she may designate to assist him/her, to remove, take possession of and copy (image) and/or conduct a complete search of the following computer systems, electronic data storage devices, computer data storage diskettes or CD-ROMs, or any other electronic equipment capable of storing, retrieving and/or accessing data or necessary to assist in the accessing of said electronic data pertinent to their investigation, belonging to me. I understand that a complete search may include the recovery of deleted files, and the bypassing or cracking of passwords or encryption. This specific consent applies to the following items:

_____

_____

_____

I further authorize the law enforcement officer(s) / official(s) to copy and keep any documents, images, or data found on the computer equipment described above that are determined by the officer to be pertinent to the criminal investigation.

I give specific consent for the aforementioned official to have possession of said equipment for:

    ☐ a period of _____ business days

    ☐ an unlimited number of days

to make a forensic copy (image).

I further give specific consent for a forensic analysis of the copy (image) of the aforementioned equipment for:

    ☐ a period of_____ business days.

    ☐ an unlimited number of days

I give my specific consent freely and voluntarily without fear, threat, coercion or promises of any kind. I understand and acknowledge that I have an absolute right to refuse to give my consent and I hereby voluntarily waive this right.

I am also aware that if I wish to withdraw my consent at any time during the seizure and / or search of the equipment / data, it will be respected.

This specific consent is given by me this _____ day of _____, 20_____, at _____ am/pm.

Printed name: _____

Signature: _____   Witness name: _____

Address: _____   (LEO) Signature: _____

_____   Agency/Address: _____

Phone: _____

Figure 4-1. *Consent to search form created by RCFL (www.rcfl.gov/san-diego/ documents-forms/consent-to-search/view)*

Subpoena

When you do not have a permit from the device owner to search and seize digital equipment related to the case at hand, you can ask to have a court order or a permit. Special care should be taken when asking for such permission, as the suspect will have enough time to destroy digital evidence because s/he will know in advance your request for a court permit to search/seize the digital devices of interest.

Subpoena is usually used when it is unlikely that informing the device owner will result in destroying digital evidence. For example, many organizations (e.g., banks) require permission from the court before handling any information to investigators. This does not mean that these organizations are refusing to cooperate with investigators; rather, their applied policies and internal regulations prevent them from handing over such information without a proper court order.

Search Warrant

This is the most powerful search and seizure procedure; investigators use this when there is a high probability that informing the subject person (e.g., when he is the owner of the digital device or is involved with the suspect) will result in destroying digital evidence. A search warrant will be executed without prior notice to the suspect, so he cannot do anything to destroy or hide digital evidence.

Bear in mind that search warrants are only available to law enforcement officers; if you are an independent digital forensic investigator, you cannot request this permission from courts.

Courts usually do not give search warrants easily; investigators should have reasonable clues that a specific person and specific computing devices related to him in some way are a part of a criminal activity in order to be issued such a warrant.

We can differentiate between two types of search warrants:

1. Electronic storage device search warrant: This allows seizing digital storage devices like computers, flash drives, external hard drives, CD/DVD from suspect premises, and so on.

2. Service provider search warrant: If the suspect has committed his crime through the Internet, digital forensic investigators need to investigate this through external providers like the suspect ISP, cloud storage providers, and online merchants.

First Responder Toolkit

After obtaining the consent/search warrant paper, the first responder will head into the crime scene; it is advisable for the first responder to know as much about the incident and the crime scene as possible beforehand; this will allow him/her to prepare needed equipment and software before arriving at the crime scene.

In general, the following items must be present in a first responder's bag before investigating any crime scene that involves electronic evidence:

1. Crime scene tape.

2. Stick-on labels and ties.

3. Color marker pens.

4. Notepad.

5. Gloves.

6. Magnifying glass.

7. Flashlight.

8. Sealable bags of mixed size; should be antistatic bags to preserve evidence integrity.

9. Camera (can capture both video and images and must be configured to show the date/time when the capture happens).

10. Radio frequency-shielding material to prevent some types of seized devices (e.g., smartphones and tablets with SIM cards) from receiving calls or messages (also known as a Faraday shielding bag). This bag will also protect evidence against lightning strikes and electrostatic discharges.

11. Chain of custody forms.

12. Secure sanitized external hard drive to store image of any digital exhibits.

13. USB thumb drives (at least two).

14. USB hub.

15. Bootable CDs.

16. Network cables.

17. Different cables/connectors for computer.

18. Hardware write blocker.

19. RAM capturing tool.

20. Hard drive capture tool.

21. Forensics software to perform elementary analysis on the captured data if needed.

22. Power adapters of different sizes.

23. Multi protected power strip.

24. Specialized screwdrivers.

25. Standard pliers.

26. Wire cutters.

27. One laptop, in addition to portable forensic workstation.

28. VPN solution to protect the communications of the first responder.

29. Access to secure online repositories where more forensic tools are stored if needed at the crime scene.

30. Packing material.

It is also advisable for the first responder to carry a list of contacts for expert professionals with relevant experience in other computing domains like database, mobile, and networking, so s/he can seek their help in case s/he needs assistance during the initial investigation.

First Responder Tasks

After securing the crime scene and preventing unauthorized access, the first responder must follow general principles for the correct acquisition of digital devices holding the digital evidence. The following steps should be implemented in the correct order, considering the circumstances at the crime scene:

REMEMBER!

- As we already mentioned, an official search warrant or consent from the owner of the digital device must be available before the search/seizure of the suspect computing device.

- It is advisable to have a trained computer forensics examiner to acquire digital evidence from the suspect device to avoid leaving—or even destroying—any traces without investigation.

- Photograph the entire crime scene before searching and seizing any digital device.

- Safety is a key consideration when investigating a crime scene: the safety of the first responder's team and law enforcement officers and all people at the crime scene should be a top priority.

1. Upon arriving, if there was a surveillance camera, make sure to disconnect it before doing anything; you can also cover it if you cannot stop it instantly.

2. Sometimes, the computer might be destroying evidence (e.g., executing a specialized software to wipe clean hard drive and consequently destroy digital evidence). If you suspect something like that is happening (e.g., if the hard drive LED light is lighting continually and the fan is moving fast, then there is a high probability that read/write operations are being conducted on the drive), shut down the computer immediately. Do this by pulling the power cord (if the suspect computer is a laptop with nonremovable battery, press down and hold the power button till laptop is powered OFF. If the laptop has a removable battery, remove the battery first, then unplug the power cord).

3. If the computer is OFF, do not turn it ON. Just seize it in antistatic bag and transport it securely to the forensic lab.

4. If the computer is ON and there are no clues that a destruction program is working, do the following:

   a. If the computer screen shows a login window (password prompt), power off the device by removing the power cord from the wall (perform hard shutdown); you can also try to crack the device's password if necessary to obtain the volatile memory (more on this in the next chapter).

   b. If the computer screen is dark or showing a screen saver, move the mouse slowly, without pressing any buttons or rotating the mouse wheel, to show the screen.

   c. Photograph the computer screen to show running programs and opened files/folders, and to record system date/time.

   d. Acquire its volatile memory (RAM) using specialized tools, as we are going to see in the next chapter (acquiring RAM memory is also known as live memory dump). Capturing RAM memory is a key step before powering OFF the machine as it can contain a wealth of information like cryptographic keys, IM chat logs, unencrypted contents, clipboard contents, and process information, among other things.

   e. If the computer was attached to a networking device (router or switch), try to acquire its networking information first (IP address, open sessions, open ports, routing table, LAN addresses, broadcast address, and network interface card number). Some digital forensics experts argue that you should unplug the network cable to prevent any remote connection to the suspect device; however, this may destroy important evidence especially if the case was to investigate a network intrusion. Acquiring network information from the suspect computer (e.g., listing the active connections) can reveal other computers on the network which may possess evidence. Furthermore, the disconnecting target computer from the network may seriously impact business operations; for instance, disconnecting an e-mail server may bring great losses to the victim company. Handling a network computer should be done on a case-by-case basis; for instance, to stay safe, it is better to acquire networking information quickly. Then, if you see suspicious traffic through the network, you can disconnect the network cable to prevent unauthorized remote access. For servers that cannot get disconnected easily (e.g., Web and e-mail servers), you should conduct a risk assessment and seek expert knowledge.

f.   Perform a hard shutdown (unplug the power cord from the wall socket). If the device is a laptop, remove the battery first and then unplug the power cord. If you cannot remove the laptop battery, press down and hold the power button for 20 seconds to power it OFF.

g.   Finally, document all steps taken to seize the suspected computer device so it is available if someone asks for it later.

5.   When seizing a portable device with wireless communication capabilities, make sure to put it in an impermeable bag that can block wireless communications to the device.

HOW TO TURN-OFF SUSPECT COMPUTING DEVICE WHEN IT IS ON

When the suspect computing device is ON, you need to power it OFF before moving it to the forensic laboratory. From a digital forensic perspective, there are two methods to power off devices with varying consequences and effects on the target computing device. Select the one that best fits your needs, taking into account the following considerations.

1.   Hard shutdown (remove battery/power cord): This will preserve system files, prevent wiping programs from activating upon shutdown, and prevent changes to files' time stamps and other attributes. However, this method will remove unsaved open files and may corrupt system files and the user's open documents.

2.   Graceful shutdown (powering off the computer using the ordinary preferred way): The advantages of this method include discovering open files and programs upon shutting down and preventing any corruption to system files in addition to allowing running applications to write any artifacts to hard drive so

we can recover them later. The disadvantages include: launching destructive programs configured to run at shutdown, overwriting data on the hard drive, activating user-created scripts that can perform different tasks like removing system logs, clearing system pagefile (if the computer is configured to do so upon normal shutdown), and changing some attributes of files.

Note!   If the subject computer was running and you suspect there is an FDE implemented, make sure to acquire an HDD image before shutting down the computer.

Other important notes to consider when investigating the crime scene:

1. Identify any clues that can reflect suspect knowledge of computing technology; for example, if a suspect has a book about "digital steganography" on his/her bookshelf, you should suspect that this suspect may employ such techniques to hide incriminating data.

2. Photograph the area surrounding the suspect computer to show all devices that were connected to it (e.g., USB thumb drives, printer, scanner, USB camera, and microphone). You should also search for any handwritten notes around the computer or pasted on its screen; some people store their passwords on such notes, and finding a password in this way can save you a lot of effort if the suspect was using encryption to protect his data. Bear in mind that handwritten notes relative to the investigation should be documented in a similar way to any other digital evidence.

3. Physical evidence should not be compromised during crime scene documentation (e.g., use gloves when touching the suspect computing device to avoid destroying any existing fingerprints). The first responder should image the storage device (acquire digital forensic image) before sending it to the crime lab for DNA and fingerprint investigation.

4. If the crime scene contains advanced IT equipment that exceeds the first responder's expertise, s/he should seek advice/help from an investigator with greater expertise.

5. Do not move an electronic device while it is ON; this may damage/corrupt digital evidence within it.

Note!   Some digital media devices (like USB thumb drives) are designed to look like toys, pen, keys, jewelry, and so forth to conceal their true purpose. First responders performing digital media seizure must take note of this to avoid leaving important clues behind.

Order of Volatility

It is the job of the first responder to determine the order in which the digital evidence will be collected. They should begin with the most volatile and go to the least volatile. The following order is suggested by many digital forensic processes, beginning with the most volatile:

1. CPU, registers, and system cache.

2. Routing table, ARP cache, process table, kernel statistics.

3. RAM memory.

4. Temporary file systems.

5. Swap space or virtual memory (named "pagefile" in Windows OS). This is a file on the hard drive that extends the amount of RAM available to a computer.

6. Hard drive and/or other removable media storage.

7. Remote logging and monitoring data.

8. Physical configuration, network topology.

9. Backup data and printouts.

Remote data existing on networking devices (like proxy servers, routers, intrusion detection systems, and firewalls) will also have a volatility order. For instance, it is worth mentioning that network caches and remote logs can be volatile and should be acquired by the first responder if it is accessible and related to the case in hand.

Documenting the Digital Crime Scene

As a digital forensics investigator, you should keep in mind that approaching a crime scene with digital evidence is similar to a traditional crime scene; hence, you need to document the crime scene in detail using photos and notes. This will effectively help you avoid leaving any evidence behind and will aid you in preparing your final report and in remembering the crime scene when testifying in court later. The following key points should be documented clearly:

1. When you entered the crime scene, how long you stayed there, and with whom.

2. Name all people who accessed the crime scene and list each one's role. For example, who took photos of the crime scene? Who seized the computing device? At what time was the evidence obtained? Did you capture volatile memory (if the computing device was ON), and if so, by what method/tool?

3. The first responder must also document all items related to the case in hand that have been discovered at and acquired from the crime scene; each acquired item must be fully documented in a chain of custody form as we already described in Chapter 1.

4. Create a sketch of the crime scene showing where the digital devices were located in addition to any attached peripherals; the sketch can also include other details like computing device type and model number.

5. Photograph all areas of the crime scene; you can also use video for this purpose. Photography should be conducted twice, once upon entering the scene and the second before leaving (after seizing the digital device[s]).

6. Write notes describing everything related to the case at hand in detail; these notes will help you remember what you have seen at the crime scene when testifying in court later.

7. If the laws prohibit the first responder from searching and seizing some digital devices, he should mention this in the documentation of the crime scene.

As a final note, everything you see at the crime scene is worth documenting; an investigator should not leave the crime scene without documenting everything.

Packaging and Transporting Electronic Devices

After you have finished documenting the crime scene and you shut down the digital device (if it was ON), you are ready to package and transport it to the lab.

Start by unplugging the cables, but before doing this make sure to put a tag that contains a number on each cable and on the corresponding port on the computer. Finally, photograph the cables before unplugging them so you know later where each cable was attached. This will help investigators to reconstruct the system again in the lab if needed.

Begin the packaging process by putting a tape over the power switch, so the device will not power on accidentally while in transit, and then put the digital device in antistatic bags. Finally, put the acquired device(s) in a suitable evidence bag, seal it using tape, and record your name and date/time on it. The evidence bag must contain a panel that holds the following details about its contents:

1. Contents of the bag.

2. Names of investigators who:

   a. Seized the evidence.

   b. Photographed evidence and crime scene.

   c. Created the crime scene sketch diagram.

   d. Packaged the evidence in the bag.

3. Location where evidence was found and seized.

4. Suspect information and criminal record if applicable.

5. Date and time of seizure.

6. Passwords of seized devices (if available).

7. Any additional notes.

Note!   For digital devices that can receive network signals (like smartphones and other mobile communication devices), use a Faraday bag to prevent this.

Do not forget to seize the power adapters and cables of the acquired digital devices.

While transporting the electronic evidence bags, make sure to put them securely in the back seat of the car and tie them down to avoid exposing the bags to physical shock and vibration. The climate in the transportation vehicle should be dry, cool, and away from magnetic sources (e.g., speaker magnets, radio transmitters, and heated seats in cars) and dust. Do not leave the evidence bag exposed to high temperature or humidity because you may damage digital evidence within it. Finally, document the transportation of digital evidence in the chain of custody forms and make sure that these forms remain in a safe location while in transit, so all movement of digital evidence can be tracked back to maintain its integrity in a court of law.

Conducting Interview

Upon receiving a call from the reporting person/company about the subject incident, a first responder will have to ask questions to clarify the case s/he is going to investigate. In this section, we will put the most common questions that should be asked by the first responder before arriving at the crime scene and after arriving and talking with witnesses (e.g., site custodians and administrators) and possible suspects.

First Responder Questions When Contacted by a Client

When a client contacts the first responder to investigate an incident, the client should be asked the following initial questions by the first responder:

1.   What is the problem?

2.   If the client is a company, who is responsible for handling digital crime incidents in the target company?

3.   What is the location of the incident?

4. Under which jurisdiction (authority) will the evidence be searched and seized?

5. What types of computing devices are going to be seized at the crime scene?

6. What tasks are expected to be performed at the scene? For example, do we need to perform live memory capture/analysis? Have there been any networking devices involved in the incident that need to be searched and/or seized?

7. What type of Internet access does the target organization have?

8. What is the ISP name?

9. Has there been any offsite storage?

Witness Interview Questions

Different digital crimes require different interview questions; for instance, questioning witnesses and possible suspects about a child pornography incident is different from the questions asked when the incident is related to fraud or hacking.

Upon arriving at the crime scene, the first responder should take as much information as he can from the people who were available at the time when the incident took place. People who were at the crime scene should be questioned about the following:

1. What they saw, and also where and how.

2. The names of all people who were at the crime scene, in addition to their phone numbers, e-mail addresses, and roles/jobs in the target organization.

3. Their work account usernames and passwords (jurisdiction rules apply here).

4. Social profiles and IM chat screen names for all employee of interest.

5. Identity of any administrator/site manager who can identify devices and custodians at the crime scene.

6. The number, types, and models of devices involved in incident.

7. The type of digital data (e.g., e-mail, databases, images, documents, etc.) expected to be involved in the incident.

8. The type of operating system involved in the incident.

9. Whether any of the digital data owned by target organization is stored outside its premises (e.g., cloud storage, remote locations, etc.).

10. Identity of any contractors who have remote access ability to target the organization's network.

11. Whether data access restriction is in place.

12. Any suspicious about who may have conducted the attack (e.g., a disgruntled ex-employee).

After returning to the lab and analyzing the primary information collected, more questions can be prepared to ask the possible suspects/witnesses.

Witness Signature

Sometimes a witness signature is required to verify the information collected from the crime scene; this procedure is not applied in all jurisdictions, especially if the person collecting the digital evidence is a law enforcement officer. However, take this point into consideration where applicable.

Chapter Summary

The purpose of this chapter is to present the mission and services provided by the first responder for any investigation that involves digital evidence.

A first responder is the first person who appears at the crime scene: his main duty is to identify, collect, preserve, and transport digital evidence to the forensic lab following a predefined digital forensic methodology, so that acquired evidence is admissible in a court of law.

Before a first responder can search or seize any digital device from the crime scene, he needs to have a legal permit from the court or from the owner of the digital device; this permit is named a "consent to search" when it is voluntary or a "search warrant" when it is forced by the law. Without this legal paper, any acquired evidence is considered inadmissible in a court of law.

First responders can come from different work backgrounds: the majority are network or system administrators. However, they all must be trained in proper procedure in the digital forensics field and understand relevant enforced criminal law before searching or seizing any evidence.

The complexity of today's digital crime scene and the different types of computing and networking devices can make this work very challenging, and the first responder may need assistance from different professionals with more expertise.

Now that we understand the role of the first responder in digital investigation, it's time to begin learning how to collect digital evidence from computing devices, and this is what we are going to cover in the next chapter.

CHAPTER 5

Acquiring Digital Evidence

How to acquire volatile and nonvolatile memory

The main task of a computer forensics investigator is to acquire and analyze computing devices' memory images. In a nutshell, a memory image—widely known as a forensic image—is a static snapshot of all or part of the data on a computing devices' secondary storage (e.g., HDD, SSD), attached storage device (e.g., USB thumb drive, external hard drive, magnetic tape), or RAM memory (when performing live acquisition on running systems). We can think of this image as a container of data, where you can store individual files or the whole drive/live memory files in one image file.

A forensics image will contain the digital evidence that must be retrieved and analyzed in order to identify indications of security incidents, fraud, and other illegal practices that target information systems. Keep in mind that forensics images may be used in a court of law, so the tools and techniques used to acquire and analyze them should be legally accepted.

In this chapter, we will cover techniques and tools to create forensics images from both running systems (volatile memory, RAM) and hard drives (HDD, SSD, flash thumb, and any similar digital storage media), we will defer the discussion of how to analyze acquired images of deleted files and other interesting artifacts till the next chapter.

Let us begin by talking about the different file formats that a forensics image uses to store information.

© Nihad A. Hassan 2019
N. A. Hassan, *Digital Forensics Basics*, https://doi.org/10.1007/978-1-4842-3838-7_5

Forensic Image File Format

A forensic image can have different file formats; some are free and others are proprietary formats developed by the company behind the forensic software used to create the forensic image. The following are the main one used in the industry.

Raw Format

The most used file format, Raw format is a bit-by-bit copy of the raw data of the drive under investigation, and it can be used to image either the complete drive or a single volume (partition) within it. Raw file format's main advantages lie in its ability to ignore minor read errors from the source drive in addition to its fast data transfer. Raw format cannot store metadata within it; however, some applications store such metadata (e.g., hash value of the image file, drive serial number, etc.) in a separate file. Raw format is supported by most computer forensics software and it is the default file format for the output generated from the famous Linux/UNIX dd command. Raw format has several naming schema (extensions), such as 001, dd, dmg, raw, and img. The main shortcoming of Raw format is that it requires the same storage space as the source drive, because you cannot compress data when it is in Raw format and this could be a problem when acquiring large hard drives.

AFF

Advanced forensic format (AFF) is an open source extensible file format for forensics images; its source code can be freely integrated into other open source and propriety programs. AFF supports two compression algorithms: zlib and LZMA. You can also split the resulting forensic image file into multiple files. AFF supports encryption of drive images (beginning from AFF V2.0), so you can protect your acquired image with a password. AFF allows wide arrays of metadata info to be stored within the image file itself; this should effectively reduce the hassle and allow for one file that stores all information related to the acquired forensic image (e.g., a metadata file can contain the chain of evidence or audit trail). The last version is AFF4 while AFF3 and AFFLIBv3 have been deprecate and should not be used for new projects. The following computer forensics software supports newer versions of AFF: Sleuthkit, Autopsy, OSFMount, Xmount, FTK Imager, and FTK. AFF uses the ".afd" extension for segmented image files and ".afm" for AFF metadata.

Expert Witness (EnCase)

This is a propriety file format created by Guidance Software (now OpenText) for their famous product "EnCase Forensic," which is widely used by law enforcement in criminal investigations around the globe.

This file format can be used to store different types of digital evidence; it is compressible and searchable and the resultant image can be split into multiple files. Metadata can be associated with the same image file; however, the quantity and type of metadata are limited compared with the AFF file format.

The EnCase file format has the extension ". E01"; however, when EnCase captures hard drives, it will automatically divide the resultant image into a chunk of 640 MB. Because of this division of forensic image data, file extensions will change according to chunk number (e.g., first chuck extension ".e01," second chunk extension ".e02," etc.).[1]

Other File Formats

There are other less popular file formats for forensics images; these are proprietary formats used by some computer forensics suites (like Safeback by NTI, ILook Imager, and ProDiscover).

Forensics Image File Validation

Acquired forensics image files must be validated to ensure their authenticity; validation ensures that the acquired image is 100% identical to the source and that it has not been altered during the acquisition process. Hashing is the acceptable standard in the computer forensics industry to validate acquired forensics images. Hash value is considered as an electronic fingerprint of the resultant image file.

Most computer forensics software will automatically produce a hash value of the captured data upon completion; however, you can use third-party tools or the standard utility, available in modern Windows versions through PowerShell (we already covered how to do this in Chapter 2), to calculate the hash value of any piece of data.

---

[1]Forensicsware, "E01 (Encase Image File Format)," August 5, 2018. www.forensicsware.com/blog/e01-file-format.html

---

Note!   The current industry standard for hashing digital evidence is the MD5 algorithm.

Acquiring Volatile Memory (Live Acquisition)

Although it has not drawn much attention until recently, live acquisition has become an integral part of any digital investigation type. For instance, there are many types of digital artifacts which only reside on RAM memory, with nothing written to the hard drive to indicate its presence.

Data is considered volatile when it will be lost when a device is turned off or rebooted. Please note that such data will also get overwritten during normal computing device use (e.g., when closing a specific application on a PC, the reserved data space will disappear from RAM memory, allowing other applications to use its space for operation).

Capturing a live memory requires specialized software (and in some cases, hardware) tools. Analyzing volatile data forensic image contents also requires specialized software, as RAM does not store data in the same way as hard drives do. These two reasons make capturing and analyzing volatile memory more difficult than the traditional acquisition of hard drives.

Volatile memory is not only limited to computers; for example, networking devices like routers and switches can also have volatile data stored in their logs. The process of capturing data from volatile memory is known as dumping, and acquiring it differs according to each operating system type. In this book, we focus only on computers running Windows OS.

TYPES OF INFORMATION THAT CAN BE FOUND IN RAM MEMORY

The following are types of information that can be found in RAM memory:

1.   Cryptographic keys

2.   Processes running

3.   Executed console commands

4.   Clipboard contents

5. Network information

6. Decrypted contents

7. Registry hives

8. Text files and images

9. Deleted files

10. Web browsing logs

11. Open/active registry keys

12. Internet account passwords (e.g., e-mail, social media, and cloud storage)

13. Instant messages

14. Exploit-related information

15. Malware (rootkits and Trojan horses)

16. Evidence of activity not typically stored on the local hard disk

Acquiring volatile memory is similar to acquiring hard drive data; however, it uses different tools, because unlike hard drives, data are not stored in a structured way in the RAM memory.

Before we begin talking about how to capture RAM memory, let us first cover some concepts related to volatile memory that should be understood by any digital forensics examiner.

Virtual Memory (Swap Space)

Pagefile.sys (also called virtual memory) is a file created by Windows to compensate for the limited capacity of RAM memory. It usually resides in *C:\pagefile.sys* by default. Normally, Windows sets the initial virtual memory paging file equal to the amount of RAM you have installed; however, a user or system administrator can usually change its size. This feature works by allowing Windows to use machine hard drive space as memory when your machine RAM begins to fill up. Parts of RAM files are moved from it into the virtual memory to free up more space. Now when the operating system needs to process any of the files that are already sent to virtual memory, it cannot do this directly. It will therefore need to send additional files to virtual memory in order to free up more space in order to be able to retrieve the files it wants to process from virtual memory into RAM again. This process, called swapping or paging, is transparent to the user.

Acquiring virtual memory is a very important part of the forensic acquisition, as it can contain valuable information transferred from the RAM memory like user passwords, encryption keys, web browser activity, and other important artifacts. Some RAM capture tools can acquire virtual memory along with the RAM (e.g., FTK Imager).

The Challenges of Acquiring RAM Memory

Acquiring live memory will pose some challenges to the forensic examiners. The following are the main considerations that should be kept in mind when doing live acquisition.

Note!   Capturing a physical memory should be conducted only by a well-trained technician (or under his supervision if the first responder is doing the job); this technician should have the proper authorization from the appropriate government/ corporate authority before proceeding.

Windows Is Locked

In Chapter 4, we mentioned that if we come across a running computer with a login screen (locked computer), it is advisable to perform a hard shutdown. However, some experts argue that we can bypass the Windows login page with no reboot by using some tools/techniques to avoid losing RAM contents:

1. Use CaptureGUARD and Phantom Probe hardware accessories (www.windowsscope.com) to access live memory and encrypted disks without needing a password.

2. Perform a direct memory access (DMA) attack to extract the password from RAM to log in to the system.

Always keep in mind that using such techniques will leave traces in RAM memory and may not be successful in some cases, so make a risk assessment to decide whether forensic live acquisition is worth the effort, and always consult a professional examiner when you are in doubt.

USING DMA TO UNLOCK LOCKED COMPUTERS

DMA is a method of computer systems that allows some hardware components to interact directly with the computer's physical memory (RAM) and transfer data to/from it without processing it first using the computer CPU. This technique is used to speed up processing time and to increase computer throughput, as the data will be transferred directly from RAM memory without processing it first in the CPU.

This technique can be exploited by computer forensics to access sensitive data on the target machine, bypassing all OS security mechanisms and any lock screen and antivirus software. The scenario works as follows:

A digital forensics examiner will connect his/her device (mobile forensic workstation), which has special cracking software to the suspect machine, and the cracking software will search the suspect PC's RAM memory for interesting artifacts like cryptographic keys, passwords, or decrypted files.

In order for this method to work, the suspect PC should have ports that support DMA. Such ports include: FireWire, Thunderbolt, PCMCIA, PCI, PCI-X, and PCI Express. USB ports do not support the DMA feature.

Administrative Privileges

Most software tools used to capture RAM memory need administrative privileges in order to work. If you come across a running PC with limited user permission (e.g., user account) you can then use a hardware acquisition tool (needs a small driver to be installed on the target machine) or perform a DMA attack to acquire RAM memory.

Capturing Tool Footprint

The capturing tool used to acquire the RAM memory will leave traces on the suspect machine. Computer forensic software vendors claim that their tools will leave a very small footprint on the acquired system; this means some data may be overwritten as a result of acquiring live memory. Hardware acquisition tools will also need a small driver to be installed on the target machine in order to work. These changes should be well documented in the investigation's final report to avoid making your evidence inadmissible in a court of law. Live acquisition will usually make the following modifications to any Windows machine:

1. Registry changes

2. Memory entries (overwrite data in RAM)

3. May write a very small amount of data to a disk drive

Courts are usually forgiving with small footprints left by RAM capturing tools; however, make sure to document each interaction with the suspect computer while capturing RAM memory in your final report, and also make sure to use legally accepted tools to perform the job.

Now, we will begin our practice on creating RAM memory dumps using different imaging tools, beginning with a simple, portable utility created by MoonSols called DumpIt.

Capturing RAM Using the DumpIt Tool

DumpIt is a tiny portable tool for acquiring RAM memory for computers running Windows OS (32 or 64 bit). To use this tool, follow these steps:

1. Go to https://my.comae.io/login and register for a free account first in order to proceed to the download section.

2. Put the tool on a USB drive (if you plan to execute the tool from within a USB drive); keep in mind that this USB drive will hold target computer RAM memory, so make sure it is large enough to hold the file that is created. For example, if you want to capture an 8-GB RAM memory, your USB drive should have 9 GB of free space.

Warning!   A USB drive—and any other portable storage media—used to store the acquired forensic image must be sanitized (wiped clean) first before using it.

---

3. Double-click the DumpIt tool to launch it and type "y" to confirm that you want to have a copy of the target computer's (Windows) RAM memory (see Figure 5-1). The captured RAM file will be stored in the same location where DumpIt resides. Note that the captured image is bigger than the acquired RAM (in this case, we're capturing a PC with 8 GB of RAM; the image size is about 8.269 GB).

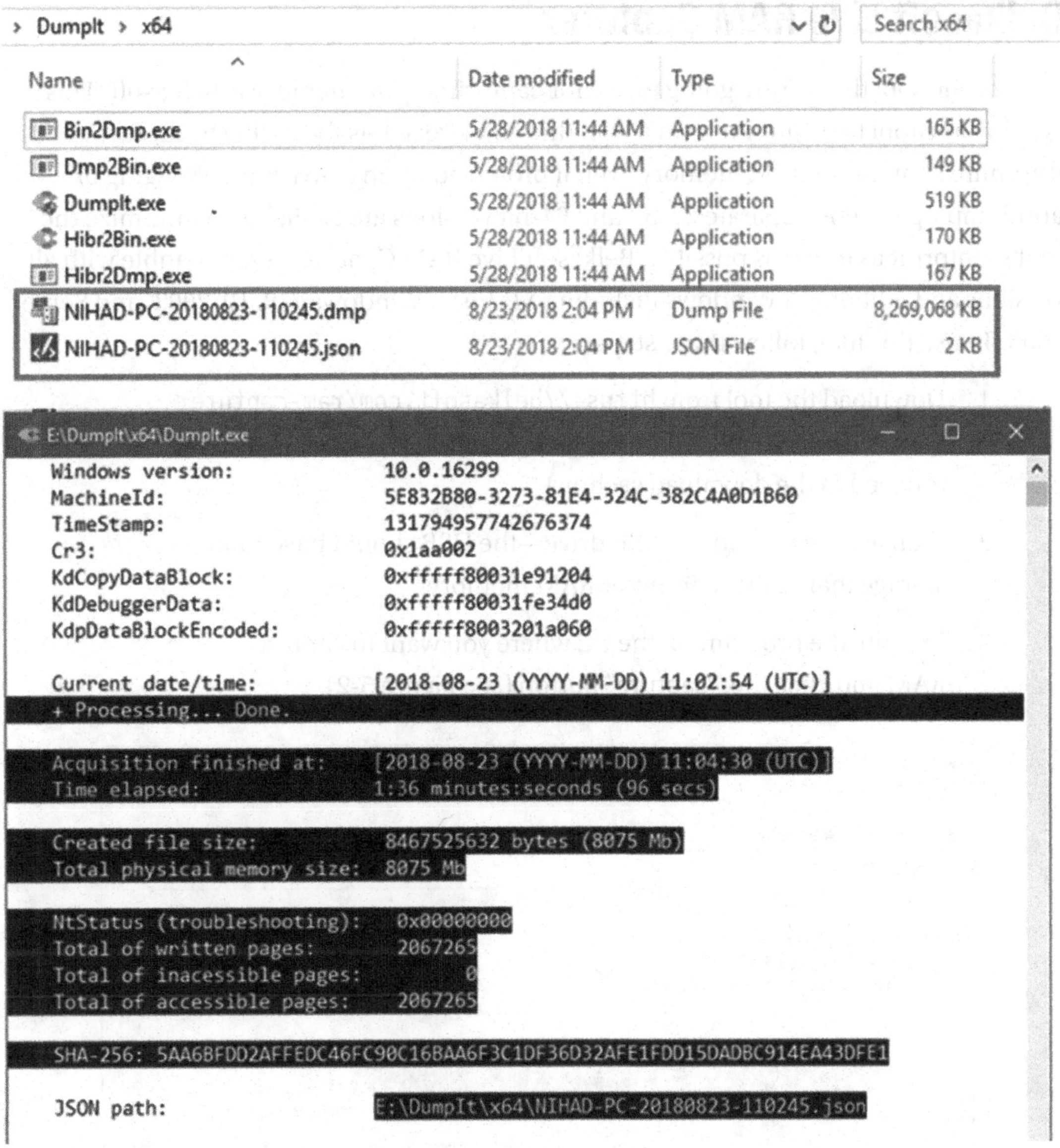

Figure 5-1. *Using the DumpIt tool to make a copy of RAM memory of the current device; the captured image has a .dmp extension*

As we note from Figure 5-1, DumpIt produces two files after finishing the acquisition: a file with the DMP extension, which holds the RAM image, and a file with the JSON extension, which contains important technical information about the captured machine like machineInfo (architectureType, machineName, maxPhysicalMemory, username), osVersion, and serviceInfo.

Belkasoft Live RAM Capturer

The second tool that we are going to use for capturing RAM memory is Belkasoft. This is a tiny free tool that can run from a USB thumb drive; it has the ability to capture the entire contents of RAM memory even if protected by an active antidebugging or antidumping system. Separate 32-bit and 64-bit versions are available to minimize the tool's footprint as much as possible. Belkasoft Live RAM Capturer is compatible with all versions and editions of Windows including XP, Vista, Windows 7, 8, 10, 2003, and Server 2008. To use this tool, follow these steps:

1. Download the tool from `https://belkasoft.com/ram-capturer`
    (you will need to fill out a simple registration form first in order to
    proceed to the download section).

2. Transfer the tool onto a USB drive—the USB should have more
    storage than target computer RAM memory.

3. Execute the program on the PC where you want to capture its
    RAM and click the "Capture" button (see Figure 5-2).

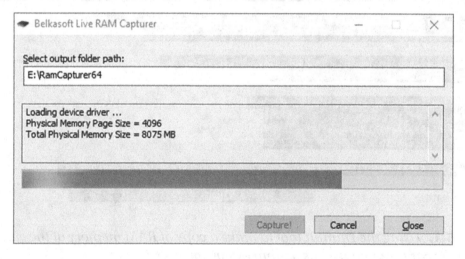

Figure 5-2. *Capturing RAM memory using the Belkasoft tool; the captured image has **.mem** extension*

Capture RAM with Magnet

Magnet, another portable tool for RAM capture, it claims its small footprint on the target machine and supports nearly all Windows OS versions: Windows XP, Vista, 7, 8, 10, 2003, 2008, and 2012 (32 and 64 bit). Using this tool is quite simple; go to `www.magnetforensics.com/free-tool-magnet-ram-capture/` and fill out a small form, and the download link will appear.

Put the tool in your USB thumb drive and attach the USB to the target machine; now execute the tool and select where you want to store the resulting RAM image. Finally, click the "Start" button to begin the capturing process (see Figure 5-3).

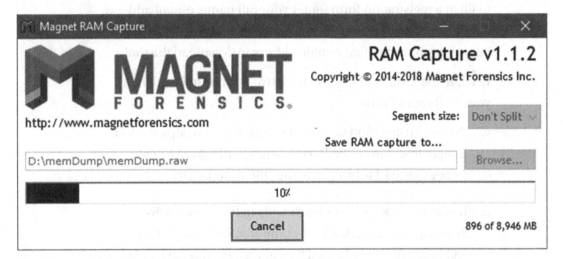

Figure 5-3. Dumping RAM memory using "magnet RAM capture"

Capture RAM with FTK Imager

FTK Imager is a data preview and imaging tool; it is used to create forensic images of target computer data without making any changes to the original evidence. By using this tool, you can create forensic images of local hard drives, floppy diskettes, zip disks, CDs, DVDs, entire folders, or individual files from various places within the media. FTK Imager can also be used to perform jobs other than acquiring images, like the following:

1. Mounting an image for read-only,

2. Previewing the contents of forensics images,

3. Exporting files/folders from forensics images,

4. Acquiring Windows registry,

5. Recovering deleted files.

The tool can be either installed locally on where it will be used or run from within a USB thumb drive connected to a machine in the field (the latter is preferred when conducting live forensics on running systems).

Before we begin using this tool, we will demonstrate how to install it on a portable media device (e.g., USB thumb drive):

1. Go to `https://accessdata.com/product-download` and select which version of "FTK Imager" you want to download. You need to fill in a registration form (enter your full name, e-mail address, and job title, among other details); after that, a download link will be sent to your specified e-mail address to download the tool.

2. Execute the installer. Now you have two options to install it on your USB thumb drive:

    a. Run the installation on a local computer, then copy the FTK Imager folder from the **[Drive Letter]:\Program Files\ AccessData\FTK Imager** to the USB thumb drive.

    b. Install the FTK Imager files directly to the thumb drive, avoiding installing to a local computer first. The installer will unzip the downloaded files to the portable drive; after then, that USB can be connected to any computer running a Windows OS, and the program file (FTK Imager.exe) can be executed from the portable USB device.

To use this tool for RAM capture, do the following:

1. Launch FTK Imager from the USB thumb drive (if you select to install it on a USB as we already demonstrated). Navigate to File ➤ Capture Memory. A new window appears showing options for capturing the RAM memory of the current machine (see Figure 5-4).

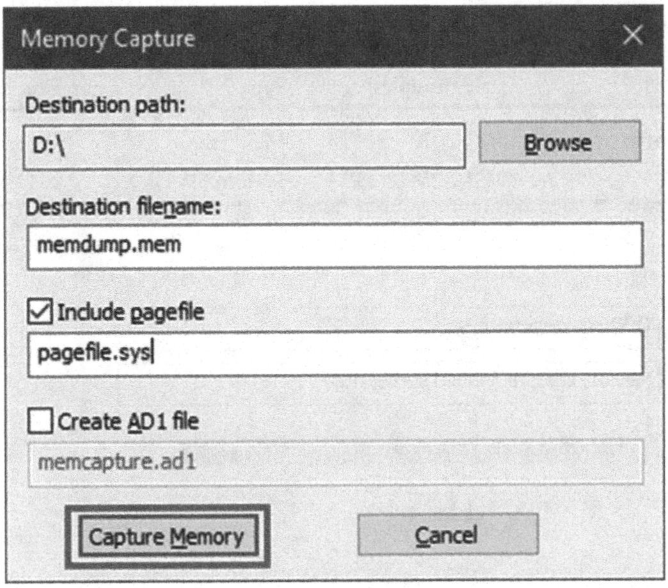

Figure 5-4. *Capture RAM memory using FTK Imager*

2. The opened window will prompt the user to select the destination where s/he wants to store the resulting RAM image; you can also select whether you want to include the *pagefile* (pagefile.sys). When everything is set, click the "Capture Memory" button.

3. Now, the capture will begin and a progress bar will appear showing the capture progress. Once the capture is complete, the open window will announce whether or not the memory dump completed successfully.

Browse to the folder where you saved the memory dump. You should find two files, memdump.mem (or whatever you named it) and pagefile.sys, if you select to acquire it (see Figure 5-5). These two files contain the entire contents of RAM memory when the dump was processed.

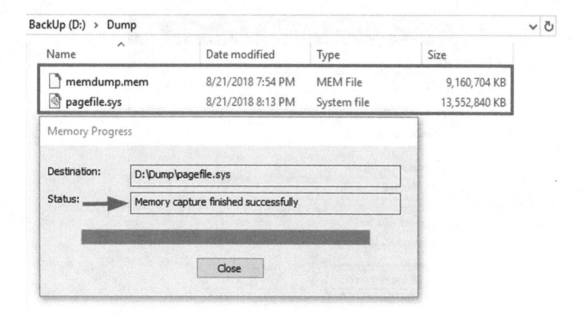

Figure 5-5. *RAM and pagefile.sys (virtual memory) dump acquired by FTK Imager*

In this section, we've demonstrated how to capture a volatile memory (Windows RAM) using four well-known free programs. The captured RAM image can be further analyzed to extract important information like passwords, temporary Internet files, deleted files, and other important artifacts, as we are going to see in the next chapter. In the coming section, we will continue our discussion of forensic image acquisition and cover how to acquire hard drives and related digital storage media images.

Acquiring Nonvolatile Memory (Static Acquisition)

As we have already discussed in Chapter 2, nonvolatile memory includes all storage media that can retain data for long time, even after power is turned off. The main types include hard drive and flash memory (thumb drive).

Capturing hard drive images is considered the main part of any computer forensic investigation, as most data that may contain inculpatory or exculpatory evidence will most probably be residing there. In this section, we will cover how to acquire a hard drive image in a forensically sound manner to be used in a court of law.

There are many tools that can be used to acquire hard drive images in Windows OS: FTK Imager, Pro Discover, EnCase, and X-Ways Forensics all offer such capability.

Note that before acquiring the hard drive image, you need to write-protect the suspect hard drive before attaching it to your forensic workstation. Write-protection can be done using hardware tools or software programs. Many investigators prefer to boot from CD/DVD using a Linux forensic distribution that is preconfigured to disallow automatic disk mounting like CAINE (www.caine-live.net) and DEFT (www.deftlinux.net), and then attach a suspect drive without any danger of manipulating it with data from external sources. If you are using a Windows OS for your forensic workstation and you want to know how to write-protect your investigated hard drive to safely acquire its image, check the author's guide at www.darknessgate.com/computer-forensic/computer-forensic-prerequisites/windows-os-write-protection-with-usb-devices.

Tip!   A hardware write blocker is preferred over the software solutions.

Hard Drive Acquisition Methods

There are different static acquisition methods to use during investigations. Before deciding which one to go with, you need to consider the following factors:

1. Size of the source (suspect) drive. (acquiring large-capacity hard drives requires large storage units to hold the resultant forensic image and can be time consuming during analysis).

2. Timeframe available to conduct the acquisition (if time is limited, you cannot spend hours on acquiring the entire hard drives of suspect computer[s]).

3. Can you take the suspect digital media (e.g., hard drive) with you to the lab or should you perform the acquisition at the crime scene?

4. Can you shut down the target machine in order to acquire its drive data or is this impossible due to various considerations (e.g., shutting down e-mail server may bring significant business loss)?

After considering these and other factors, you can select the acquisition method that best suits the case at hand. The following are the three main acquisition methods of forensics images.

Physical Acquisition

Also known as a bit-stream image, in this method, we create a bit-by-bit/sector-by-sector copy of a hard drive. File system metadata, deleted files, fragments of deleted files, and unallocated space will also get captured using this method. The resulting image will be a complete duplication of the source (the exact copy); in other words, if we are making a forensics image of a 500-GB hard drive, the resulting image will be exactly 500 GB, unless compression is used during the acquisition process.

Bit-stream images can be read by any computer forensics software, and as we insisted before, you need to attach the suspect hard drive that you want to image to a hardware write blocker, so that the forensic workstation used to acquire the image will not write any data to the suspect hard drive during the acquisition process.

We can differentiate between two types of physical acquisition, according to where the captured data is stored:

1. Bit-stream disk-to-image file: Captured data is stored in an image file. This is the most used method in investigation. It allows you to create an exact bit-by-bit replication of the source drive and store it in an image file. The main advantage of this method is that you can create many copies of a suspect drive while maintaining the original media untouched.

2. Bit-stream disk-to-disk: In this method, we are copying data (bit by bit) from the source drive to a newer drive which has the same storage capacity or slightly more. This method is not widely used, but you still need it in some circumstances, for example, when acquiring an old HDD. There are some computer forensics tools (e.g., EnCase and X-Ways forensics) that can adjust the new hard disk (destination) drive geometry so that the captured data will have the exact same location of the source (suspect) disk drive.

Logical Acquisition

In this method, we are capturing only a selected set of active data. By "active data," we mean the data present in front of us when dealing with our computing device. Unallocated space, file system data, and deleted and partially erased files will not get captured using this method; nor will hidden data or all unused space. For example, performing a logical capture of a 500-GB drive that has only 100 GB of active data will result in imaging only the 100 GB.

Logical acquisition is feasible when the target (suspect) drive is too large (e.g., RAID storage) and the first responder does not have time to make a full volume (physical) acquisition onsite. It is also feasible when we want to perform selected acquisition of a specific file(s) (e.g., acquire e-mail files only from the target machine or when we want to capture all photo files existing on a suspect drive).

Logical acquisition could be the only feasible solution when dealing with some types of civil litigation (e-discovery). You can also use search terms to search for a specified keyword(s) within huge datasets and then acquire the results only.

WHAT IS A RAID SYSTEM?

Redundant array of independent (formerly "inexpensive") disks (RAID) is a computer configuration (virtualization technology) that allows multiple physical hard drives (two or more) to work in parallel as if they were one logical unit. Major computer forensics suites (e.g., AccessData FTK, ProDiscover, EnCase, X-Ways forensics) can acquire RAID systems.

Sparse Acquisition

This method is similar to logical acquisition, as it captures only specific files which are related to the investigated case; however, in sparse acquisition, deleted data and fragments thereof are also acquired during the capturing process. This method is commonly used when performing static acquisition on RAID systems or on one for which the suspect was not tech savvy enough to have employed advanced antiforensic techniques.

Warning!   Forensic disk imaging is different from disk backup; do not use backup software to image suspect hard drives.

Now that we know the different methods of hard drive acquisition, it's time to begin acquiring hard drive images. There are many types of software that can perform hard drive acquisition; however, we cannot cover them all in this book, so we will opt to use a free reliable tool, FTK Imager.

Warning!   The destination HDD should be forensically clean (completely wiped) before using it to store the acquired forensics image(s). An example of such a wiping tool is Moo0 Anti-Recovery (`www.moo0.com/software/AntiRecovery`)

Using FTK Imager to Capture Hard Drive

We have already used this tool to capture RAM memory; capturing hard drive with it is similar.

1. If you did not download and install the tool yet, go to this chapter's section titled "Capture RAM with FTK Imager" and read the relevant instructions.

2. Launch AccessData FTK Imager and go to File ➤ Create Disk Image...

3. A new window appears (see Figure 5-6); here you will need to select the source evidence type. You have five options:

   • Physical Drive: This is the most commonly used option. A physical drive will allow you to capture all data (bit by bit) on a hard drive; unallocated space and deleted files will get captured too.

   • Logical Drive: Select a specific partition within a drive to capture; for example, capture the D:\ drive only.

   • Image File: Here you can select an image file as a source.

   • Contents of a Folder: Select a folder as a source.

   • Fernico Device: Restore forensics images from multiple sources (multiple CD/DVDs).

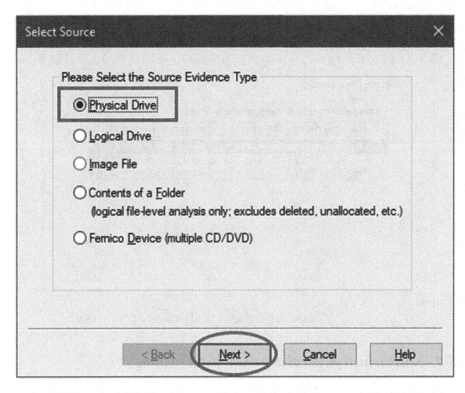

Figure 5-6. *FTK Imager "Select Source" window allows you to select the type of acquisition you want to perform*

4. Select "Physical Drive" and click the "Next" button; you will go to the window to choose which physical drive you want to image (see Figure 5-7). In our case, we want to capture an image for \\.\ PHYSICALDRIVE2.

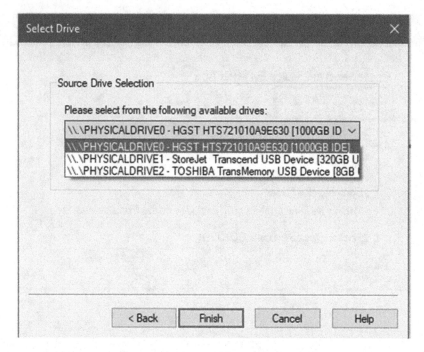

Figure 5-7. *Select which physical drive you want to image*

5. Click the "Finish" button to move to the next window; here you
    will be asked where you want to save the drive image. Click the
    "Add" button and a new dialog will appear asking you to choose
    the image format (see Figure 5-8).

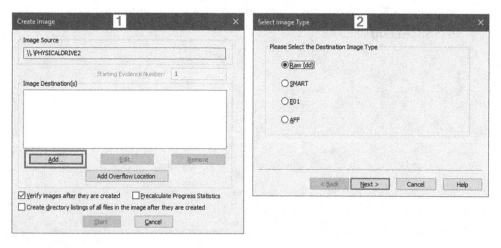

Figure 5-8. *FTK Imager "Create Image" window allows you to select image
location and image type*

6. In our case, we will select "Raw (dd)"; click the "Next" button
    and a new window will appear asking you to enter evidence
    information, which includes case number, evidence number,
    unique description, examiner, and notes. All fields are optional
    (see Figure 5-9). Click "Next" to continue.

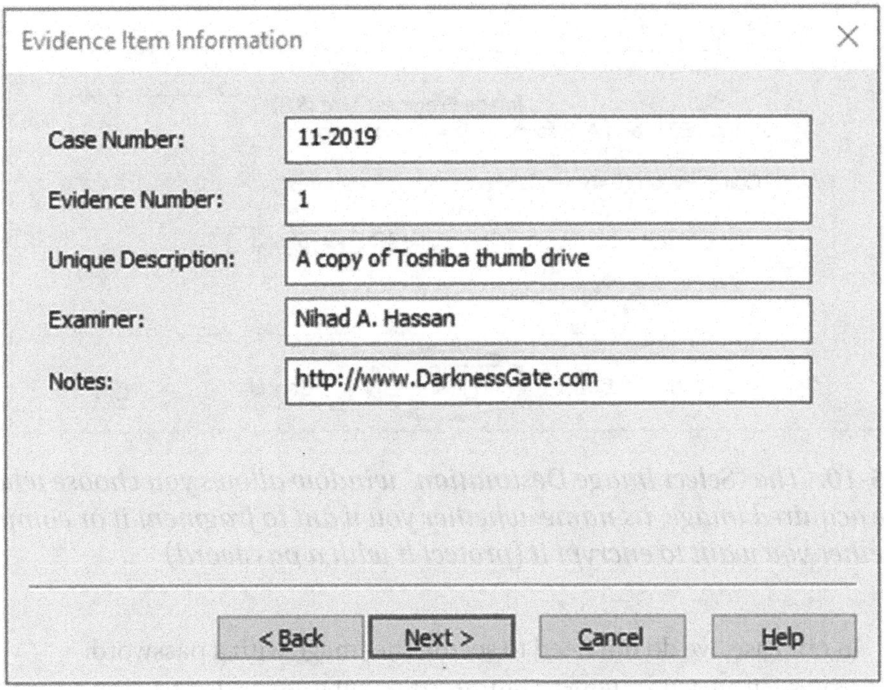

Figure 5-9. Enter evidence item information in FTK Imager

7. The next window will allow you to select where you want to store
    this image; you can also specify the file name to use and whether
    or not you want to split the image up into multiple fragments
    (fragment size is measured in megabytes). Remember that you
    cannot split a forensic image that has a Raw file format. If you
    want to secure the image with a password, tick the option "Use AD
    Encryption" and enter a password twice after clicking the "Finish"
    button. FTK Imager uses AES-256 encryption algorithm to secure
    the image (see Figure 5-10).

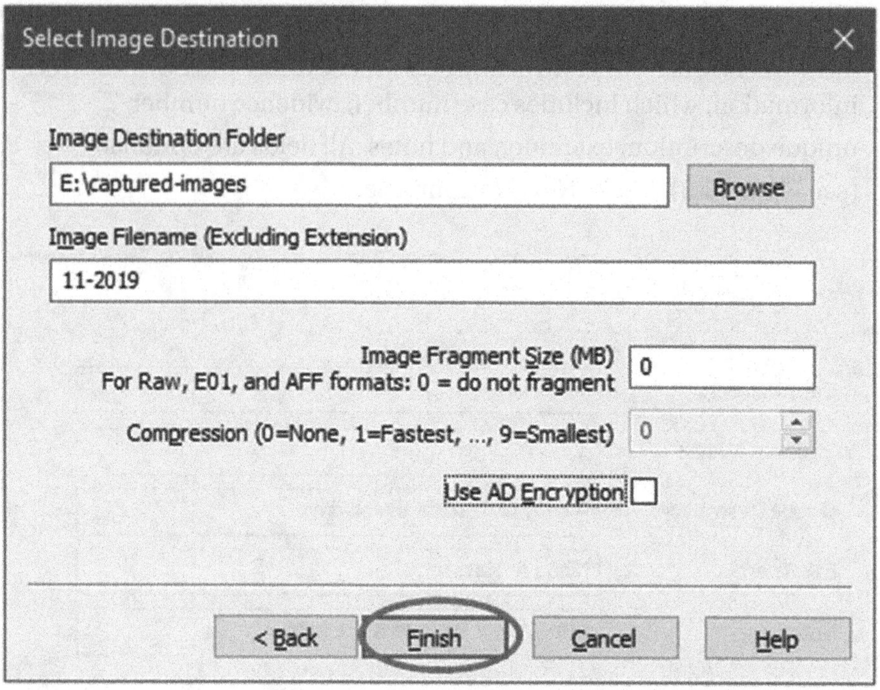

Figure 5-10. *The "Select Image Destination" window allows you choose where to store the acquired image, its name, whether you want to fragment it or compress it, and whether you want to encrypt it (protect it with a password)*

8.   In our case, we do not need to secure the image with a password, so we will click the "Finish" button. This will bring us back to the original "Create Image" screen with the "Start" button enabled (see Figure 5-11).

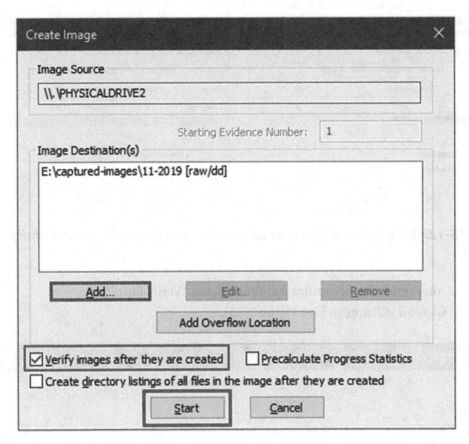

Figure 5-11. *FTK Imager "Create Image" window ready to start the acquisition process*

9. Make sure the option "Verify images after they are created" is checked so that you can ensure that the source drive and the resultant image are 100% equal. Now, after everything is settled, press the "Start" button to begin the acquisition process.

10. A window with a progress bar will appear showing you the acquisition progress. Once the image has been created, the verification process begins (see Figure 5-12).

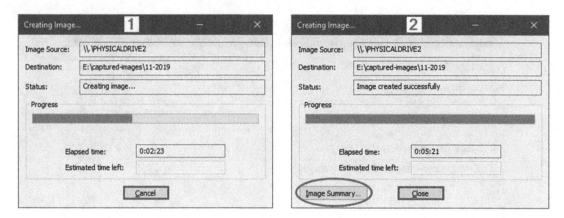

Figure 5-12. *Image acquisition is underway (left) until finishing successfully (right)*

11.   After finishing the verification process, the "Verify Results" window will appear (see Figure 5-13).

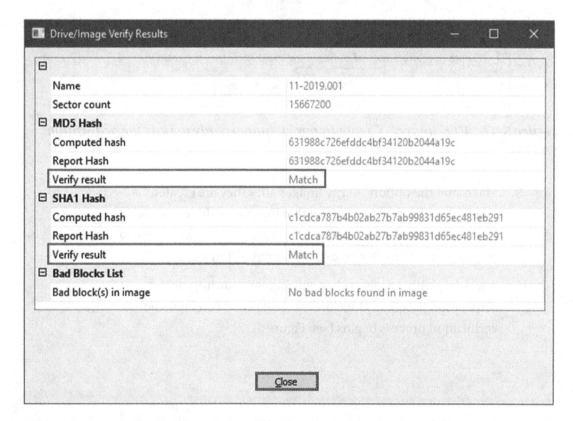

Figure 5-13. *Verify Results window: Hash value of the captured data is identical to the resultant image file hash value*

Go to the folder where you choose to store the acquired image. There, you should find two files (see Figure 5-14): the image file and the associated metadata file (text file). FTK Imager has created a separate metadata file for the image because we selected to store the image in Raw format. If we select another file format (e.g., **.e01** file format), we will have only one file, namely, the image file, and the metadata will be associated with it.

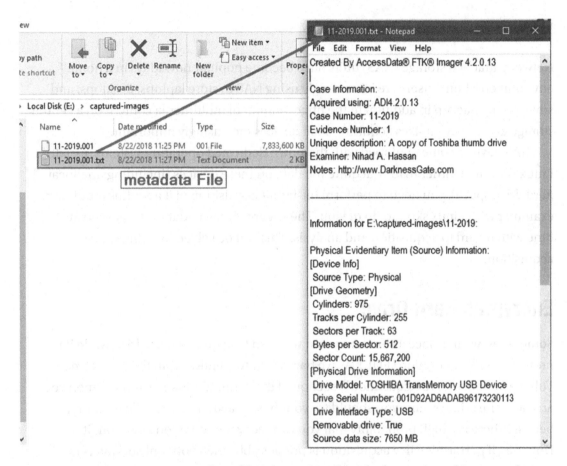

Figure 5-14. *Separate metadata file is associated with the captured image when using the Raw file format for acquiring the image file*

Hard Drive Imaging Risks and Challenges

In Chapter 1, we have listed the obstacles that can frustrate—and even stop—digital forensic examiners while acquiring digital evidence. In this section, we will describe in some detail the most common obstacles faced by forensic examiners when acquiring digital evidence from various locations.

Acquiring hard drive images is not always a straightforward task, as we have already demonstrated; sometimes problems may arise that frustrate the examiner or make the acquisition process more difficult and time consuming. In this section, we will list the most common challenges that investigators may face when conducting forensic image acquisition.

NAS

Network attached storage (NAS) units have become popular nowadays in a home environment; home users are increasingly using NAS to store laptops, desktops, and smartphone backup in addition to the huge amount of multimedia content on a central storage device. This makes acquiring such devices increasingly important.

NAS devices come equipped with their own dedicated operating systems, usually a Linux variant. In order to fully acquire the data on these devices (including unallocated hard drive space), you need to perform bit-by-bit acquisition of it and thus require an examiner with Linux skills to do the job. The sheer volume of data will also consume time with regard to acquisition and analysis. This can be solved by using sparse acquisition.

Encrypted Hard Drive

Sometimes, we may face a situation when we need to acquire a hard drive while it is protected with encryption (FDE). As we have already mentioned in the "Acquiring Volatile Memory (Live Acquisition)" section, if the computer is still running upon your arrival at the crime scene, you should try your best to acquire its volatile memory, because there is a high probability that you can recover encryption keys from it. However, if performing live acquisition is not possible, then your only option is to acquire the encrypted hard drive and after that try to decrypt it using the appropriate tools (you cannot guarantee successful password using such tools) or simply ask for the password from the hard drive owner if possible.

Corrupted or Physically Damaged Hard Drive

If there is physical damage to the suspect hard drive, you will not be able to acquire its data unless it gets fixed first by a hardware technician. There are many specialized companies that can recover data forensically from damaged hard drives; advanced police labs can also do this job. However, keep in mind that whatever the damage to the suspect hard drive, you should not abandon it; make sure to take it to a professional technician, because there is a chance that the data on it can be recovered.

Cloud Data Acquisition

The advent of cloud computing in recent years has changed the way many IT services are created, delivered, accessed, and managed. For instance, corporations and individuals are increasingly using cloud services to simplify the sharing of data and reduce IT infrastructure costs. According to Gartner, by 2020 IT spending on cloud service will exceed $1 trillion. This clearly shows where a great portion of digital investigations will need to take place in the near future.[2]

The nature of cloud computing architecture makes traditional digital forensics practice impracticable in a cloud environment. The dynamic nature of cloud computing and its wide dependence on virtualization technology in addition to the distribution of cloud computing components (e.g., servers, networks, applications, and services) across different geographical areas will bring serious legal (multiple jurisdictions), technical (e.g., tools needed to acquire digital evidence), and logistics challenges to forensic examiners.

Network Acquisition

Network forensics have similar challenges to cloud forensics; for instance, e-crime, which involves using networked computers, is increasing rapidly. As a forensic examiner, you can expect to face the following challenges when working on criminal cases involving the use of computer networks.

1. You will usually need to acquire and analyze large volume of data (e.g., acquisitions of redundant array of independent disks [RAID], which involves two or more hard drives).

2. You will need technical skills, as the evidence can be spread across different device types in the target network.

---

[2]Gartner, "Gartner Says by 2020 'Cloud Shift' Will Affect More Than $1 Trillion in IT Spending," August 24, 2018. www.gartner.com/newsroom/id/3384720

3. There will be organizational issues imposed by the corporations which request the investigation; for example, you cannot stop a specific service because it is crucial for the business.

4. The presence of multiple jurisdictions may pose challenges; for instance, there have been times when a storage server resided in Europe, while the investigation—or the breach—took place in New York. How you will handle this legally? Other legal issues arise when different jurisdictions impose different privacy regulations; for instance, in a network breach, private information (e.g., about customers, partners, or employees) may be exposed to the examiner, and such data could be protected by different privacy regulations.

Forensic Tool Limitations

Some forensics acquisition software cannot copy or access data in HPA and DCO; these two places may hold incriminating data and must be acquired for analysis. Always consult the acquisition tool documentation for such ability: if the tool lacks this capability, it is advisable to use a hardware acquisition tool instead.

Warning!   Some acquisition tools cannot acquire bad sectors from an HDD. Bad sectors should be captured, as they can store incriminating information hidden in this way. Always consult a professional examiner and tool documentation for this issue. Using the Raw file format may result in not acquiring bad sectors from a suspect HDD, and this should be taken into consideration also.

Other Challenges

Other challenges when acquiring digital evidence include steganography (data hiding), covert channels, antiforensics techniques, and attacking the forensics tools themselves. We will cover these issues in more detail in Chapter 9.

Chapter Summary

The main task during any digital forensics investigation is to capture a computer memory image. There are different methods to acquire digital images: the most common one is a bit-stream image where all data in the suspect drive—including deleted files, fragments of deleted files, and unallocated space—is copied into a forensic image file that can be analyzed later for digital evidence.

We can differentiate between two main types of image acquisitions:

1. Volatile memory (live acquisition): Here we capture RAM memory and other volatile data like network information.

2. Nonvolatile memory (static acquisition): Here we capture HDD, SSD, flash thumb, and other similar digital storage media.

Acquired forensics images must be validated to ensure their integrity; a hash value is used to ensure that an acquired image is 100% identical to the source and that it has not been altered during the acquisition process.

It is advisable to create multiple replications of the acquired image file; in this way you will preserve the original media untouched while having multiple images to work on safely in case something goes wrong (e.g., image modified accidentally) during the analysis phase.

We thoroughly covered how to capture a RAM memory using four tools, and discuss the various considerations and challenges associated with this process. Hard drive acquisition methods are covered thoroughly and we demonstrate how to capture an HDD using the famous tool FTK Imager.

Now that we have acquired a suspect hard drive and RAM memory image, it's time to begin the analysis process, and this is what we are going to cover in the next chapter.

CHAPTER 6

Analyzing Digital Evidence

Analyzing forensic image file contents

In the previous chapter, we've covered how to capture/create a forensic image of both RAM and hard drive memories. Now, we are ready to move on to the next part of forensic work, which is analyzing acquired images for interesting leads.

All analysis work should be conducted on the forensics image only; forensic examiners should not interfere with the original suspect device to avoid damaging original evidence accidentally and thus making the entire investigation useless in a court of law.

Analyzing Hard Drive Forensic Images

The hard drive is the premier form of data storage used in a computer system: the majority of computer users' and corporations' data is stored on it. When a hard drive becomes a part of a legal investigation, it should be legally acquired, as we saw in the previous chapter, and analyzed for information that can help in solving the subject incident.

Hard drives today are large and usually contain a massive volume of data; it is the role of the forensic examiner to investigate this data and connect the dots to solve a crime or to understand what happened during an incident.

In this chapter, we will learn how to mount and analyze acquired hard drive forensics images using different tools, focusing on the open source and free tools.

141

© Nihad A. Hassan 2019
N. A. Hassan, *Digital Forensics Basics*, https://doi.org/10.1007/978-1-4842-3838-7_6

Arsenal Image Mounter

Arsenal Image Mounter is a free, open source program. It can mount a forensic image as complete disks in Windows (real SCSI disks), allowing investigators to browse image contents as if they were browsing any directory of files. While the free version can mount any forensic image, the paid one supports more rich features.

This tool supports forensic images in Raw and EnCase file format, and it also supports all file systems used by the Windows OS like NTFS and FAT32.

Using this tool is very simple: go to `https://arsenalrecon.com/` and download the program to your PC. Arsenal Image Mounter is a portable program, so just execute the program and then click the "Mount Image" button in the main program window to select the image file; now, the tool will ask you for mount options (see Figure 6-1). Check the first option, "Read only," and then press the "OK" button.

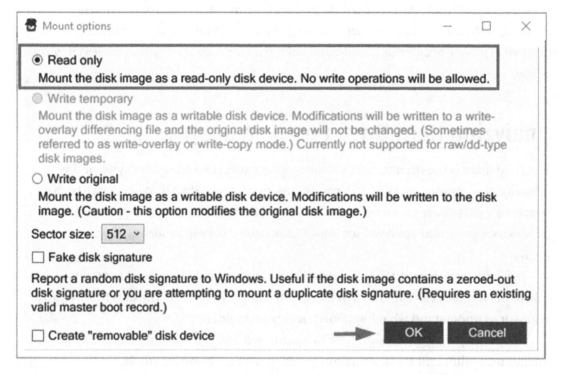

Figure 6-1. *Image mount options: use "Read only" to avoid writing data to suspect image*

Now, the forensic image will get mounted (see Figure 6-2) as a virtual drive in
Windows (you can access it from Windows file explorer) as if it were a local drive.

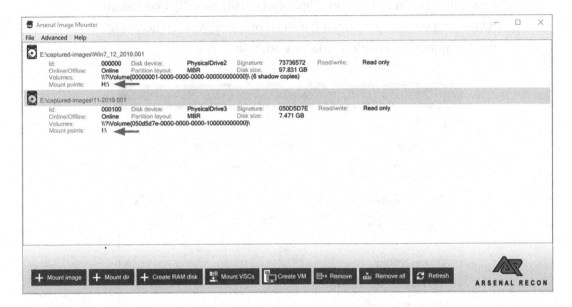

Figure 6-2. *Two forensic images mounted using Arsenal Image Mounter: you can
access them using Windows File Explorer*

OSFMount

This is another program for mounting the forensic drive image as local Windows drives;
OSFMount supports mounting images of CDs in .ISO format. It also supports the
creation of RAM disks (a disk mounted into RAM). Supported image file formats include,
among others, AFF, Raw, split Raw, and EnCase.

To use this program, follow these steps:

1. Go to `www.osforensics.com/tools/mount-disk-images.html`
   and download the tool that corresponds to your current Windows
   version (32 or 64 bits).

2. Install the program as you do with any Windows program.

3. When the program successfully launches, click the "Mount new" button; a new dialog will then appear where you can select the image file and set other mount options (see Figure 6-3). OSFMount will mount the image by default as read only and you can access it from Windows File Explorer like any other local drive.

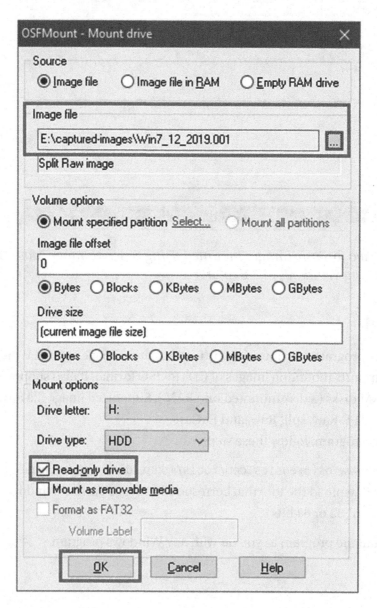

Figure 6-3. *OSFMount "Mount drive" options*

Autopsy

Autopsy is a graphical user interface (GUI) program that allows easy access to the command-line tools and the C library included in the Sleuth Kit and other digital forensics tools. The tools included in the Sleuth Kit—and other digital forensics tools—will allow Autopsy to automate much of the forensics analysis tasks required in most investigations, such as recovering deleted files, analyzing Windows registry, investigating e-mail messages, investigating unallocated disk space, and many more. Autopsy provides additional features that help examiners to be more productive during their analysis work.

In this section, we will describe the main features of Autopsy and demonstrate how to create a case, add a forensic image to it, and conduct basic forensic analysis on this image. Autopsy is a robust forensic platform used by thousands of users around the world; it has active support from a volunteer community in addition to commercial support for paid users. Autopsy features can be extended with customized modules (Autopsy names them "ingest modules") that can be developed using Python (Jython) or Java programming language. Covering all Autopsy functions in detail will require more than a chapter; however, this section will give you everything you need to know to start using this powerful tool efficiently to investigate your cases.

Launching the Wizard and Creating Your First Case

Before we launch the Autopsy wizard, we need to download and install it first on our forensic workstation.

1. Go to `https://sleuthkit.org/autopsy/download.php` and download the version that matches your forensic workstation operating system (Autopsy is supported on Windows, Linux, and OS X).

2. Install Autopsy as you do with any Windows application (assuming you are installing it on Windows OS)

3. And you are ready to go!

Now, it's time to create our first case in Autopsy. Follow these steps:

4.   The first time you launch Autopsy, the wizard appears (see Figure 6-4); click the "New Case" button to begin the wizard. A case is a container that holds information related to one investigation. Each case must have at least one forensic image associated with it; however, you can add more images to the case when needed. Always make sure that each case holds information about one investigation only, and all acquired images related to this investigation should be attached to this case only.

Figure 6-4. *Autopsy welcome window appears after launching the program: the current Autopsy version is 4.8.0*

5. The next window, entitled "New Case Information," appears; here
    you need to enter "Case Name" and the location (directory) where
    you want to save case database files (see Figure 6-5). After filling
    this info, click "Next" to continue.

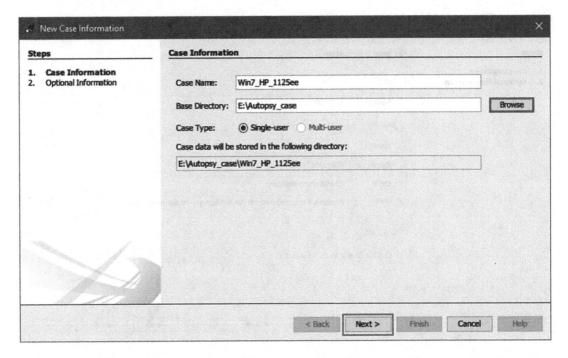

Figure 6-5. *Enter case name and base directory where case files are stored*

6. The next window allows you to enter additional information about
    the case, like number and examiner info (name, phone, e-mail,
    notes). This is optional information; discard or supply the info and
    then press the "Finish" button (see Figure 6-6).

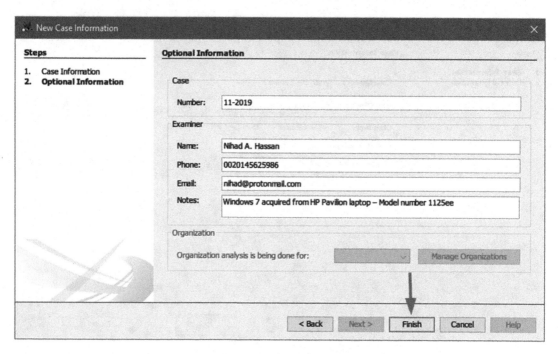

Figure 6-6. *Enter additional optional case information*

7. Now, Autopsy will create a case database and store it in your
    specified location. Then the wizard will display the "Add Data
    Source" window, where you can add an acquired forensic image
    that you are going to investigate/analyze. Select "Disk Image or
    VM File" and then click "Next" to continue (see Figure 6-7).

AUTOPSY DATA SOURCE TYPES

Autopsy supports the following data source types:

1. Disk image (the most used option)—an acquired disk or hard drive image.

2. Local disk—Like local hard drive and storage attached to the current system like USB thumb drive.

3. Logical files—Like single files or folders.

4. Unallocated space image file—Autopsy will search within the unallocated space of an image file for deleted files.

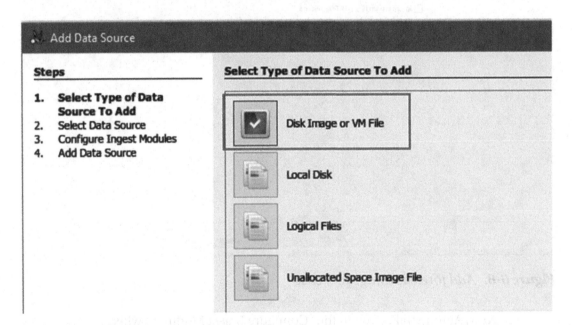

Figure 6-7. *Select "Disk Image" as a data source*

8. In the next window, you need to add the forensic image file,
    click the "Browse" button, navigate to the directory on your
    computer/network drive where the image is stored, and select it
    (see Figure 6-8). You can change the time zone of the image if the
    examiner—the one who acquires the image—resides in a different
    time zone. Leave other options as they are and click "Next" to
    continue.

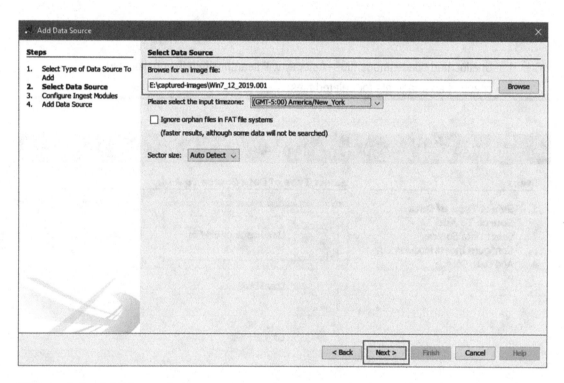

Figure 6-8. *Add forensic image to a case*

9. Now, Autopsy takes you to the "Configure Ingest Modules," where
    you can set the options for forensic image analysis. Each module
    is responsible for one forensic analysis task (see Figure 6-9). This
    step will be covered in some detail.

Note!   Autopsy supports Raw and EnCase "E01" file format for supplied disk image files.

Autopsy is an automated forensic program; hence, when adding a forensic image to it, Autopsy will automatically extract the most common information used in digital forensic analysis from this image without needing to do this manually. Autopsy provides default ingest modules for analyzing a provided data source (e.g., forensic image); it is up to you to select/deselect any module during the case creation wizard. As we've already mentioned, each ingest module is specialized in analyzing one type of data in the provided data source.

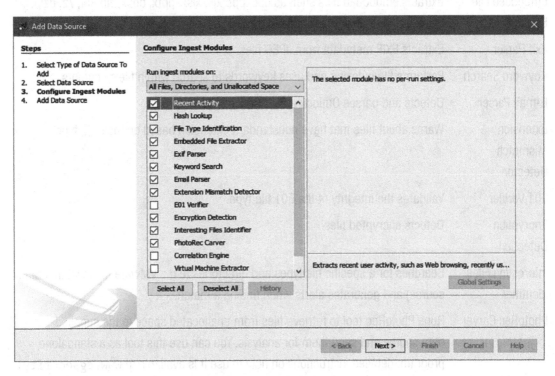

Figure 6-9.   *"Configure Ingest Modules" window*

Currently, we are using Autopsy version 4.8.0, which has the following default ingest modules available during the case creation wizard (see Table 6-1):

Table 6-1. *Autopsy Default Ingest Modules (Version 4.8.0)*

Module Name	Function
Recent Activity	Extracts recent user activity, such as web browsing and recently opened documents and installed programs. This module supports Windows OS only.
Hash Lookup	Identifies known and notable files using supplied hash sets, such as the NSRL hash set. A premade index of NSRL releases (`www.nist.gov`) can be downloaded from `https://sourceforge.net/projects/autopsy/files/NSRL/`.
File Type Identification	Matches file types based on their signatures (not extension) and reports them based on MIME type.
Embedded File Extractor	Extracts embedded files such as doc, ppt, xls, xlsx, pptx, docx, zip, tar, 7z, gzip, bzip2, arj) and analyzes their contents.
Exif Parser	Extracts EXIF metadata from JPEG files.
Keyword Search	Performs file indexing and uses keywords to search within file's contents.
E-mail Parser	Detects and parses Outlook and Thunderbird e-mails.
Extension Mismatch Detector	Warns about files that have nonstandard extension based on their file type.
E01 Verifier	Validates the integrity of the E01 file type.
Encryption Detection	Detects encrypted files.
Interesting Files Identifier	Searches for a specific file types and directories (e.g., VMware files within a data source) and generates alerts when finding a match.
PhotoRec Carver	Runs PhotoRec tool to retrieve files from unallocated space in the supplied data source and send them for analysis. You can use this tool as a standalone program; detailed instructions on how to use it is available at `www.cgsecurity.org/wiki/PhotoRec_Step_By_Step`.
Correlation Engine	Saves properties to the central repository for later correlation.
Virtual Machine Extractor	Extracts virtual machine files and adds them to a case as data sources.
Android Analyzer	Extracts and views Android system and other third-party application data.

How Long Should It Take to Finish the Data Source Analysis Process?

The size of the acquired forensic image under investigation and the number/type of ingest module you select during the initial case creation will determine how long it will take to finish analyzing image contents. Sometimes, analyzing image contents may take too long, especially if you are using a computer with low hardware specifications.

For now, let us return to "Configure Ingest Module." Check the modules you want to use to analyze image contents. For instance, if you are unaware of the needed modules, you can select all, but this may take too much time if the forensic image is big. Click "Next" to continue.

1. Autopsy will now add the specified forensic image into the case (see Figure 6-10).

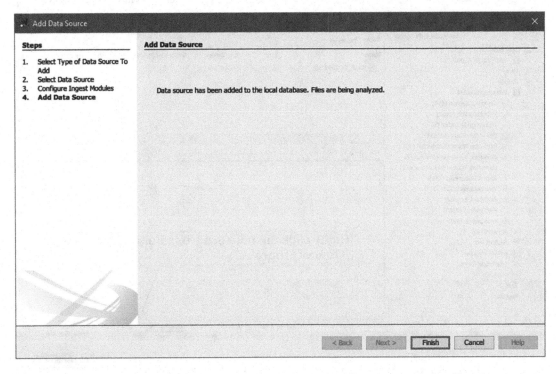

Figure 6-10. *Image added successfully to the case; the ingest process begins to analyze image contents*

2. Click "Finish" to close the wizard.

Now, Autopsy will begin analyzing the contents of the forensic image; we can show the progress of image analysis in the bottom right corner of the Autopsy main window. While working, you can see the results appear gradually on the left side of the window (Data Explorer pane).

If you want to cancel the analysis process at any time before completion, right-click the blue progress bar in the main window and then click "Cancel Process" (see Figure 6-11). Autopsy will issue a prompt window asking you to confirm. Click "Yes." A second prompt will appear asking if you want to cancel only the currently running ingest module operation or the entire module; in our case, we want to cancel all modules and begin the process again.

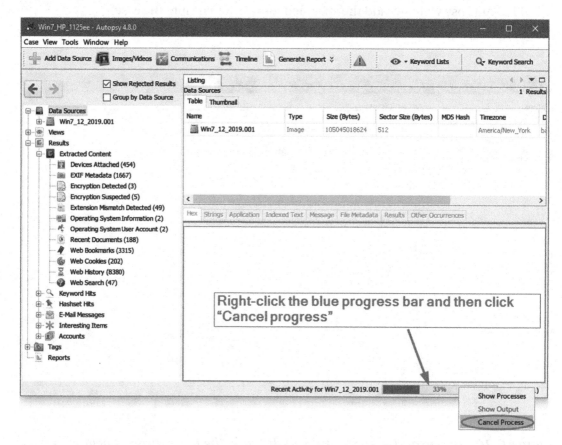

Figure 6-11. *Canceling Autopsy's current analysis process*

The cancellation can be beneficial for a first-time user of Autopsy for many reasons; for example, a beginner user of Autopsy may opt to select all default ingest modules when creating his/her case for the first time. As we already mentioned, if we select all ingest modules and the forensic image file was big, Autopsy will need a considerable amount of time to finish analyzing image contents. Here comes the benefit of canceling the process and reinitiating the analysis, as we will see in the following steps:

1. After successfully canceling the analysis process of the current case, go to Autopsy Data Explorer, right-click over the image you want to process, and then click "Run Ingest Modules" (see Figure 6-12).

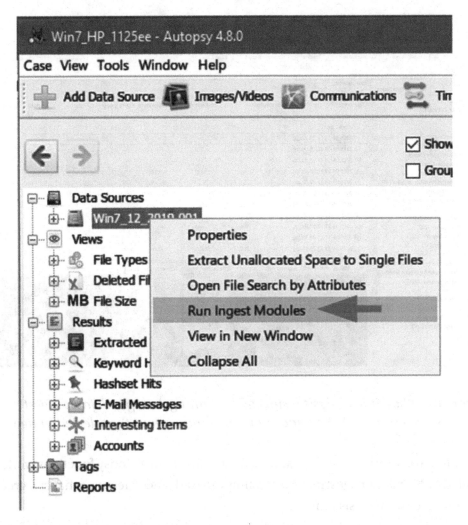

Figure 6-12. *Restart ingest module of an existing case*

2. The "Configure Ingest Modules" window will appear again; select
    only the modules needed for your investigation, then click the
    "Finish" button.

3. Now, Autopsy will return to analysis of selected image contents
    again using only the selected ingest modules.

Autopsy will begin analyzing image contents immediately after running "Ingest
Modules" again; analysis results will appear in the directory tree window on the left side
(also known as Data Explorer pane) of the main window. You can click each node in the
tree to expand its results (see Figure 6-13).

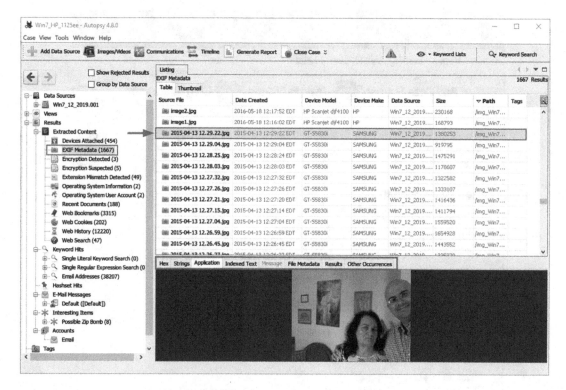

Figure 6-13. *Showing analysis results after running Autopsy default ingest
modules; screen shows EXIF metadata information about the selected image*

Now that we have a fair understanding of how the main Autopsy functions work
for analyzing forensic images, let us try testing some advanced features that can greatly
reduce the forensic analysis time.

HOW TO RECOVER DELETED FILES FROM THE SUPPLIED DATA SOURCE

To recover deleted files from the supplied data source (e.g., forensic image), go to the Data Explorer pane on the left. Select Views ➤ Deleted Files. To recover a file(s), right-click over it, select Export File(s), and select a destination where you want to save it (see Figure 6-14).

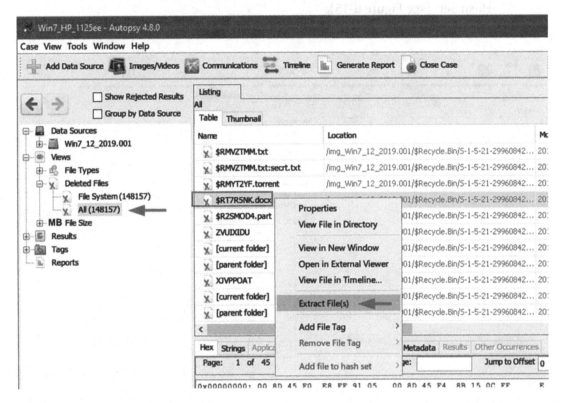

Figure 6-14.   *Recover deleted files*

Importing a Hash Database

The hash database ingest module allows an examiner to compare forensic image files' hash values to a precompiled hash value (Autopsy uses MD5 hashing) of known (good) or bad files. The known files are usually those belonging to the operating system itself and popular applications like MS Office files. By ignoring these files, Autopsy can reduce the time needed for analyzing image contents significantly. The bad file types include malware files and the like, and this type requires special attention from the examiner.

To use the hash database feature in Autopsy, follow these steps (you must enable the hash ingest module first before proceeding):

1. Go to Autopsy Tools menu ➤ Options; the options window should appear.

2. From the options window, select Hash Sets and then click "Import Hash Set" (see Figure 6-15).

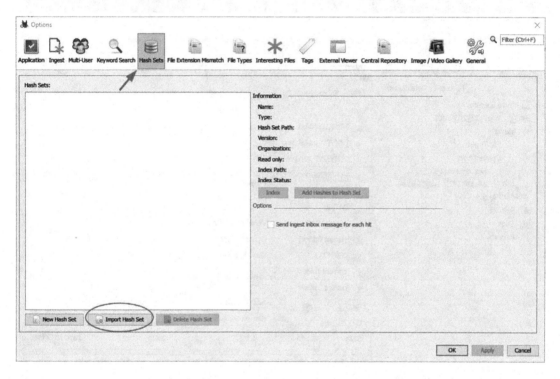

Figure 6-15. *Access hash dataset window*

3. The "Import Hash Set" window appears; click the "Open" button to browse to where the hash data set is stored on your computer, select it, and Autopsy will update the hash data set box automatically to show the name of the hash data set you have selected (see Figure 6-16).

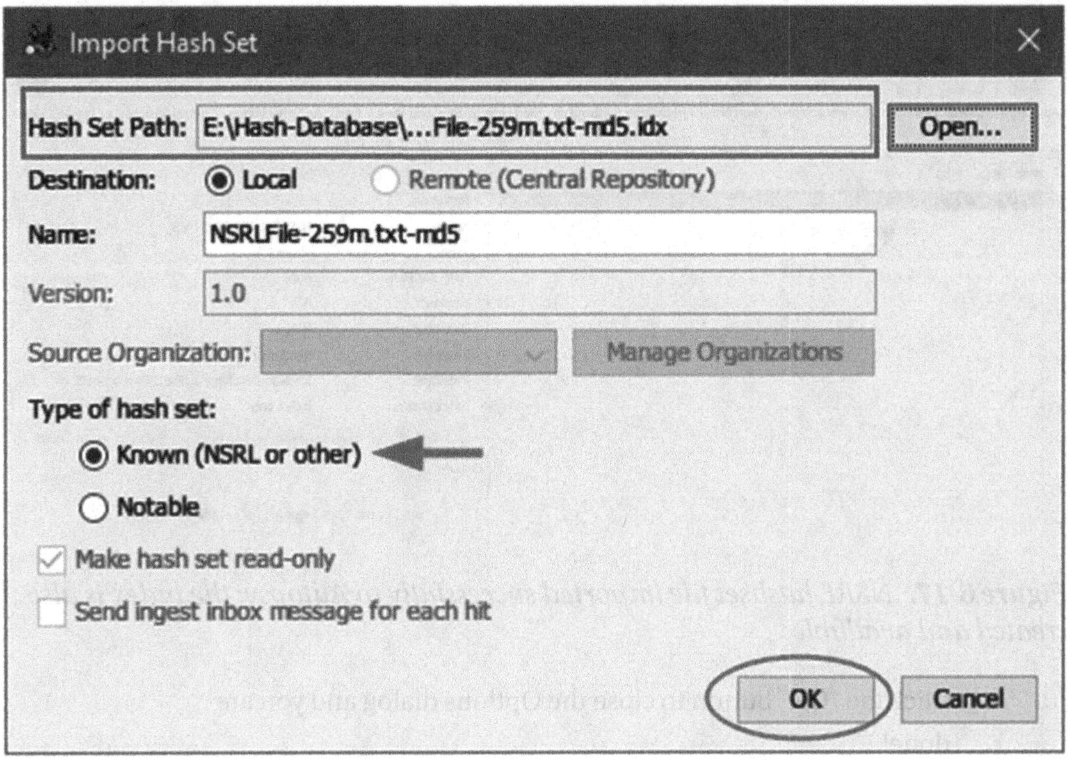

Figure 6-16. *Import hash set dialog*

In Figure 6-16, you can designate the imported hash set as known file (can be safely ignored from Autopsy analysis) or notable (dangerous or bad files that raise suspicions like malware); for instance, we are using an NSRL hash database, so we will select "Known." Click the "OK" button after setting all options in the "Import Hash Set" dialog.

Note!   If it is already zipped, the imported hash data set should be unzipped first before importing it to Autopsy.

---

4. Now, the Options window appears again; if the imported hash set has an index associated with it, the "Index Status" will display this (see Figure 6-17); otherwise, the "Index" button will be active so that you can click it to let Autopsy create an index for you.

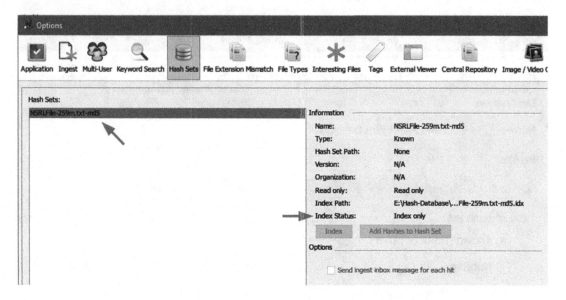

Figure 6-17. *NSRL hashset file imported successfully to Autopsy; the index is also created and available*

5. Click the "OK" button to close the Options dialog and you are done!

Now, you have successfully added a hash set to Autopsy; you need to run the ingest modules again in order to use the newly added hashset. To do this, follow these steps:

1. Cancel image analysis process as we did before if it is ongoing.

2. Right-click over the image you want to process and then click "Restart Ingest Modules" as we did before.

3. Now, make sure to select "Hash Lookup" and the hash database that you want to use during the analyzing (on the right pane of the window) (see Figure 6-18).

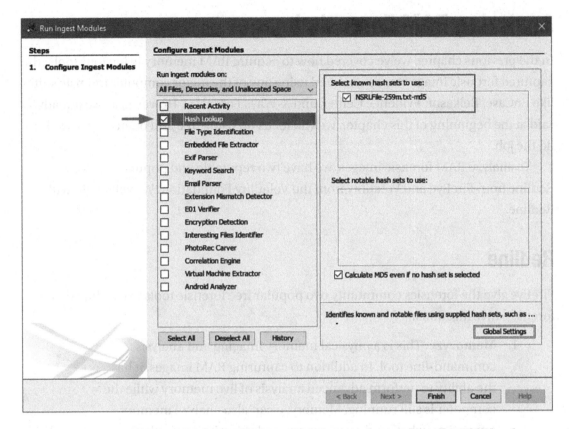

Figure 6-18. *Configure Hash Lookup module to use the imported NSRL hash database*

We cannot cover all Autopsy functions in this book; however, we showed you the main features of this platform. To learn more about Autopsy features, check the following:

1. Autopsy User's Guide (https://sleuthkit.org/autopsy/docs/user-docs/4.5.0/index.html)

2. The author's InfoSec Portal (www.DarknessGate.com)

Analyzing RAM Forensic Image

In the previous chapter, we've covered how to acquire RAM memory using four tools: the captured forensic image can be analyzed using any of the major computer forensic suites like EnCase, Belkasoft Evidence Center, and X-Ways Forensics. However, as we already said at the beginning of this chapter, we will focus on using free and open source tools to do the job.

To analyze RAM forensic images, we have two reputable and popular free tools: Redline from FireEye and Volatility from the Volatility Foundation. We will begin with Redline.

Redline

FireEye give the forensics community two popular free forensic tools to conduct digital forensics investigations:

1. **Memoryze**: This is a physical memory imaging and analysis command-line tool. In addition to capturing RAM images, it has the ability to perform advanced analysis of live memory while the computer is still running. Memoryze can also analyze memory image files, whether they were acquired using it or any other forensic software (DD-format). However, the analysis will give more comprehensive results when the forensic image is acquired by the Memoryze tool itself.

2. **Redline**: This is a Windows program for conducting a memory investigation of malicious artifacts in Windows physical memory. With Redline, you can:

   - Capture memory images, running processes, opened files, and registry data.

   - Filter (narrow) results according to many predefined criteria (such as a given timeframe of compromise events [when it started, which files were touched, and how long the compromise persisted]) and/or filter known valid data based on precompiled MD5 hash values of well-known files.

> **Note!**   Memoryze also comes embedded in Redline. Redline allows you to use Memoryze functions with an easy-to-use GUI instead of the original command-line interface, so it is highly advisable to use Redline only for both capturing and analyzing memory images.

This chapter can only examine the analysis of forensics images; however, to see the full features of Redline when investigating RAM memory image files, we will use it first to acquire a RAM image of a suspect machine (capturing RAM image with Redline will acquire more data compared with the standard Raw image format) and then show you how to analyze this image using the rich features available with Redline.

Capturing a RAM Memory Using Redline

Before we can use Redline to capture memory, we need to download it first.

1. Go to www.fireeye.com/services/freeware/redline.html; you need to fill in a simple registration form and the download link will send to the specified e-mail address.

2. Install the program on your Windows machine as you do with any other Windows application. Redline is supported on almost all versions of Windows: Windows XP, Windows Vista, Windows 7, Windows 8 (32 and 64 bit), Windows 10.

3. Launch the program, and the main window will appear (see Figure 6-19). From the "Collect Data" pane, select "Create a Comprehensive Collector."

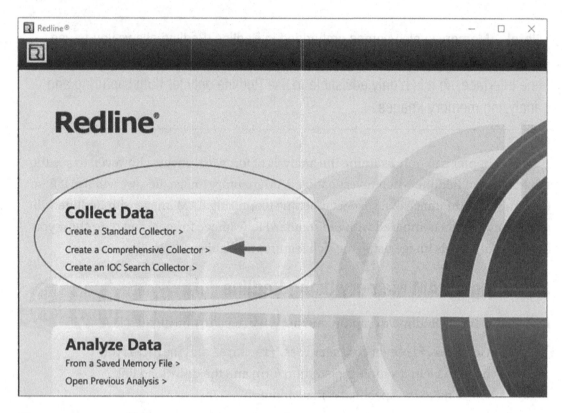

Figure 6-19. *Redline program main window*

Before we move on, let us give a brief description of available options when using Redline to collect (capture) data from a suspect Windows computer.

Redline has three types of collectors:

- Standard Collector: This type gathers the minimum amount of data (mainly process and loaded driver information).

- Comprehensive Collector: This type collects most of the data that Redline needs during its analysis process. This type of collection is very recommended and this what we are going to use during this experiment.

- IOC Search Collector: This type collects only the data that matches selected Indicators of Compromise (IOCs).

4. In our case, we will select "Comprehensive Collector"; click it, and
    the collector configuration window appears. From this window,
    you can configure what you are going to capture by clicking "Edit
    your script"; you should also check the option "Acquire Memory
    Image" to acquire the target memory image (see Figure 6-20).

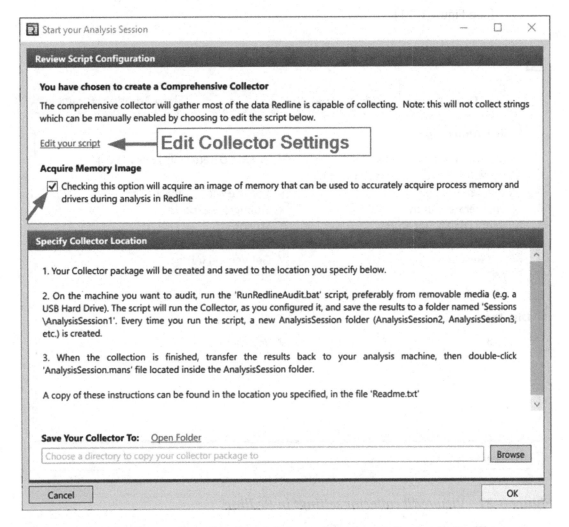

*Figure 6-20. Configure Standard and Comprehensive Collector in Redline;
please note that both collectors share the same window but with different default
configurations*

5.   The Redline Collector script (you can access it from "Edit Your
     Script") has memory, disk, system, network, and other options
     preselected. You can modify these options within any collector
     type. For instance, the comprehensive collector type (which we
     have chosen to select for this example) has most options already
     checked by default, so you can go safely with the default settings
     (see Figure 6-21).

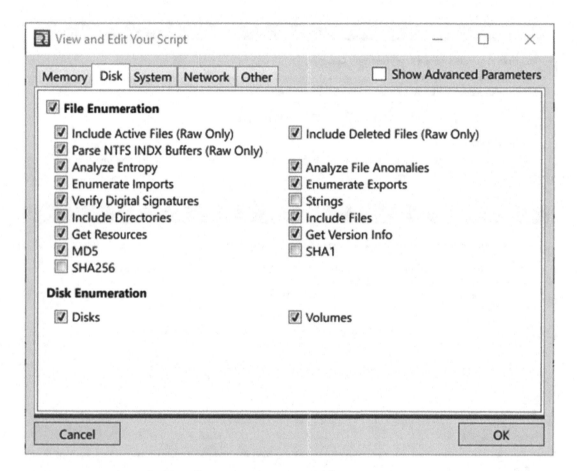

Figure 6-21. *View/edit collector settings in Redline*

6. Now, from the collector configuration window, click "Browse" under "Save Your Collector To" and select an empty directory where you want to save this collector. For instance, we will store it on a USB thumb drive, so that we can use it later to acquire a memory image from suspect machine. Click "OK" to begin writing to the Redline collector (see Figure 6-22).

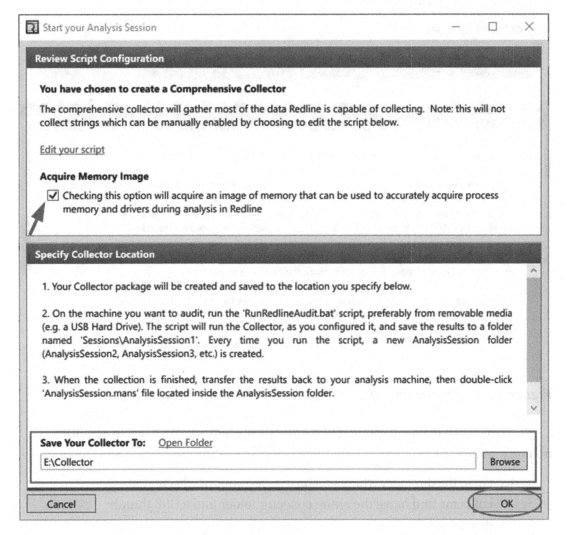

Figure 6-22. *Select the destination where you want to store your collector files*

7. When Redline finishes creating the collector, a success window will pop up, showing you important information on how to use this collector to acquire memory data from potentially compromised systems (see Figure 6-23).

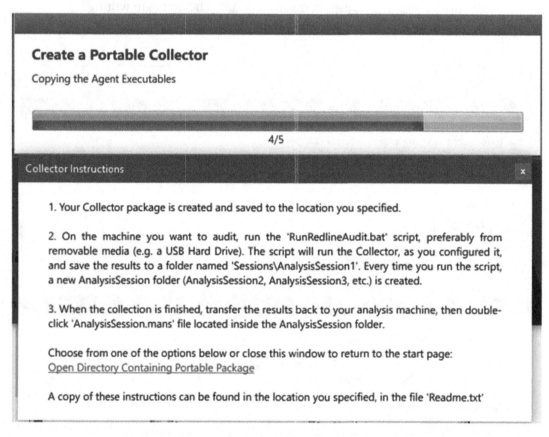

Create a Portable Collector

Copying the Agent Executables

4/5

Collector Instructions   x

1. Your Collector package is created and saved to the location you specified.

2. On the machine you want to audit, run the 'RunRedlineAudit.bat' script, preferably from removable media (e.g. a USB Hard Drive). The script will run the Collector, as you configured it, and save the results to a folder named 'Sessions\AnalysisSession1'. Every time you run the script, a new AnalysisSession folder (AnalysisSession2, AnalysisSession3, etc.) is created.

3. When the collection is finished, transfer the results back to your analysis machine, then double-click 'AnalysisSession.mans' file located inside the AnalysisSession folder.

Choose from one of the options below or close this window to return to the start page:
Open Directory Containing Portable Package

A copy of these instructions can be found in the location you specified, in the file 'Readme.txt'

Figure 6-23. *Redline showing collector instructions after creating it*

Now that we have created our collector, let us see how we can use it to acquire memory images:

1. Go to the directory where you have saved your newly created collector, and move the entire collector folder into a USB thumb drive.

2. Attach the USB thumb drive into the target machine.

3. Execute the script named "RunRedlineAudit.bat" in the collector folder to run the collector (see Figure 6-24).

Collector			
Name ^	Date modified	Type	Size
x64	8/31/2018 4:22 PM	File folder	
x86	8/31/2018 4:22 PM	File folder	
elevate.cmd	6/7/2018 8:40 AM	Windows Comma...	2 KB
elevate.vbs	6/7/2018 8:38 AM	VBScript Script File	4 KB
finishAnalysis.js	6/7/2018 8:38 AM	JavaScript File	2 KB
getNextSessionFolder.js	6/7/2018 8:38 AM	JavaScript File	1 KB
getPath.js	6/7/2018 8:40 AM	JavaScript File	3 KB
Helper.bat	6/7/2018 8:39 AM	Windows Batch File	3 KB
MemoryzeAuditScript.xml	8/31/2018 4:22 PM	XML Document	21 KB
Readme.txt	6/7/2018 8:39 AM	Text Document	1 KB
RunRedlineAudit.bat	6/7/2018 8:39 AM	Windows Batch File	1 KB

Figure 6-24. Running the collector to begin acquiring RAM memory of the target machine

4.   The collector should begin its collection work by showing a CMD window (see Figure 6-25), and it will store acquired data to a folder named 'Sessions\AnalysisSession1' in the same directory. Every time you run the script, a new AnalysisSession folder (AnalysisSession2, AnalysisSession3, etc.) is created.

```
C:\WINDOWS\System32\cmd.exe
Ensuring the proper working directory
".\x64\xagt.exe" -o "E:\captured-images\Collector\\Sessions\AnalysisSession1\Audits" -f "MemoryzeAuditScript.xml"
```

Figure 6-25. CMD window appears while the collector is running; upon finishing, the CMD should disappear without showing any message

5.   After the Collector completes the collection, the CMD window should disappear without showing any message. Now, go into the AnalysisSession folder, and you will see an Audits folder and an AnalysisSession1.mans file (see Figure 6-26).

> Collector > Sessions > AnalysisSession1

Name	Date modified	Type	Size
Audits	8/31/2018 3:30 AM	File folder	
AnalysisSession1.mans	8/31/2018 3:30 AM	Mandiant Analysis File	1 KB

Figure 6-26. *Collector data (XML files) are stored within the Audits folder*

Now that we have acquired suspect machine volatility data (in addition to other important data like Prefetch folder information), it's time to begin the analysis process using Redline.

Memory Forensics Using Redline

To analyze memory data collected by the Redline collector, follow these steps:

1. Move the Sessions folder from the Collector folder into the forensic machine that you want to perform the analysis on. Of course, Redline should be installed on this machine first.

2. Open Sessions ➤ AnalysisSession1 (there could be more than one analysis session if you run the collector more than once) and you will see an Audits folder and an AnalysisSession1.mans file.

3. Double-click the 'AnalysisSession1.mans' file to create your session in Redline. This automatically imports the data into Redline (see Figure 6-27).

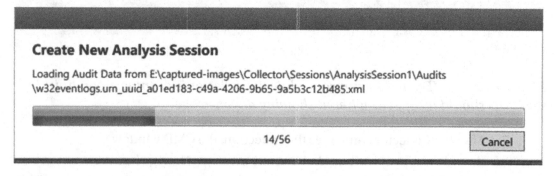

Create New Analysis Session

Loading Audit Data from E:\captured-images\Collector\Sessions\AnalysisSession1\Audits
\w32eventlogs.urn_uuid_a01ed183-c49a-4206-9b65-9a5b3c12b485.xml

14/56   Cancel

Figure 6-27. *Create new analysis session in Redline to investigate acquired image data*

4. Importing data into Redline will take some time (from minutes to hours); the time needed will depend on the size of the captured memory image and the acquired memory operating system type.

5. Once the data has finished loading into the new analysis session, the Redline analysis session window will appear. Redline groups data by type; you will see these groups on the left side of the Analysis Data frame (see Figure 6-28).

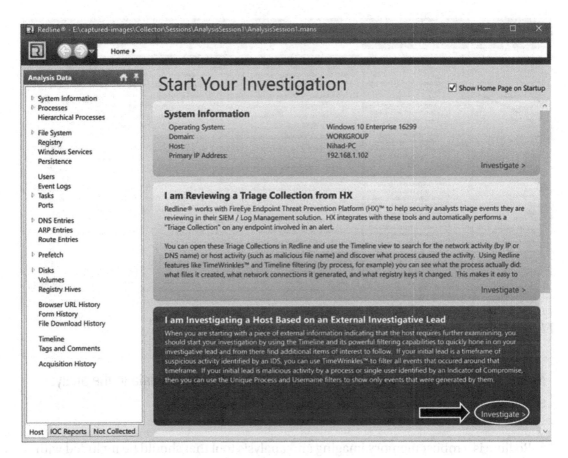

Figure 6-28. *Redline analysis session window*

6. You have different options to start your investigations; for instance, we will use the option "I am Investigating a Host Based on an External Investigative Lead."

7. A new window will appear (see Figure 6-29); click any data type in the "Analysis Data" (corresponds to number 1) pane to see all related acquired information on the right pane. The middle pane allows you to set some filters (corresponds to number 2) on the data to limit the number of returning data, while the third pane displays the sum of filtered information according to what a user has selected in pane 2.

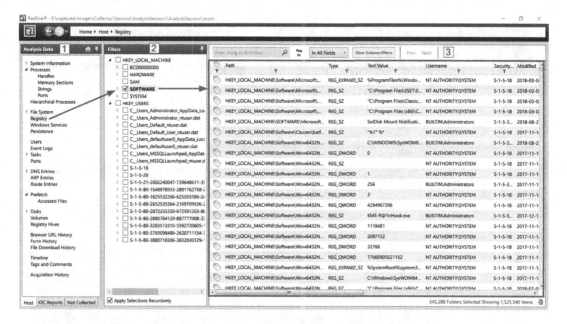

Figure 6-29. *Analysis memory image data using Redline*

Note!   The data types available for analysis depend upon the data in the analysis session.

Redline is a robust memory imaging and analysis tool that should be included with any digital forensic examiner toolkit. In this section, we tried to give an overview of how we can use this tool to capture RAM memory and how to start our analysis of the captured image.

Volatility Framework

Volatility is another famous tool for analyzing RAM forensic images; it is a research project that has emerged from published academic research papers in the field of advanced memory analysis and forensics.

It is a free, open source, and cross-platform program written in python; its development is now supported by a nonprofit organization known as the Volatility Foundation.

Volatility comes already installed with many Linux security distributions like Kali; however, this tool is also supported on Windows machines (a standalone portable application). The latest version is 2.6, and you can download it from `www.volatilityfoundation.org/26`.

We will not demonstrate how to use Volatility in detail as we did with Redline; however, it is useful to know its main features and how you can begin using it.

Volatility uses a set of plug-ins to do its functions; these plug-ins are similar to Autopsy modules, in that each one will perform one analysis function in the supplied forensics image file.

Let us now practice using this tool to analyze a RAM image using a Windows machine:

1. Download Volatility (Windows version) and extract the zipped file.

2. Launch the command-line prompt; change the command prompt to where Volatility resides (use the CD command switch).

3. Type the name of the Volatility file into the prompt, followed by -h switch to see the available options (see Figure 6-30).

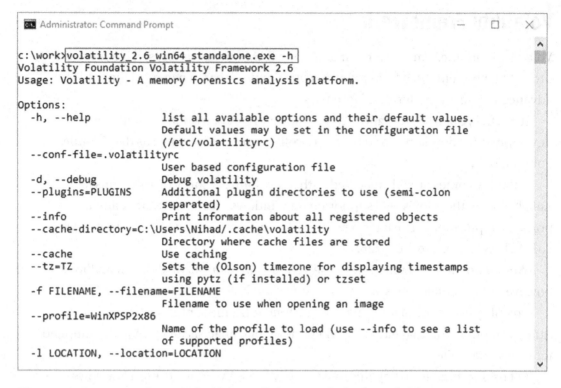

```
Administrator: Command Prompt                                    —    □    ×

c:\work>volatility_2.6_win64_standalone.exe -h
Volatility Foundation Volatility Framework 2.6
Usage: Volatility - A memory forensics analysis platform.

Options:
  -h, --help              list all available options and their default values.
                          Default values may be set in the configuration file
                          (/etc/volatilityrc)
  --conf-file=.volatilityrc
                          User based configuration file
  -d, --debug             Debug volatility
  --plugins=PLUGINS       Additional plugin directories to use (semi-colon
                          separated)
  --info                  Print information about all registered objects
  --cache-directory=C:\Users\Nihad/.cache\volatility
                          Directory where cache files are stored
  --cache                 Use caching
  --tz=TZ                 Sets the (Olson) timezone for displaying timestamps
                          using pytz (if installed) or tzset
  -f FILENAME, --filename=FILENAME
                          Filename to use when opening an image
  --profile=WinXPSP2x86
                          Name of the profile to load (use --info to see a list
                          of supported profiles)
  -l LOCATION, --location=LOCATION
```

Figure 6-30. *Launching Volatility and showing help (available options and default values)*

4. Before you can start analyzing any memory image, you need to know the operating system type that the specified image belongs to; this allows Volatility to know which commands to use during the analysis process. **Imageinfo** is the plug-in used by Volatility to perform this task (see Figure 6-31).

    Type the following in the command prompt:

    volatility_2.6_win64_standalone.exe -f NIHAD-PC-20180830-111531.dmp imageinfo

    - volatility_2.6_win64_standalone.exe (this is to launch Volatility)

    - -f NIHAD-PC-20180830-111531.dmp— "-f" is the file name parameter followed by image file location/name

    - Imageinfo (this is the name of the plug-in used by Volatility to know which operating system this image belongs to)

```
Administrator: © www.DarknessGate.com 2019                                    —  □  ×

C:\work>volatility_2.6_win64_standalone.exe -f NIHAD-PC-20180830-111531.dmp imageinfo
Volatility Foundation Volatility Framework 2.6
INFO    : volatility.debug    : Determining profile based on KDBG search...
          Suggested Profile(s) : Win7SP1x86_23418, Win7SP0x86, Win7SP1x86 (Instantiated with WinXPSP2x86)
                     AS Layer1 : IA32PagedMemoryPae (Kernel AS)
                     AS Layer2 : WindowsCrashDumpSpace32 (Unnamed AS)
                     AS Layer3 : FileAddressSpace (C:\work\NIHAD-PC-20180830-111531.dmp)
                      PAE type : PAE
                           DTB : 0x185000L
            KUSER_SHARED_DATA : 0xffdf0000L
        Image date and time : 2018-08-30 11:15:33 UTC+0000
  Image local date and time : 2018-08-30 14:15:33 +0300

C:\work>_
```

Figure 6-31. *Learn image OS profile type by typing -f switch followed by image file location and then imageinfo*

5. Suggested Profile(s) show the operating system that this image belongs to. Always begin from the first suggestion and move on.

6. Now, to extract process names that were running at the time of the capture from the image file, use the Pslist command.

   volatility_2.6_win64_standalone.exe -f NIHAD-PC-20180830-111531.dmp profile=Win7SP1x86 pslist

   • profile= Win7SP1x86 (this is taken from "Suggested Profile(s)" in Figure 6-11)

7. In the same way, to display the list of loaded dlls for each process, use the **DllList** plug-in:

   volatility_2.6_win64_standalone.exe -f NIHAD-PC-20180830-111531.dmp profile=Win7SP1x86 dlllist

As we said at the beginning, we will not delve into how to use Volatility in various scenarios; however, keep in mind that this tool is excellent for conducting forensic investigations on physical memory images, and it is already used by law enforcement, military, academia, and commercial investigators throughout the world.

To find more resources on how to use Volatility in your investigation, check these links:

- Volatility Wiki (https://github.com/volatilityfoundation/volatility/wiki)

- Volatility Documentation Project (https://github.com/volatilityfoundation/volatility/wiki/Volatility-Documentation-Project)

VOLATILITY WORKBENCH

Do you prefer to use a GUI for the Volatility tool, in which you can select all Volatility command parameters visually (using a drop-down menu) without the need to remember them? Fortunately, one has been developed by PassMark software.

Volatility Workbench (www.osforensics.com/tools/volatility-workbench.html) is an open source GUI for the Volatility tool; it runs in Windows and offers an easy-to-use interface so that even novice users can run Volatility easily (see Figure 6-32).

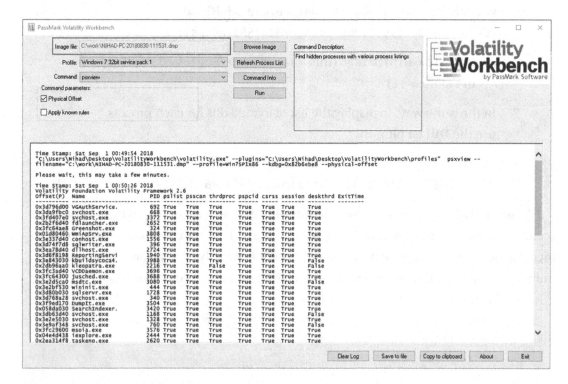

Figure 6-32.   *Volatility Workbench: a GUI for the Volatility tool*

Chapter Summary

In this chapter, we showed you how to analyze acquired forensics images from both hard drives and RAM memory. The focus was on using free and open source software to do the analysis job. Many popular open source forensics softwares are used by thousands of investigators worldwide, and they have proven records in official investigations throughout the world; however, keep in mind that despite this fact, commercial software will usually have more rich features when investigating some types of digital devices, and some of these tools are officially enforced by law enforcement agencies in some countries.

As a forensic examiner, you should practice using different forensics tools, both free and commercial, as in the computer forensics domain, there is no one tool that can perform all needed tasks. There are always some tools that are better than others in performing some functions.

In the next chapter, we will continue our analysis work and will cover how to build in-depth digital forensics knowledge of Microsoft Windows operating systems by knowing where forensics artifacts can be found and how we can analyze them to solve the case at hand.

CHAPTER 7

Windows Forensics Analysis

Investigating Windows OS for forensics artifacts

In July 2018, the market share of the Windows operating system (desktop version) range stood at 82.88%.[1] This means that the majority of personal computers worldwide run using this operating system (using its different versions) (see Figure 7-1). Obviously, a world running on Windows computers certainly means that most of our digital forensic work involves investigating this type of OS; knowing how to find your way using Windows is a must for any digital forensics practitioner.

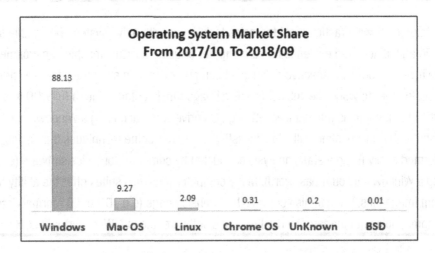

Figure 7-1. *Operating system market share (October 2017 to September 2018). Data source: www.netmarketshare.com/operating-system-market-share.aspx.*

---

[1]Statista, "Global Operating Systems Market Share for Desktop PCs, from January 2013 to July 2018," September 14, 2018. (www.statista.com/statistics/218089/global-market-share-of-windows-7/

© Nihad A. Hassan 2019
N. A. Hassan, *Digital Forensics Basics*, https://doi.org/10.1007/978-1-4842-3838-7_7

The ultimate goal of any digital forensic examination is investigating the action of a person(s) conducted on his/her computing device. For instance, operating system forensics help examiners to correlate events conducted using the suspect device's operating system to other actions/events that have happened in the real world.

Almost any event or state change on a system is considered a result of a user action. A Windows user will leave traces while using it; actually, Windows is notorious for leaving too many traces at different places as a part of its normal use, compared with other operating system types. Advanced Windows users—who know how to delete and cover their traces—will not always succeed in deleting all these traces, leaving valuable evidence for digital forensic examiners to retrieve.

This book is about teaching readers how to conduct digital forensics investigations using Windows OS, so this chapter will introduce the different types of artifacts left by Windows users/operating system functions and the forensics significance of these artifacts.

In the previous chapter, we've covered how to configure Autopsy to conduct basic searches within supplied data source—hence the forensic image file. In this chapter, we will continue demonstrating how to use different tools, in addition to many functions supplied by Autopsy, to capture and analyze Windows artifacts.

BOOTING FROM A FORENSIC IMAGE

In this chapter, we will practice most forensics techniques with a live system. Being able to boot an image of acquired evidence into a computer or using a virtual machine environment will give investigators a perspective on suspect computer usage in an entirely forensic manner. Of course, in order to work, the subject forensic image must contain either a full HDD image or the partition that contains the installed OS (e.g., C:\ drive when acquiring a Windows machine). In addition to this, live booting will allow investigators to use some techniques that cannot be performed easily using a static analysis conducted by computer forensics software (e.g., cracking a Windows account password). Many computer forensics suites offer the ability to boot from image files. You can also convert the forensic image (e.g., DD or E01 format) into a format compatible with the target virtual machine software (e.g., VMWare, VirtualBox, Hyper-V).

Timeline Analysis

Timeline analysis is considered an important element in most digital forensics investigations, as it gives a holistic view about the succession of events that have happened to the system of question and is used to answer a main question in any investigation: when did a specific activity take place? Timeline analysis allows investigators to save their investigation time by reducing the volume of data that needs to be investigated to a specific timeframe (e.g., after the incident took place). Timeline analysis is very important when investigating malware incidents to identify when a system state has changed because of a malware attack.

Creating a Timeline Using Autopsy

Recent versions of Autopsy (3.0.5+) come equipped with an advanced timeline interface that groups different artifacts found within the supplied forensic image according to their timestamps.

Note!   Timestamp information exists for each file in the forensic image. A file's time attributes include when the file was created, changed, modified, and accessed. Please note that each operating system type treats the "Change" and "Create" time attributes of files differently. For instance, in Windows, the file creation and change times indicate when the file's content has changed, while UNIX file systems do not store the creation time attributes and consider a file to be changed when its metadata get changed, regardless of the file's content change.

To generate a timeline of events for your case using Autopsy, follow these steps:

1. Launch Autopsy and create a new case (as we did in the previous chapter) or launch an existing one.

2. Go to the Tools menu ➤ Timeline.

3. Autopsy will need some time (depending on the supplied forensic image size) to populate the data for the timeline (see Figure 7-2).

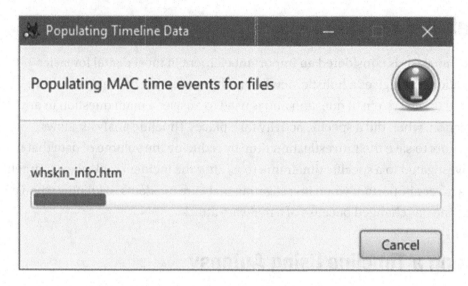

Figure 7-2. *Autopsy population of timeline data in progress*

4. After finishing timeline data population, Autopsy can present data using three view modes:

- Bar chart (counts) mode: This mode offers less detail and is intended to answer questions about how much data alteration occurred in a given timeframe.

- Detail mode: This mode will give you details about events and present those events to you using a unique clustering approach (e.g., grouping all files in the same folder as one event and showing all URLs that belong to one domain as one event).

- List mode: Similar to detail mode, but it shows the results in a list organized from oldest to newest.

Regardless of the display mode, Autopsy allows investigators to view the forensic image file contents using different viewer programs (see Figure 7-3).

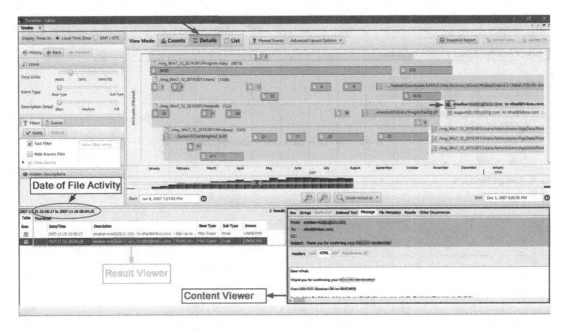

Figure 7-3. *Timeline analysis in detail mode using Autopsy; file content can be viewed in the bottom right corner of the main window*

Generate a Timeline Report Using Autopsy

Autopsy allows you to generate a report—in HTML, Excel, text, and other formats—that contains time information of every file in the supplied forensic image. This feature opens possibilities to use such information in other programs outside Autopsy. To generate a timeline report using Autopsy, follow these steps:

1. Go to Tools menu ➤ Generate Report. The Generate Report wizard appears; the first window allows you to select the report format (see Figure 7-4).

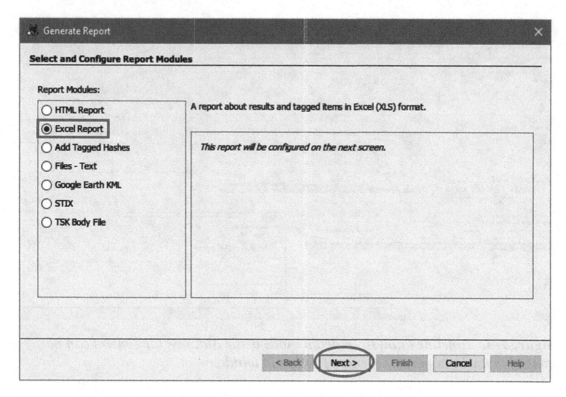

Figure 7-4.   Select report format for your generated timeline in Autopsy

2.   In our case, we select "Excel Report," so we can play with the
     data using the MS Excel spreadsheet program or any other
     alternative program that can read Excel files like Apache
     OpenOffice (www.openoffice.org). Click "Next" to continue.

3.   The next window asks you to configure the returned results. You
     have two options: All Results and Tagged Results. In our case, we
     will select all results and click "Finish"; then, Autopsy will begin
     the report generation process (see Figure 7-5).

Figure 7-5.   Report Generation Progress window

4. After it finishes generating the report, Autopsy will show you the link where your generated report is saved; click over this link to open the file using your default program (see Figure 7-6).

5. Finally, click "Close" to close the Report Generation Progress window.

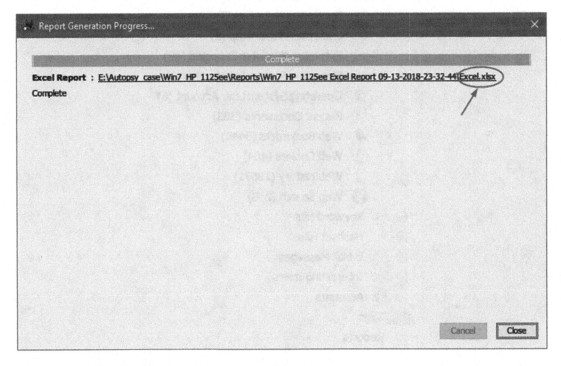

Figure 7-6. *The location of Autopsy-generated report*

RETRIEVING LAST SEVEN DAYS OF ACTIVITY USING AUTOPSY

Please note that as a part of Autopsy's initial analysis, it will list the last seven days of activity—of web browsers (including web searches), installed programs, operating system, and recent changes to registry hives—of the supplied forensic image files in the Data Explorer panel under the "Extracted Content" section (see Figure 7-7). Remember that you need to activate the "Recent Activity" ingest module in order to retrieve this result.

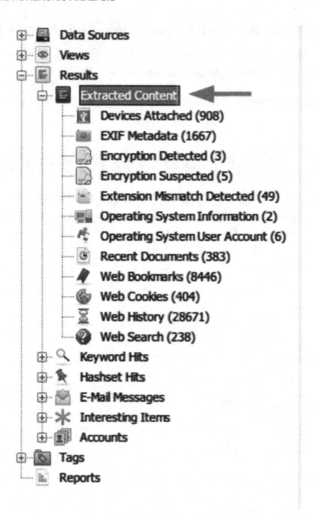

Figure 7-7. *Viewing the results of "Recent Activity" module: you must activate the "Recent Activity" ingest module to view this info*

File Recovery

Analysis of deleted files is a key task in any type of digital forensic investigation. To become a successful digital forensic examiner, you must know how Windows deletes files; where such files can be located, even after they are deleted; and methods/techniques to investigate these files (e.g., retrieving deleted files' metadata to support a criminal investigation). In this section, we will list some tools and techniques to recover critically important documents and file fragments that can help us solve the case at hand.

Undeleting Files Using Autopsy

In the previous chapter, we talked about how to use Autopsy to recover deleted files from supplied forensic image files' slack space. Actually, using Autopsy to recover deleted files does not require any interference by the forensic examiner. All you need to do is just to create the case as we did previously and select the "PhotoRec Carver module" from the ingest modules (make sure that "Process Unallocated Space" is selected); then, you are ready to go. Autopsy will automatically retrieve data from unallocated space of the supplied data source and show them in the Data Explorer pane under Views ➤ Deleted Files.

The PhotoRec tool (www.cgsecurity.org/wiki/PhotoRec) is a free, open source application that can be used as a standalone application to recover files from different digital media devices like HDDs, USB drives, SD cards (e.g., those in smartphones and digital cameras), and CD-ROMs.

PhotoRec can be used with TestDisk (www.cgsecurity.org/wiki/TestDisk, from the same developer); this is another open source program that is specialized in recovering lost partitions and/or fixing the problem of nonbooting disks, making them bootable again.

A step-by-step tutorial on how to use TestDisk is available at www.cgsecurity.org/wiki/TestDisk_Step_By_Step. Another tutorial for using PhotoRec can be found at www.cgsecurity.org/wiki/PhotoRec_Step_By_Step.

Windows Recycle Bin Forensics

The Windows recycle bin—first introduced in Windows 95—contains files that have been deleted by users but still exist within the system. For instance, when a user deletes a file (using the standard delete button on the keyboard after selecting the target file OR selecting a file, right-clicking it, and choosing "Delete" from the pop-up menu), Windows moves the subject file to the recycle bin without deleting it permanently. This is the default behavior of Windows; however, a user can configure the recycle bin settings to permanently delete files without moving them into the recycle bin; besides, some users press and hold the Shift key when deleting a file to delete it permanently without moving it into the recycle bin. In practice, few people employ permanent deletion of recycled files (or even know about it); this makes it possible for the recycle bin to hold important recycled artifacts, which are considered a valuable source for digital evidence.

As we already said, when a user deletes a file, the default behavior of Windows is to move it into the recycle bin. Different versions of Windows have different recycle bin file names and locations. For Windows XP (formatted using the FAT file system), deleted files are stored in the "Recycler" folder in the root directory where Windows is installed (usually the C:\ drive), which in turn holds another important file named "INFO2."Both "Recycler" and "INFO2" are hidden files: you must first display hidden files—including OS files—to display them.

Inside the "Recycler" folder, we can see one or more folders; these folders are named according to each user's specific security identifier (SID) (e.g., S-1-5-21-2602240047-739648611-3566628919-501); if a system has more than one user, then each one will have its own folder that stores the deleted files belonging to that user account. There is also another important file inside each user recycle bin folder called "INFO2"; this file contains an index of all the files that have been previously deleted by the user. It also contains metadata about each deleted file like its original path, file size, and date/time when it was deleted.

Note!   When you delete a file from a removable media or mapped network path, it will bypass recycle bin and be cleared permanently.

With Vista and beyond (7, 8, 8.1, and 10), Windows has changed both the recycle bin main folder and the way deleted files are organized. For instance, deleted files are stored in a folder named "$Recycle.Bin," under which there is a subfolder for each user on the system named using that user's SID. The "$Recycle.Bin" is stored under the C:\ drive (assuming Windows is installed there). Now, in these modern versions of Windows, when a file is deleted, Windows will move it into the recycle bin as two files: one contains the actual data of the recycled file (its name begins with "$R"), while the other contains the deleted file's metadata (its name begins with "$I"). Obviously, this discards the need for the "INFO2" file from older Windows versions, which was used to store recycled a file's metadata.

Note!   The Windows recycle bin has limited storage capacity with regard to the volume of deleted files that it can accommodate. In Windows XP, the recycle bin is configured by default to hold 10% of hard drive; if it fills up to maximum capacity, it will delete the old files to make room for incoming deleted files. In newer Windows versions like Vista and later, the default size is 10% of the first 40GB of the drive and 5% of the remaining storage space that is above 40GB.

Now, let us experiment with deleting a file and analyzing it using Windows 10 and a free tool called $I Parse.

Open a command-line prompt; use the CD command to change the working directory into the $Recycle.Bin folder under the C:\ drive. Display the folder contents using the DIR command followed by the /a switch (to display hidden system files). These commands are displayed in Figure 7-8.

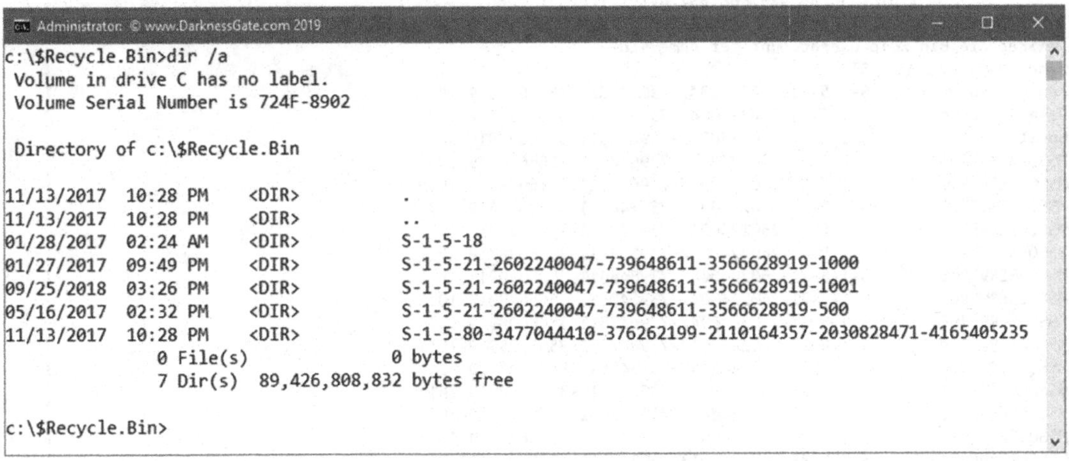

```
Administrator © www.DarknessGate.com 2019                                              —    □    ✕
c:\$Recycle.Bin>dir /a
 Volume in drive C has no label.
 Volume Serial Number is 724F-8902

 Directory of c:\$Recycle.Bin

11/13/2017  10:28 PM    <DIR>          .
11/13/2017  10:28 PM    <DIR>          ..
01/28/2017  02:24 AM    <DIR>          S-1-5-18
01/27/2017  09:49 PM    <DIR>          S-1-5-21-2602240047-739648611-3566628919-1000
09/25/2018  03:26 PM    <DIR>          S-1-5-21-2602240047-739648611-3566628919-1001
05/16/2017  02:32 PM    <DIR>          S-1-5-21-2602240047-739648611-3566628919-500
11/13/2017  10:28 PM    <DIR>          S-1-5-80-3477044410-376262199-2110164357-2030828471-4165405235
               0 File(s)              0 bytes
               7 Dir(s)  89,426,808,832 bytes free

c:\$Recycle.Bin>
```

Figure 7-8. *Viewing $Recycle.Bin contents under Windows 10 using DOS prompt*

As we note from Figure 7-8, the $Recycle.Bin contains four subfolders: these are SID subfolders and correspond to the SID of the user who deleted the file. Each subfolder is created the first time a user deletes a file that is sent to the recycle bin.

Now, to learn the name of the user account which owns a specific SID subfolder, we need to use the following command:

wmic useraccount get name,sid

This will display all user accounts on the target machine, so now we can learn which SID subfolder in the Recycle.Bin belongs to the target user (see Figure 7-9).

```
Administrator: © www.DarknessGate.com 2019                                                    —    □    ×

 Directory of c:\$Recycle.Bin

11/13/2017  10:28 PM    <DIR>          .
11/13/2017  10:28 PM    <DIR>          ..
01/28/2017  02:24 AM    <DIR>          S-1-5-18
01/27/2017  09:49 PM    <DIR>          S-1-5-21-2602240047-739648611-3566628919-1000
09/25/2018  03:26 PM    <DIR>          S-1-5-21-2602240047-739648611-3566628919-1001
05/16/2017  02:32 PM    <DIR>          S-1-5-21-2602240047-739648611-3566628919-500
11/13/2017  10:28 PM    <DIR>          S-1-5-80-3477044410-376262199-2110164357-2030828471-4165405235
                 0 File(s)              0 bytes
                 7 Dir(s)  89,426,808,832 bytes free

c:\$Recycle.Bin>wmic useraccount get name,sid
Name                    SID
Administrator           S-1-5-21-2602240047-739648611-3566628919-500
DefaultAccount          S-1-5-21-2602240047-739648611-3566628919-503
Guest                   S-1-5-21-2602240047-739648611-3566628919-501
MSSQLSERVER01           S-1-5-21-2602240047-739648611-3566628919-1009
MSSQLSERVER02           S-1-5-21-2602240047-739648611-3566628919-1010
MSSQLSERVER03           S-1-5-21-2602240047-739648611-3566628919-1011
MSSQLSERVER04           S-1-5-21-2602240047-739648611-3566628919-1012
MSSQLSERVER05           S-1-5-21-2602240047-739648611-3566628919-1013
MSSQLSERVER06           S-1-5-21-2602240047-739648611-3566628919-1014
MSSQLSERVER07           S-1-5-21-2602240047-739648611-3566628919-1015
MSSQLSERVER08           S-1-5-21-2602240047-739648611-3566628919-1016
MSSQLSERVER09           S-1-5-21-2602240047-739648611-3566628919-1017
MSSQLSERVER10           S-1-5-21-2602240047-739648611-3566628919-1018
MSSQLSERVER11           S-1-5-21-2602240047-739648611-3566628919-1019
MSSQLSERVER12           S-1-5-21-2602240047-739648611-3566628919-1020
MSSQLSERVER13           S-1-5-21-2602240047-739648611-3566628919-1021
MSSQLSERVER14           S-1-5-21-2602240047-739648611-3566628919-1022
MSSQLSERVER15           S-1-5-21-2602240047-739648611-3566628919-1023
MSSQLSERVER16           S-1-5-21-2602240047-739648611-3566628919-1024
MSSQLSERVER17           S-1-5-21-2602240047-739648611-3566628919-1025
MSSQLSERVER18           S-1-5-21-2602240047-739648611-3566628919-1026
MSSQLSERVER19           S-1-5-21-2602240047-739648611-3566628919-1027
MSSQLSERVER20           S-1-5-21-2602240047-739648611-3566628919-1028
Nihad                   S-1-5-21-2602240047-739648611-3566628919-1001
WDAGUtilityAccount      S-1-5-21-2602240047-739648611-3566628919-504
```

Figure 7-9. *Knowing the owner of a specific SID subfolder within $Recycle.Bin*

After knowing which recycle bin belongs to the target account, we can access it using the CD command. Use the DIR command with the /a switch to display its contents (see Figure 7-10).

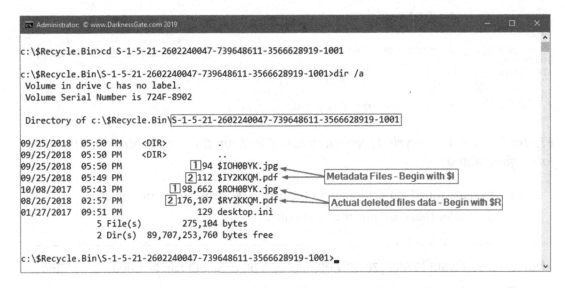

Figure 7-10. *Viewing target recycle bin: contents display two deleted files*

From Figure 7-10, we can note that the target recycle bin has four files belonging to two deleted files (see Figure 7-11). As we already said, each deleted file has two files in the recycle bin, a metadata file and the actual data (recoverable data) of the deleted file.

Name	Original Location	Date Deleted	Size	Item type	Date modified
1 Diala.jpg	C:\Users\Nihad\Desktop	9/25/2018 5:50 PM	97 KB	JPG File	10/8/2017 5:43 PM
2 NihadHassan_CV.pdf	C:\Users\Nihad\Desktop	9/25/2018 5:49 PM	172 KB	Adobe Acrobat Document	8/26/2018 2:57 PM

Figure 7-11. *Two deleted files in the recycle bin*

Now, let us investigate the deleted file's metadata, also known as index files (begin with $I), in the recycle bin of Windows Vista and later using a free tool called $I Parse. To use this tool follow these steps:

1. Go to `https://df-stream.com/recycle-bin-i-parser/` and download the tool and extract its contents (if it is zipped).

2. To use this tool, we need first to extract the recycled file metadata file. To do this, type the following in the command prompt (see Figure 7-12): `copy $I* \users\nihad\desktop\recover`

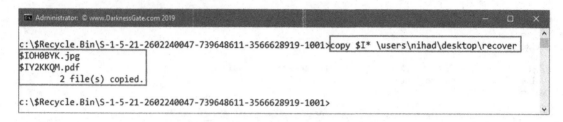

Figure 7-12. Copy recycled files' metadata files from the recycle bin into another folder for analysis

3. Execute the $I Parse tool, go to **File** menu ➤ **Browse...**, and select the folder that contains metadata files.

Note!   If you want to analyze only one file at a time, select File ➤ Choose... instead.

---

4. From the main program menu, click the Choose... button and select where to save the output file (a file with CSV extension that will hold parsing results) (see Figure 7-13).

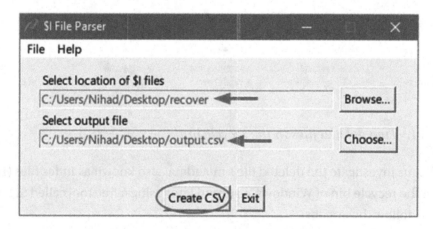

Figure 7-13. Parse all metadata files in the target directory

5. Finally, click "Create CSV"; a success window will appear after parsing all files is finished, and you are done!

Now, go to where you have saved the output file (in our case, it's named **output.csv**) and open it to view a list of all recycled files names in the target recycle bin along with all file metadata information (original path, deletion date/time, and file size) (see Figure 7-14).

	A	B	C	D	E	F	G	H	I	J
1	$I File Name	$R File Name	Size (Bytes)	Timestamp (UTC)	Original File Name With Path	Original File Name	MD5 Hash			
2	$IOHOBYK.jpg	$ROHOBYK.jpg	98662	09-25-2018 14:50:	C:\Users\Nihad\Desktop\Diala.jpg	Diala.jpg	4ccca460bb5ea964a85241e04a5d1ae9			
3	$IY2KKQM.pdf	$RY2KKQM.pdf	176107	09-25-2018 14:49:	C:\Users\Nihad\Desktop\NihadHassan_CV.pdf	NihadHassan_CV.pdf	66d355c6801d2c91d471520c531ca389			
4										
5										

Figure 7-14. *output.csv shows that information existed within subject recycled files' metadata files*

To extract information from the recycled files' metadata files (INFO2 files) under Windows XP (and other ancient versions of Windows like 95, NT4, and ME since 0.7.0), you can use "Rifiuti2" (`https://abelcheung.github.io/rifiuti2`).

Data Carving

Data carving is an advanced type of data recovery, usually used in digital forensic investigations to extract a particular file (using file's header and footer information) from unallocated space (raw data) without the assistance of any file system structure (e.g., MFT).

Data carving can be the only method to recover important evidence files and fragments of files in a criminal investigation where the file system that was originally responsible for organizing these files on the hard drive is missing or corrupted. Data carving is also needed when extracting a file(s) from a captured network traffic stream.

Data carving is an advanced technique in digital forensics and is beyond this book's scope. However, you should know that expert forensic examiners can extract (recover) structured data, and hence a file like a document or photo, out of nonstructured data or raw data using data carving techniques.

FILE CARVING WITH A HEX EDITOR

File carving can be conducted using only a Hex editor; however, there are some tools that can aid examiners. The following are some free tools for conducting file carving:

1. Foremost (`http://foremost.sourceforge.net`)

2. Scalpel (`https://github.com/sleuthkit/scalpel`)

3. Jpegcarver (`www.seedstech.net/jpegcarver`)

4. List of data recovery (including some file carving) tools from forensics wiki
   (`www.forensicswiki.org/wiki/Tools:Data_Recovery`)

Attributing an Action to Its Associated User Account

Sometimes, a suspect Windows PC can have more than one account, for example, one for Nihad, another for Rita, and the third for Susan. For each account on a Windows PC, there is a unique number that distinguishes it called the SID. By using this SID, a digital forensic examiner can know which user account conducted which action or when a particular user account triggered a specific event. The MS-DOS command (`wmic useraccount get name,sid`) can show us the available user accounts and their associated SIDs of any Windows machine (see Figure 7-9).

Windows Registry Analysis

The registry is considered the heart of Windows OS; it contains critical information needed by the operating system and installed applications in order to function. Almost every action conducted by a Windows user is stored in its registry in one way or another; this makes the Windows registry a rich source of evidence that can be extremely valuable for any digital forensic investigation.

Architecture of Windows Registry

The registry is a hierarchical database that stores Windows system configuration settings for hardware, software applications, and the operating system in addition to the user's preferences and the computer's and applications' usage history.

Registry data is structured in a tree format, where each node in the tree is called a key. A key can contain other keys (subkeys) in addition to data values (see Figure 7-15).

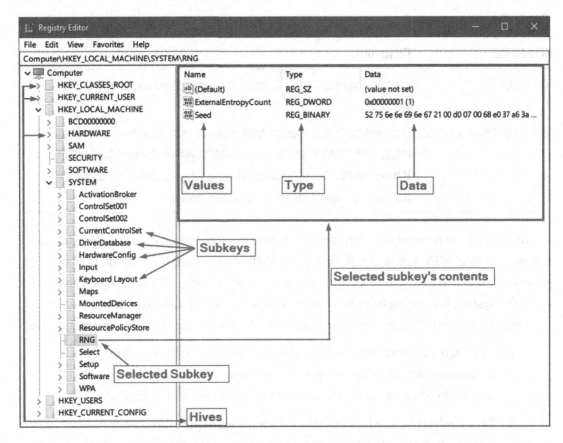

Figure 7-15. *Windows registry structure*

The Windows registry contains five root folders (also known as hives). Hives are the first folders in the registry and appear on the left side when you first open the registry editor and all other keys are minimized (see Table 7-1).

Table 7-1. *Windows Registry Root Folders (Hives)*

Hive Name	Contents
HKEY_CLASSES_ROOT	Contains file association information (configuration information that tells Windows which program to use to open files).
HKEY_CURRENT_USER	Stores configuration information (related to the installed software and operating system) to the currently logged-in user.
HKEY_LOCAL_MACHINE	Contains the majority of the configuration information for currently installed programs and the Windows OS itself.

(continued)

Table 7-1. (*continued*)

Hive Name	Contents
HKEY_USERS	Contains configuration information (user profiles) for all active users on the system.
HKEY_CURRENT_CONFIG	Does not store information itself; instead, acts as a pointer to another registry key (**HKEY_LOCAL_MACHINE\System\CurrentControlSet\ Hardware Profiles\Current**). This hive keeps information about the hardware profile of the local computer system.

Root hives are divided into two types with regard to their data persistence: volatile and nonvolatile. HKEY_LOCAL_MACHINE and HKEY_USERS keys are nonvolatile and are stored on the hard drive, while the remaining hives are volatile and should be captured while the system is running in order to acquire useful information from them.

Digital forensic investigators can examine the Windows registry using two methods:

1. The registry is contained within a forensic image. In this way, the computer forensic program will be used to investigate registry files as you do when browsing files/folders using Windows File Explorer.

2. Live analysis (e.g., when booting up from the suspect forensic image). In this method, you can access the registry as you do with any computer using the Windows built-in registry editor.

If we are examining the Windows registry using a captured forensic image, it is necessary to know where the registry files are stored. Registry hives are located in **Windows\System32\Config** folder, so if your OS is installed on the **C:** drive, your registry files will be located in the **C:\Windows\System32\Config** folder. After accessing this folder, you will find many files (a separate file for each root hive and a couple of supporting files for each one, except for the HKEY_CURRENT_USER hive, as this one is stored in your profile folder).

Windows comes equipped with a registry editor, which allows any user with administrative privilege to view, edit, and back up the Windows registry. To access the built-in registry editor, follow these steps:

1. Press the Windows button and the R button (Win+R) to open the Run dialog.

2. Type "regedit" and press OK.

Acquiring Windows Registry

As we saw in Chapter 5, computer forensics tools will acquire Windows registry files as a part of acquiring the target machine's system drive or when performing a complete hard drive acquisition. You can also extract only the registry files from a live system and store it separately for later analysis (this is usually referred as "Registry Image"). The following shows how we can do this using AccessData FTK Imager.

To acquire target Windows machine registry using FTK Imager, follow these steps:

1. Download AccessData FTK Imager as we did in Chapter 5 and transfer it into your USB thumb drive.

2. Attach the USB drive that contains FTK Imager to the suspect machine, open FTK Image, and go to File menu ➤ Obtain Protected Files...

3. A new dialog appears; select where you want to store obtained files, and check the option "Password recovery and all registry files" (see Figure 7-16). Finally, click the "OK" button.

Figure 7-16. *Using FTK Imager to acquire target Windows registry database*

4. A progress window will appear showing registry files' export progress; upon finishing, the window will disappear without announcing any success message.

Go to the directory where you have saved your registry files to see the resultant files; you should see the five files and one folder (see Figure 7-17).

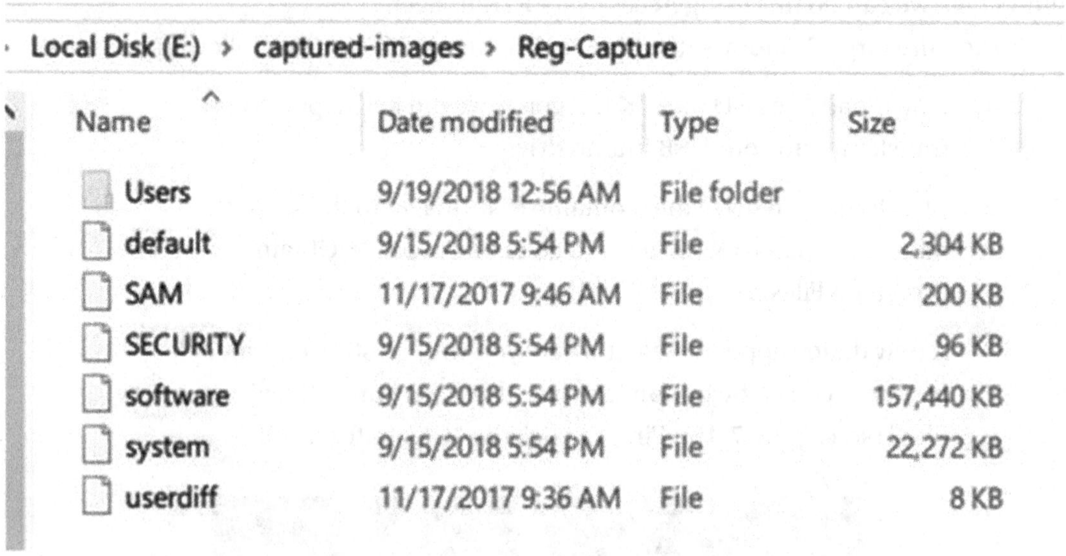

Local Disk (E:) > captured-images > Reg-Capture			
Name	Date modified	Type	Size
Users	9/19/2018 12:56 AM	File folder	
default	9/15/2018 5:54 PM	File	2,304 KB
SAM	11/17/2017 9:46 AM	File	200 KB
SECURITY	9/15/2018 5:54 PM	File	96 KB
software	9/15/2018 5:54 PM	File	157,440 KB
system	9/15/2018 5:54 PM	File	22,272 KB
userdiff	11/17/2017 9:36 AM	File	8 KB

Figure 7-17. A registry forensic image captured with AccessData FTK Imager

Now that we have successfully exported our target machine registry, we can use different forensics tools to analyze it.

Registry Examination

Most computer forensics suites have the ability to investigate the Windows registry from the acquired forensic image. There are also many programs specializing in analyzing Windows registry files alone. In this section, we will assume that we have booted up using a suspect forensic image to perform various forensic analyses on it. Some dedicated tools for investigating specific areas within the registry will get covered too where applicable.

Automatic Startup Locations

Windows has a feature that allows programs to launch automatically as it boots; this feature is necessary for some applications like antivirus software that must run first to stop any malicious software before Windows gets booted completely.

Malicious software like keyloggers and botnets can add entries to the Windows registry in order to launch automatically with each Windows boot. The Windows registry stores a record of every program boot with Windows. A list of autobooted programs can be found in the registry keys listed in Table 7-2.

Table 7-2. *Common Windows Registry Startup Location Keys*

No	Registry key
1	HKEY_LOCAL_MACHINE\System\CurrentControlSet\Services
2	HKEY_LOCAL_MACHINE\Software\Microsoft\Windows\CurrentVersion\Explorer\ ShellServiceObjects
3	HKEY_LOCAL_MACHINE\Software\Microsoft\Windows\CurrentVersion\RunServicesOnce
4	HKEY_LOCAL_MACHINE\Software\Microsoft\Windows\CurrentVersion\RunOnce
5	HKEY_LOCAL_MACHINE\Software\Microsoft\Windows\CurrentVersion\Policies\Explorer\Run
6	HKEY_LOCAL_MACHINE\Software\Microsoft\Windows\CurrentVersion\Run
7	HKEY_LOCAL_MACHINE\Software\Microsoft\Windows NT\CurrentVersion\Windows
8	HKEY_LOCAL_MACHINE\Software\Microsoft\Windows\CurrentVersion\ ShellServiceObjectDelayLoad
9	HKEY_LOCAL_MACHINE\Software\Microsoft\Windows\CurrentVersion\Explorer\ SharedTaskScheduler
10	HKEY_LOCAL_MACHINE\Software\Microsoft\Active Setup\Installed Components
11	HKEY_LOCAL_MACHINE\Wow6432Node\Microsoft\Active Setup\Installed Components
12	HKEY_LOCAL_MACHINE\Software\Microsoft\Windows\CurrentVersion\Explorer\ SharedTaskScheduler
13	HKEY_LOCAL_MACHINE\Software\Microsoft\Windows NT\CurrentVersion\Drivers32
14	HKEY_CURRENT_USER\Software\Microsoft\Windows\CurrentVersion\RunOnce
15	HKEY_CURRENT_USER\Software\Microsoft\Windows\CurrentVersion\Run

(*continued*)

Table 7-1. (*continued*)

No	Registry key
16	HKEY_CURRENT_USER\Software\Microsoft\Windows\CurrentVersion\Policies\Explorer\Run
17	HKEY_CURRENT_USER\Software\Microsoft\Windows NT\CurrentVersion\Windows\load
18	HKEY_CURRENT_USER\SOFTWARE\Wow6432Node\Microsoft\Windows\CurrentVersion\Run (64 bit systems only)
19	HKEY_CURRENT_USER\Software\Microsoft\Windows\CurrentVersion\RunServices
20	HKEY_CURRENT_USER\ Software\Microsoft\Windows\CurrentVersion\RunServicesOnce
21	HKEY_CURRENT_USER\Software\Microsoft\Windows\CurrentVersion\RunOnceEx

Microsoft has a portable utility available to investigate all autorun programs called Autoruns (see Figure 7-18). This tool can be downloaded from `https://docs.microsoft.com/en-us/sysinternals/downloads/autoruns`.

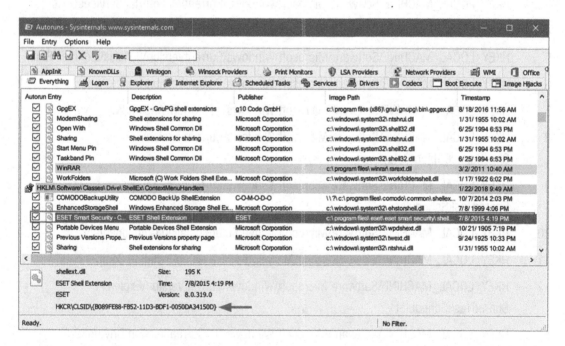

Figure 7-18. *Using Autoruns from Sysinternals to view automatic startup programs and associated registry key in Windows*

Investigating startup programs has a great forensics value in many cases; for example, a malware can control a suspect machine and launch DDoS attacks using it without the owner's knowledge. When something like this is investigated, a suspect might become very forthcoming to investigators, even though his/her PC was used to commit a crime.

Installed Program Keys in the Windows Registry

Learning what programs are currently or were previously installed on the suspect machine can be of a great value for forensic investigators. For example, the existence of steganography and encryption programs—or the leftovers belonging to such tools—will give an indication that the suspect machine may contain hidden data or simply was used to execute such programs.

Windows keeps records of all installed applications in the following locations in the registry (Table 7-3).

Table 7-3. *Registry Keys That Hold Information About Installed Programs (Current and Previous Leftover)*

No	Registry key
1	HKEY_LOCAL_MACHI NE\SOFTWARE\MICROSOFT\WINDOWS\CURRENTVERSION\UNINSTALL
2	HKEY_CURRENT _ U S E R \ S O F TWARE\MICROSOFT\WINDOWS\CURRENTVERSION\ UNINSTALL*
3	HKEY_LOCAL_MACHINE\SOFTWARE\WOW6432NODE\MICROSOFT\WINDOWS\ CURRENTVERSION\UNINSTALL**
4	HKEY _ CLASSES_ROOT \INSTALLER\PRODUCTS\<PRODUCT CODE>\SOURCELIST\NET
5	HKEY_CURRENT_USER\SOFTWARE\MICROSOFT\INSTALLER\PRODUCTS\<PRODUCT CODE>\SOURCELIST\NET

If the suspect's machine has more than one user, each user will have his/her own set of software installed on his/her own key under the (HKEY_CURRENT_USER) hive.
**For Windows X64 version.*

We can use automated tools to search for a program installed on the Windows registry or lost information such as parts of installed programs, applications left over, or any data items that could be hidden in the Windows registry.

Nirsoft offers a free tool called RegScanner (www.nirsoft.net/utils/regscanner.
html), which is a small tool used to search the Windows registry according to specific
search criteria entered by the user. The returned results appear in a list, and a user can
click any item in this list to go to the associated value in RegEdit. We can also export the
found registry values into a .reg file.

After executing this tool, a search option dialog will appear to enter your search
criteria, and you can also set some search options (see Figure 7-19).

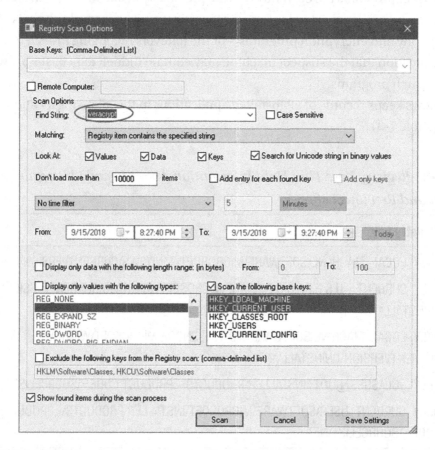

Figure 7-19. *Registry scan options used by the RegScanner tool to search within
the Windows registry*

Please note that not all programs need to install a registry key before using it; for
instance, portable applications do not need to be installed on Windows in order to run
(e.g., applications launched from a U3 USB stick).

To investigate the possibility of launching portable applications from a suspect computer, we can scan the registry for all previously connected USB devices. Another method to reveal the execution of portable programs is to check the Windows Prefetch folder for such programs. We will examine both methods later on in this chapter.

USB Device Forensics

Windows keeps a history log of all previously connected USB devices along with their connection times in addition to the associated user account which installs them. The Windows registry also stores important technical information for each connected USB device such as vendor ID, product ID, revision, and serial number.

Windows stores USB history-related information using five registry keys, where each key offers a different piece of information about the connected device. By merging this information together, investigators will have an idea of how an offender has used removable devices—such as a USB—to conduct/facilitate his/her actions.

1. **HKEY_LOCAL_MACHINE\SYSTEM\CurrentControlSet\ Enum\USBSTOR** Here you will find all USB devices that have been plugged into the operating system since its installation. It shows the USB vendor ID (manufacturer name), product ID, and the device serial number (note that if the second character of the device serial number is "&," it means the connected device does not have a serial number and the device ID has been generated by the system). See Figure 7-20 for a list of previously connected USB devices on the author's machine.

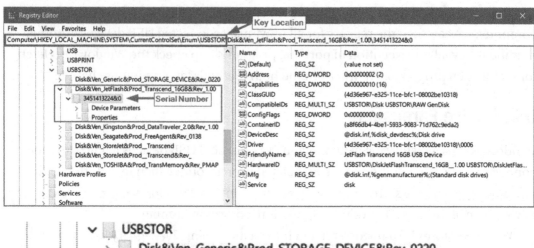

Figure 7-20. *History of USB connected devices*

2. **HKEY_LOCAL_MACHINE\SYSTEM\MountedDevices** The MountedDevices subkey stores the drive letter allocations; it matches the serial number of a USB device to a given drive letter or volume that was mounted when the USB device was inserted.

3. **HKEY_CURRENT_USER\Software\Microsoft\Windows\ CurrentVersion\Explorer\MountPoints2** This key will record which user was logged into Windows when a specific USB device was connected. The key also includes the "Last Write Time" for each device that was connected to the system.

4. **HKEY_LOCAL_MACHINE\SYSTEM\Currentcontrolset\Enum\ Usb** This key holds technical information about each connected USB device in addition to the last time the subject USB was connected to the investigated computer.

5. **Identify the first time device was connected:** Check this file at \Windows\inf\setupapi.dev.log for Windows Vista, 7, and 8, and at \Windows\inf\setupapi.upgrade.log for Windows 10. On Windows XP, this file will be located at \Windows\setupapi.log. Search in this file for a particular USB device's serial number to learn when it was first connected to the subject system (in local time).

To automate the process of finding information about the current and previous USB connected devices, you can download a free tool by Nirsoft that can perform all the tasks we just did manually; this tool is called USBDeview (www.nirsoft.net/utils/usb_devices_view.html). After executing this tool on the target system, extended information (e.g., device name/description, device type, serial number, and much more) about each connected USB device will appear.

In Figure 7-21, the Last Plug/Unplug Date represents the first time that the device was connected to the system. This date does not change when the same device is repeatedly reinserted. The "Created Date" represents the last time that the same device was attached to the system.

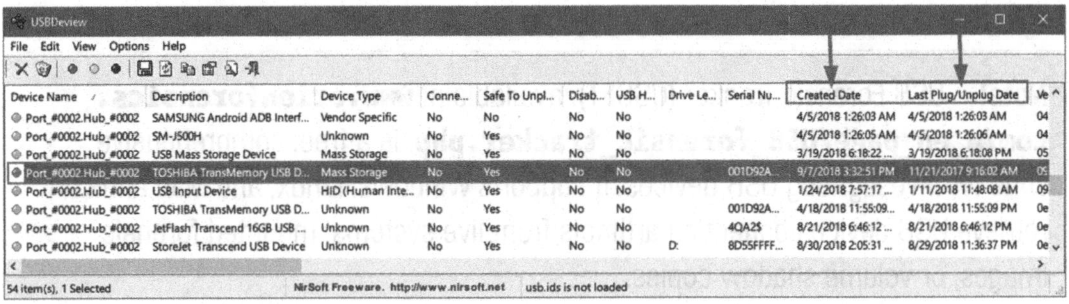

Figure 7-21. *Using USBDeview to view different artifacts about previously connected USB devices*

Unfortunately, not all USB device types will leave traces in Windows registry as we have described, for instance, USB devices that use media transfer protocol (MTP) when connecting with computers. Devices equipped with the modern Android OS versions in addition to Windows phones and Blackberry all use the MTP protocol; this protocol does not leave traces in the Windows registry when a USB device is connected to a Windows computer. This necessitates a specialized tool to handle the investigation of such artifacts.

USB Detective (`https://usbdetective.com`) supports detecting USB devices that use the MTP protocol to connect to Windows. It also offers rich features for thoroughly investigating connected USB devices, like creating timelines of all unique connection/disconnection and deletion timestamps for each device; however, you need to upgrade to the professional paid version to use all features.

To conclude this section, a USB device connected through an MTP connection needs special treatment to acquire its traces from a Windows machine; consult your computer forensic software documentation for the availability of such a feature.

ADDITIONAL READING

More information about USB devices and MTP can be found at

- SANS DFIR Summit presentation: **https://digital-forensics.sans.org/summit-archives/dfir14/USB_Devices_and_Media_Transfer_Protocol_Nicole_Ibrahim.pdf**

- Nicole Ibrahim's series of blog posts about this topic: **http://nicoleibrahim.com/part-1-mtp-and-ptp-usb-device-research/**

Note!   USB Forensic Tracker (USBFT), available at **www.orionforensics.com/w_en_page/USB_forensic_tracker.php**, is a free, comprehensive suite for investigating USB devices. It supports Windows, Linux, and Mac and can retrieve USB device connection artifacts from live systems, mounted forensic images, or volume shadow copies.

Most Recently Used List

Windows keep a log of the most recently accessed files (e.g., when you open a file using Windows File Explorer or from a standard open/save dialog box, run command using the MS-DOS prompt on the registry). There are many applications that run on Windows that have most recently used (MRU) lists such as recently opened MS Office files and recently visited web pages; these applications list the files that have been most recently accessed. The most common places for storing such lists are in the registry keys shown in Table 7-4:

Table 7-4. *Common Windows Registry History List Keys: Windows 10*

No	Registry key
1	HKEY_CURRENT_USER\Software\Microsoft\Internet Explorer\TypedURLs
2	HKEY_CURRENT_USER\Software\Microsoft\Office\16.0\Word*\File MRU
3	HKEY_CURRENT_USER\Software\Microsoft\Windows\CurrentVersion\Explorer\ComDlg32\ OpenSavePidlMRU
4	HKEY_CURRENT_USER\Software\Microsoft\Windows\CurrentVersion\Explorer\ComDlg32\ LastVisitedPidlMRU**
5	HKEY_CURRENT_USER\Software\Microsoft\Windows\CurrentVersion\Explorer\RunMRU
6	HKEY_CURRENT_USER\Software\Microsoft\Windows\CurrentVersion\Explorer\RecentDocs
7	HKEY_CURRENT_USER\Software\Microsoft\Windows\CurrentVersion\Applets\Regedit

** *This key tracks the application (executable) used to open the files in the previous (OpenSavePidlMRU) key.*

- Replace "Word" with "Excel," "Access," "PowerPoint," "Outlook," or "Groove" as needed. The MRU list for each MS Office program currently installed is located under this General key. We are testing now using Windows 10 with MS Office 2016 already installed.

Note!   Further info about OpenSaveMRU and LastVisitedMRU can be found at `https://digital-forensics.sans.org/blog/2010/04/02/ openrunsavemru-lastvisitedmru`.

Nirsoft offers great tools for investigating the list of files and programs or batch files that have been previously opened/executed on the target machine.

1. ExecutedProgramsList (`www.nirsoft.net/utils/executed_ programs_list.html`): List of programs and batch files that have executed previously on the target machine.

2. OpenSaveFilesView (`www.nirsoft.net/utils/open_save_files_ view.html`): List of files that have been previously opened on the target machine using the standard open/save dialog box of Windows.

Network Analysis

Whenever a Windows user connects his/her machine to the Internet or intranet, Windows will log this action in the registry. Knowing the network connection has vital forensic value; for instance, the registry lists all network cards that have been used on the suspect machine whether it is built in or attached (e.g., via USB port). The registry will also reveal the wireless connection profile (name, IP address, subnet mask, DHCP) in addition to the date the connection was first created and the last date the connection took place.

In Table 7-5 you will find registry keys for investigating network connection information.

Table 7-5. *Common Windows Registry Keys for Storing Network Connections*

No	Registry key
1	HKEY_LOCAL_MACHINE\SOFTWARE\Microsoft\Windows NT\CurrentVersion\NetworkCards
2	HKEY_LOCAL_MACHINE\SOFTWARE\Microsoft\WindowsNT\CurrentVersion\NetworkList\Nla\Cache\Intranet
3	HKEY_LOCAL_MACHINE\SOFTWARE\Microsoft\Windows NT\CurrentVersion\NetworkList\Nla\Wireless*
4	HKEY_LOCAL_MACHINE\SOFTWARE\Microsoft\WindowsNT\CurrentVersion\NetworkList\Signatures\Unmanaged**
5	HKEY_LOCAL_MACHINE\SOFTWARE\Microsoft\Windows NT\CurrentVersion\NetworkList\Profiles***

Holds the identifier of all wireless networks to which the system was connected.

**Holds detailed information about each wireless connection on the target machine. Links the identifier of the previous key to this key to provide comprehensive information about the target connection (see Figure 7-22).*

***Holds the "Creation date" and "Last connected date" of the selected wireless connection. The values of these dates are of binary type (see Figure 7-23).*

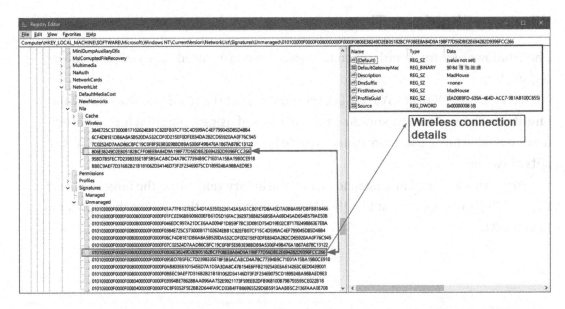

Figure 7-22. *Revealing wireless connection (access point) network properties*

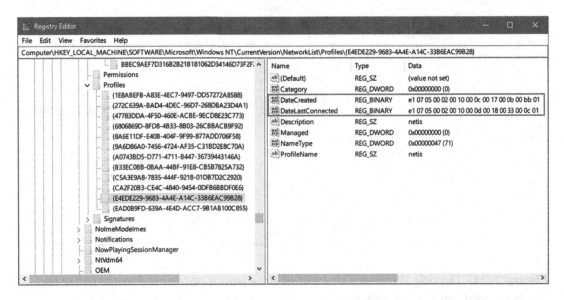

Figure 7-23. *Viewing "Creation date" and "Last connected date" of the selected wireless connection*

Windows Shutdown Time

The Windows registry records when the system was last closed down in the following registry key:

HKEY_LOCAL_MACHINE\SYSTEM\CurrentControlSet\Control\Windows under the **ShutdownTime** value. The shutdown value is stored using a binary value; to decode it to a readable form, use a tool called DCode from Digital Detective (www.digital-detective.net/dcode).

To use this tool, you first need to extract the binary value from the target key (see Figure 7-24) and then enter it into the DCode program; set the options that appear in Figure 7-24.

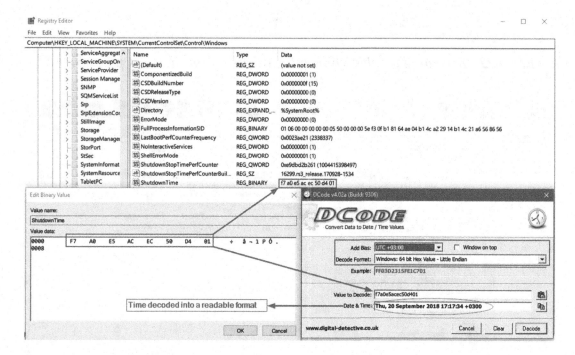

Figure 7-24. *Decode Windows shutdown time into a readable format using the "DCode" tool from Digital Detective*

UserAssist Forensics

UserAssist keeps a record of all executable programs recently launched in addition to the frequency of usage (number of executions) for each recorded program. UserAssistinformation can be found in the following registry key:

HKEY_CURRENT_USER\Software\Microsoft\Windows\CurrentVersion\Explorer\ UserAssist

---

Note!   UserAssist will only record programs launched via Windows Explorer; programs launched through the command line will not appear in UserAssist registry keys.

Information stored in UserAssist keys is encoded using ROT-13 encoding schema. To decode this information, use UserAssist-View (www.nirsoft.net/utils/userassist_ view.html), a tool by Nirsoft that can display stored info in a readable format.

Printer Registry Information

The Windows registry contains the entries for printing shown in Table 7-6.

Table 7-6. *Location of Installed Printer's Keys in Windows Registry*

Registry key	Description
HKEY_CURRENT_USER\Printers	Holds settings of the current default printer.
HKEY_LOCAL_MACHINE\SYSTEM\ CurrentControlSet\Control\Print	Contains additional subkeys that hold information about installed printer.

For instance, to view the properties of currently installed printers on the target machine, go to HKEY_LOCAL_MACHINE\SYSTEM\CurrentControlSet\Control\Print\ Printers\<printername> (see Figure 7-25).

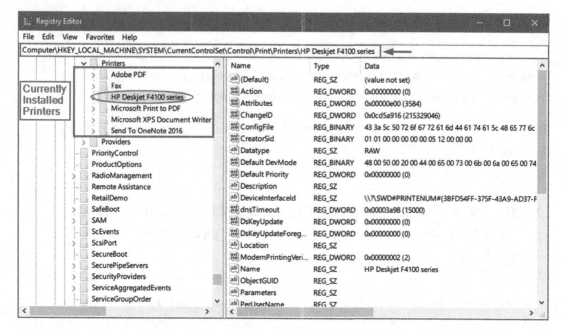

Figure 7-25. *Viewing currently installed printers' properties*

Deleted Registry Key Recovery

Recovering deleted Windows registry keys can be forensically valuable in many cases; for instance, there is a simple, portable tool developed by Eric Zimmerman to handle this task and more. To use this tool, do the following:

1. Go to `https://ericzimmerman.github.io/#!index.md` and download Registry Explorer/RECmd.

2. Double-click to execute the tool; go to File ➤ Load offline hive.

3. Browse to where the registry files are stored (we already showed you how to acquire registry files using FTK Imager) and select the file(s) you want to open. If you want to open more than one file, hold **Ctrl** and click files to select them individually.

4. Registry Explorer will recover any deleted records available during hive loading (see Figure 7-26). The option "Recover deleted files/ values" should be enabled (it is already enabled by default) to view deleted registry records. You can access this option from: Options menu ➤ Recover deleted files/values (the selector is to the right).

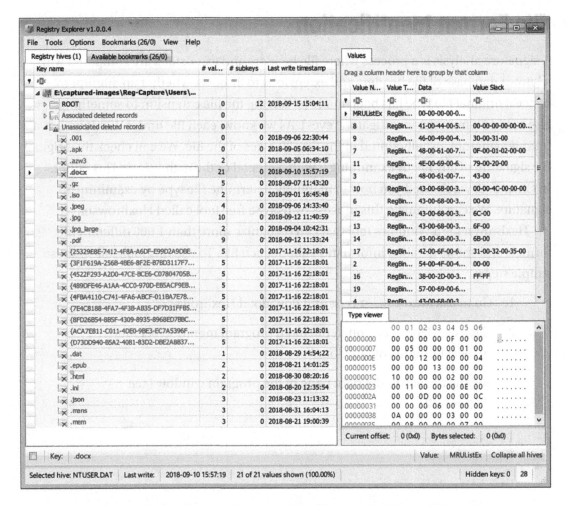

Figure 7-26. *View deleted registry keys using Registry Explorer ("Associated deleted records" are still associated with keys in the active registry, while the "Unassociated delete records" are not).*

5. Right-click over any deleted registry key to export it or to export its value (you can export recovered key value into HTML, PDF, Excel, JSON, or TSV).

File Format Identification

A signature analysis is a process where file headers and extensions are compared with a known database of file headers and extensions to discover whether an attempt to conceal original file type has been made (changing the file extension to something else to hide it from the investigators' eyes). As we know, each file under Windows has a unique signature, usually stored in the first 20 bytes of the file. We can check the original file signature of any file by examining it with Notepad or through using a Hex editor. In Chapter 2, we showed you how to manually determine file type by examining its signature. We can automate this process by using a free tool called HexBrowser.

HexBrowser is a Windows tool that can recognize more than 1,000 different file formats and shows detailed information about each file. To use this tool, follow these simple steps:

1. Go to www.hexbrowser.com and download HexBrowser.

2. Click the "Open" button in the main program menu, select the suspect file, and you are done!

3. See the results on the right pane of the program window (see Figure 7-27).

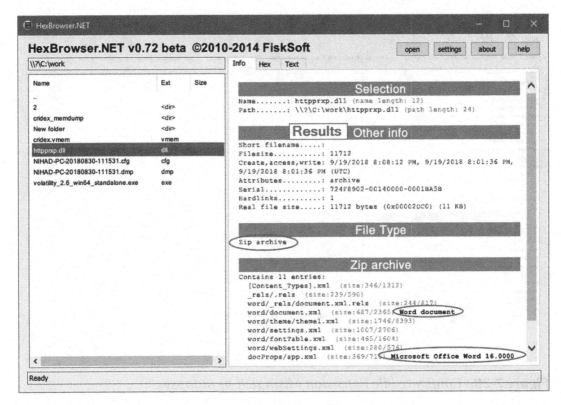

Figure 7-27. *Using HexBrowser to discover specified original file format. In this example, a file with a DLL extension was investigated, and HexBrowser discovered that the original file type is MS Word 2016.*

Autopsy has the ability to discover file extension mismatches; to use this feature, you have to enable the "Extension Mismatch Detector" module. You can further configure file mismatch search options by going to the Tools menu ➤ Options ➤ File Extension Mismatch. From here, you can add or remove extensions based on your case need (see Figure 7-28), and the results are shown in the Results tree under "Extension Mismatch Detected" (see Figure 7-29).

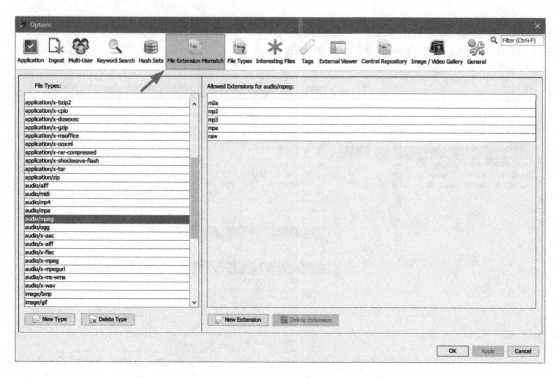

Figure 7-28. *Configure File Extension Mismatch in Autopsy*

Figure 7-29. *Discover file mismatch results using Autopsy*

Windows Features Forensics Analysis

There are many features offered by Windows OS to optimize—or to allow a user to customize—some of its functions to become more user friendly. Investigating such features is essential, as they can be a source of digital evidence. In this section, we will examine some common features of Windows for interesting artifacts.

Windows Prefetch Analysis

Prefetch is a feature used by Windows to speed up loading applications. Windows creates a Prefetch file when a user executes an application for the first time, and then it will record which files have been loaded as a part of this application execution, in addition to the last time this application was executed, so the next time a user launches it, Windows will load it quicker. From a digital forensic perspective, the Prefetch feature can tell us what program(s) was executed on the target system even though the subject program was uninstalled after executing it, as it will remain in the Windows Prefetch folder.

The Prefetcher's configuration is stored in the following Windows registry key:

HKEY_LOCAL_MACHINE\SYSTEM\CurrentControlSet\Control\Session Manager\Memory Management\PrefetchParameters

Windows stores Prefetch files at **C:\Windows\Prefetch**. Prefetch files are all named using common naming criteria. The name of the running application comes first, then comes an eight-character hash of the location where the application was run, and finally it ends with the .PF extension (see Figure 7-30).

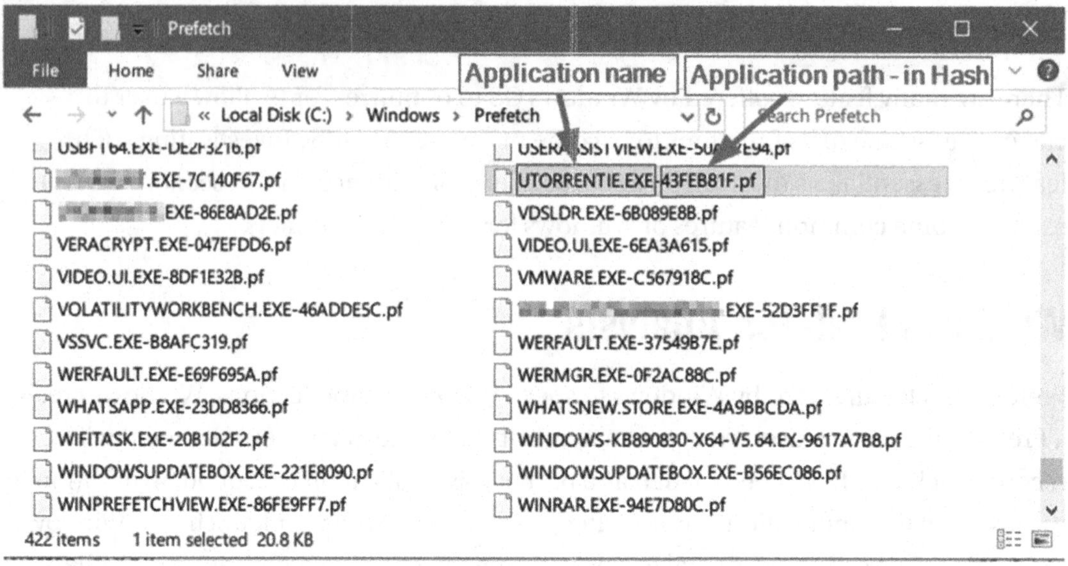

Figure 7-30. *Contents of Windows Prefetch folder; image taken from Windows 10*

WinPrefetchView from Nirsoft (`www.nirsoft.net/utils/win_prefetch_view.html`) is a simple, portable tool for reading the Prefetch files stored in the target Windows computer.

Another tool for investigating Windows Prefetch files also comes from Eric Zimmerman: Prefetch Parser (`https://ericzimmerman.github.io/#!index.md`) is a portable command-line tool for reading the information associated with each Prefetch file located in the Windows Prefetch folder.

Using this tool is simple: execute it from the command-line prompt, using the **-d** switch followed by Prefetch folder location. You can export the result directly to TXT file as we did in this experiment (see Figure 7-31).

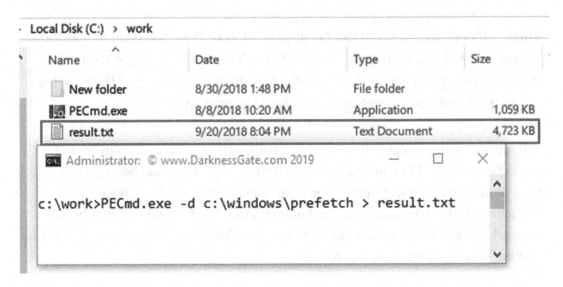

Figure 7-31. *Using Prefetch Parser and storing the output results directly in the same working directory under the name "result.txt"*

Windows Thumbnail Forensics

Windows stores thumbnails of graphics files (JPEG, BMP, GIF, PNG, TIFF) and some document types (DOCX, PPTX, PDF) and movie files in the thumbnail cache file called *thumbs.db* when a user selects to view files as thumbnail, for quick viewing at a later time.

Investigating this feature can tell examiners about previous files (e.g., images) that existed on a system even though the user has deleted them, as image thumbnails may still exist at *thumbs.db*.

Modern Windows versions (Vista+) store thumbnail previews on a central location in the system. The cache is stored at `%userprofile%\AppData\Local\Microsoft\Windows\Explorer` as a series of files with the standard name thumbcache_xxx.db (XXX refers to its size), in addition to an index file to find thumbnails in each database.

Thumbs Viewer is a portable tool for extracting thumbnail images from the Thumbs.db, ehthumbs.db, ehthumbs_vista.db, Image.db, Video.db, TVThumb.db, and musicThumbs.db database files found on all versions of Windows OS. You can download it from `https://thumbsviewer.github.io`.

Note!   *Thumb.db* files come hidden. In order to view them, you need first to show hidden files and folders by going to the Control Panel ➤ Folder Options➤ View tab and checking the option "Show hidden files, folders, and drives." Uncheck the option "Hide protected operating system files (Recommended)."

If you are looking to open thumbcache_*.db files, there is another utility from the same developer called Thumbcache Viewer (`https://thumbcacheviewer.github.io`), which allows you to extract thumbnail images from the thumbcache_*.db and iconcache_*.db database files found in Windows Vista, 7, 8, 8.1, and 10. Thumbcaches are usually located at `\Users\<USER>\AppData\Local\Microsoft\Windows\Explorer` in Windows Vista and above (see Figure 7-32).

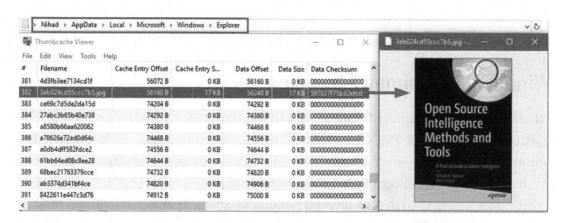

Figure 7-32. *Using Thumbcache Viewer to extract information from thumbcache_*.db and iconcache_*.db files*

Jump Lists Forensics

Beginning with Windows 7, Microsoft released a new feature for Windows users. Jump Lists is a feature that allows users to view recently viewed or accessed files for each installed application. Investigating this feature has great forensic value, as it gives deep insight into the user's computer habits and recently accessed files, especially in criminal cases when the user's activities on the computer are the focus of the investigation.

This feature is enabled by default in Windows 10; you can configure it by going to Windows Settings (Win + i button) ➤ Personalization ➤ Start.

Jump List files are created for each user on a Windows and are located at

\Users\<username>\AppData\Roaming\Microsoft\Windows\Recent\

Note!   The "AppData" directory is hidden by default; you need to view hidden files under Windows as we did previously in order to see it.

We can differentiate between two types of Jump List, automatic and custom:

AUTOMATICDESTINATIONS-MS

These files are created in \Users\<username>\AppData\Roaming\Microsoft\Windows\ Recent\AutomaticDestinations-ms and are created automatically by Windows when a user opens an application or accesses a file. Jump Lists are contained within OLE containers and are named according to the application that has opened the relevant file (see Figure 7-33).

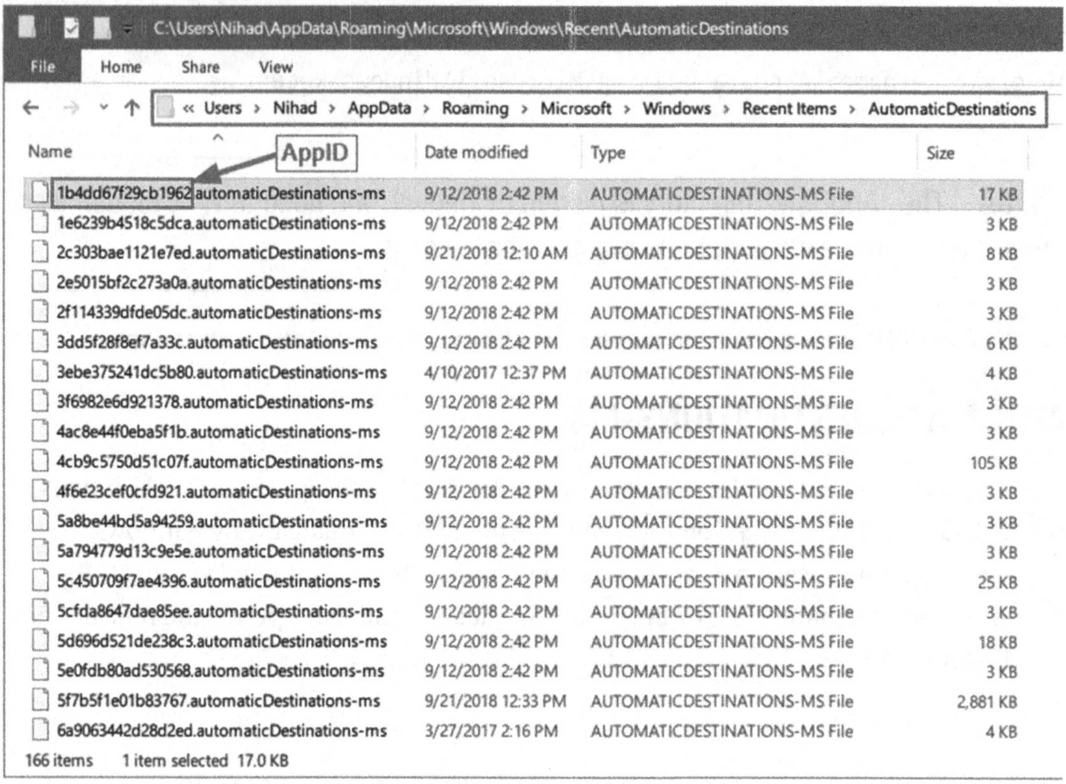

Figure 7-33. *Viewing hidden directory Users\<username>\AppData\Roaming*
Microsoft\Windows\Recent\AutomaticDestinations-ms

CUSTOMDESTINATIONS-MS

These files are created in \Users\<username>\AppData\Roaming\Microsoft\Windows\
Recent\CustomDestinations-ms when a user pins a file to the Start menu or task bar.

For both *AutomaticDestinations-ms* and *CustomDestinations-Ms*, files are named
using the relevant application name (AppID), which consists of 16 hexadecimal digits,
followed by the ".customDestinations-ms" or "automaticDestinations-ms" extensions.
These AppIDs are named by the application or the system during application runtime.

Knowing the AppID name will allow the examiner to learn the identity of the
application used to access or view the intended file in the Jump List. There are different
web sites that list Jump List IDs, like Forensics Wiki (www.forensicswiki.org/wiki/
List_of_Jump_List_IDs) and Github (https://github.com/4n6k/Jump_List_AppIDs/
blob/master/4n6k_AppID_Master_List.md).

Nirsoft offers a tool to automate the process of extracting information from Windows Jump List files. This tool, JumpListsView (`www.nirsoft.net/utils/jump_lists_view.html`), displays the information stored by the Jump Lists, like the name of the file opened by the user and the date/time when the open event took place. However, you still need to investigate the AppID manually to determine which program was used to open a subject file.

LNK File Forensics

The Windows shortcut file (LNK extension) is a shortcut file (consider it a kind of metadata file) that points to an application or file on Windows OS. Such files are commonly found at a user's desktop; however, we can also see them scattered in other locations. LNK files can be created by a user or autogenerated by Windows when a user opens a local or remote file.

LNK files hold a wealth of useful information about the computer at which the file was first created time in addition to the computer where it resides currently.

LNK files are forensically valuable because they reveal the following information:

1. MAC time attributes (Creation, Modification, and Access time) for the LNK file itself and for the linked file.

2. The user's previous activities on the computer; for example, if a suspect moves a file into a USB drive or deletes it permanently from his/computer, the associated LNK file will still exist, giving valuable information about what has executed on the target system before.

3. Linked file size.

4. Original path of the linked file.

5. The serial number and name of the volume that held the linked file.

6. The network adapter MAC address and original network path of the original computer.

Right-clicking over the LNK shortcut will reveal some information like the MAC time of the LNK file itself (see Figure 7-34) and the linked file path.

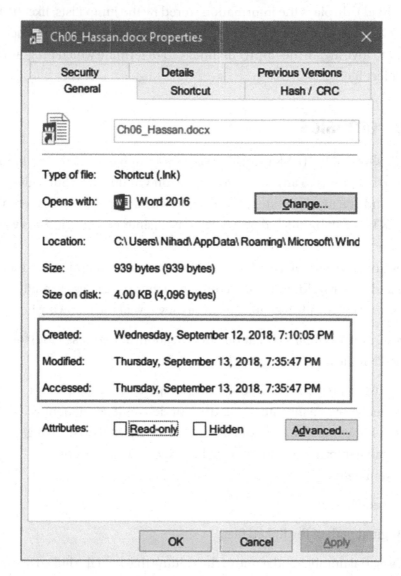

Figure 7-34. *Properties of LNK file reveal a MAC time of a LNK file in addition to the original (linked) file path, which can be found under the "Shortcut" tab*

However, there is much information that can be retrieved by using third-party tools specializing in parsing LNK files. The following are two popular tools for investigating LNK files.

Windows File Analyzer (WFA)

This program decodes and displays information extracted from special Windows files like shortcut files, Prefetch files, Index.dat, Thumbnail Database, and others. To use this tool to extract LNK file information from a specific directory, do the following:

1. Download the tool from www.mitec.cz/wfa.html (this is a portable free program).

2. Launch the tool, and go to File ➤ Analyze Shortcuts ➤ Browse and select target folder (see Figure 7-35). The program will ask you to the select target OS. Finally click the "OK" button and you are done!

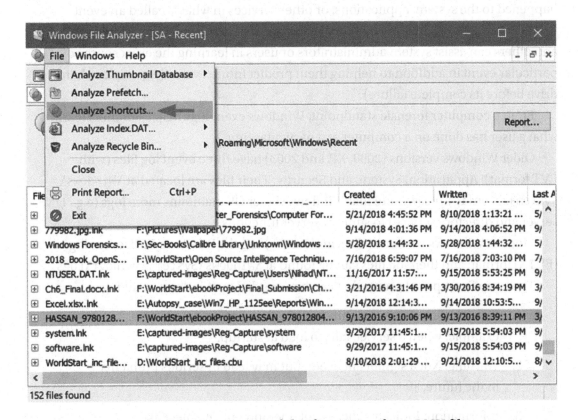

Figure 7-35. Using WFA to extract useful information from LNK files

Link Parser

Developed by 4Discovery, Link Parser (`www.4discovery.com/our-tools`) is a free portable tool for extracting information from LNK files. It can parse a single item or multiple items, a complete forensic image, or a folder and list all found LNK files in addition to their information (about 30 attributes). The gathered information can be exported into a CSV.

Event Log Analysis

Windows records important events (both hardware and software events) that have happened to the system, applications, or other services in what is called an event log. Recording events like low memory, excessive access to hard drive, failed login, and others can assist system administrators or users in learning the exact source of a particular event in addition to helping them predict future events (e.g., replace hard drive before its complete failure).

From a computer forensic standpoint, Windows event logs help examiners learn what a user has done on a computer at a particular time.

Older Windows versions (2000, XP, and 2003) have three event log files (with EVT format): Application, System, and Security. Their files are located at `\Windows\system32\config`; please note that Windows server OS maintains more logs (e.g., DNS server and directory service) to support server functions.

Modern Windows versions (Vista and newer) use the Windows XML event log (EVTX) format, and their log files can be found at `\Windows\System32\winevt\Logs`.

There are five types of events that can be recorded by Windows event log:

1. Error: Indicates that a significant problem has occurred: for example, when a service fails to load at startup.

2. Warning: Not a significant event, but may lead to serious problems in the future.

3. Information: Indicates successful operation of an object like service, application, or driver.

4. Success Audit: Points to a successful security event (e.g., successful login is recorded as "Success Audit event").

5. Failure Audit: Reverses a Success Audit (e.g., when a user fails to log in to Windows, the event is logged as a "Failure Audit event").

Note!   Microsoft recommends a list of Windows log events to be monitored because they can give a sign of compromise. You can find the list at `https://docs.microsoft.com/en-us/windows-server/identity/ad-ds/plan/appendix-l--events-to-monitor`.

The main elements of every event in a log entry are as follows:

1. User: Username of the account logged into the machine when the event occurs.

2. Event ID: A number generated by Windows that identifies event type.

3. Source: The object which caused the event to occur.

4. Computer: Name of the computer where the event occurred.

5. Date and time: The date and time when the event occurred.

6. Description: Description of what happened to launch the event.

Windows offers a simple GUI to view logged events; you can access Event Viewer by going to Control Panel ➤ Administrative Tools ➤ Computer Management (see Figure 7-36).

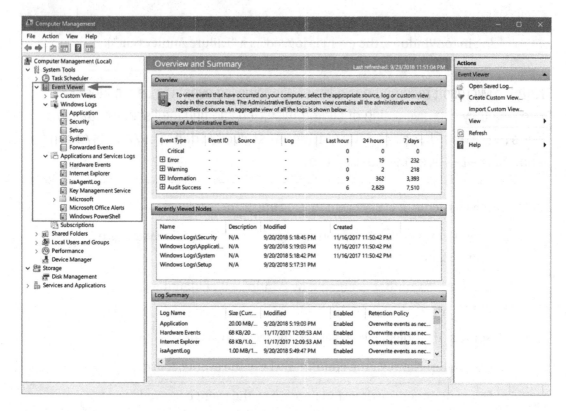

Figure 7-36. *Event Viewer using Windows 10 OS*

The built-in Windows event viewer offers an adequate interface to search and explore within available events; however, some third-party tools can offer a more convenient way to browse Windows events.

FullEventLogView (`www.nirsoft.net/utils/full_event_log_view.html`) is a portable tool developed by Nirsoft that displays all Windows event logs in one table. By using this tool, you can view events stored on a local machine or a remote computer, or you can examine an exported Windows log file with an .evtx extension. An event list can be exported into a TXT or HTML file, allowing easy manipulation of results in another program.

Using this tool is simple: after the tool is executed, it will automatically display a log of all events of the current machine in the past seven days. To change this setting, go to Options ➤ Advanced Options and change these settings to "Show events from all times."

To change the data source from which you want to parse events, go to File ➤ Choose Data Source (see Figure 7-37).

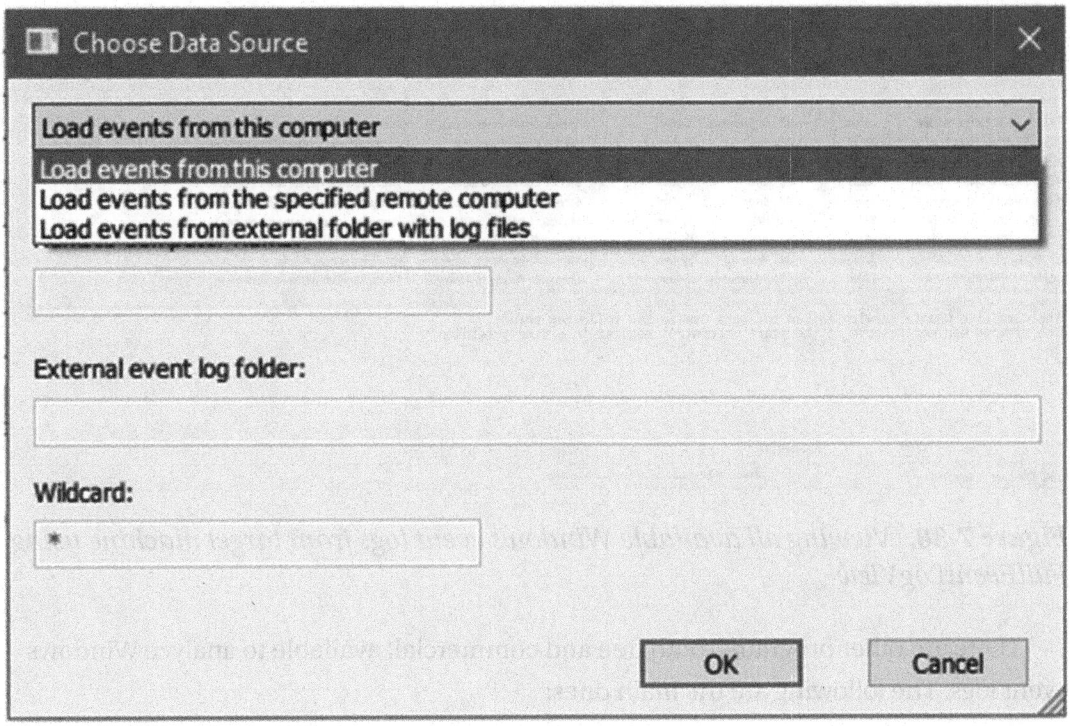

Figure 7-37. *Choosing data source in FullEventLogView*

Now, once the data source of the log has been selected and the timeframe to view log data has been updated, FullEventLogView will update its view to display all available event logs in the main window (see Figure 7-38).

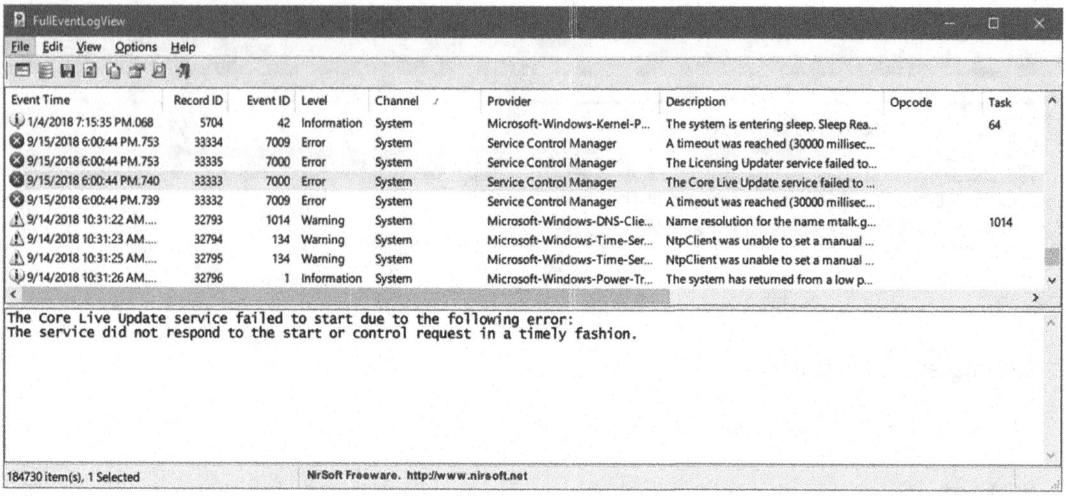

Figure 7-38. *Viewing all available Windows event logs from target machine using FullEventLogView*

There are other programs, both free and commercial, available to analyze Windows event logs. The following are the main ones:

1. Log parser (`www.microsoft.com/en-us/download/details.aspx?id=24659`). Query Windows event log using the SQL query language.

2. Log Parser Lizard GUI (`www.lizard-labs.com/log_parser_lizard.aspx`). Query software tool; it uses SQL to query Windows event log, IIS log, the registry, the file system, the active directory services, and more. This is a commercial application; a free trial is available.

Hidden Hard Drive Partition Analysis

Most hard drives (HDD and SSD) usually come divided into partitions. Dividing a partition is useful for many reasons; for example, a user can dedicate one partition for housing the OS files and another one for storing user private data.

Dividing hard drives into partitions is not only limited to end users; for instance, most computer vendors create a hidden partition to store a recovery image of an installed OS. However, hidden partitions can also contain incriminating data and other files of interest.

To check if a particular hard drive or USB stick contains hidden partitions, we can use the DiskPart command-line utility, which comes as a part of the Microsoft Windows family (Windows 10, 8, 8.1, 7, Vista, XP, and Server 2003).

To launch this tool, open a DOS prompt, type DiskPart, and press Enter. Perform the following actions to check for hidden partitions:

1. Type "List disk" to view a list of hard disks/drives connected to this PC and associated numbers.

2. To view the partitions of a selected hard drive, you first need to select it through the "select disk = n" command, where n points to the disk/drive number that appears in the first command.

3. After selecting the disk/drive, type "list partition" to see a list of partitions associated with this disk drive.

See Figure 7-39 for a complete demonstration of these steps.

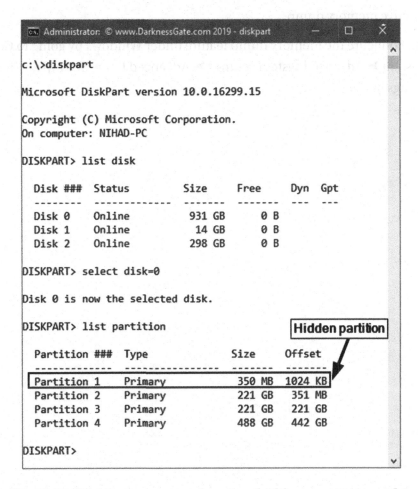

Figure 7-39. *Using DiskPart command to view hidden partitions within the Windows OS*

Windows Minidump File Forensics

When a Windows machine crashes with a Blue Screen of Death, a copy of computer memory at the time of the crash will be stored in *\Windows\minidump* or *\Winnt\ minidump* depending on the version of Windows. Windows can create different memory dumps; for instance, there are five types in Windows 10 (see Figure 7-40):

1. Small memory dump (256 KB)

2. Kernel memory dump

3. Complete memory dump

4. Automatic memory dump (default option)

5. Active memory dump

You can configure the memory dump feature under Windows by going to Control Panel ➤ System ➤ Advanced system settings ➤ Advanced tab ➤ Startup and Recovery pane – Settings button.

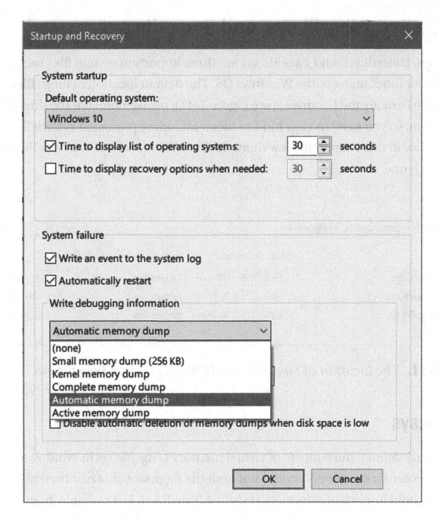

Figure 7-40. *Configuring memory dump under Windows 10*

Minidump files will usually contain the programs that were running/installed at the time of the crash; this can be very useful for digital forensic examiners. For example, if we think that a suspect was using a portable steganography tool to conceal a secret file when the crash happened, the steganography tool name will appear in the dump file, making it available for forensic investigations.

BlueScreenView is a portable by Nirsoft for investigating (`www.nirsoft.net/utils/blue_screen_view.html`). This tool will scan all your Minidump files created during crashes and display relevant information about all crashes in one table.

Pagefile.sys, Hiberfil.sys, and Swapfile.sys

Swapfile.sys, Hiberfil.sys, and Pagefile.sys are three important system files required for the proper functioning of the Windows OS. The default location of these files is in system drive (usually the C:\ drive) (see Figure 7-41); please note that the three files come hidden, so you need to view hidden files—including protected system files—as we did previously in this chapter to view them. In this section, we will discover the forensic value of each one.

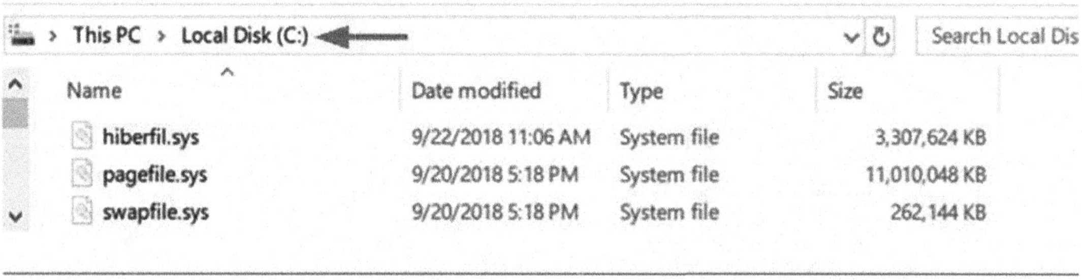

> This PC > Local Disk (C:) ◀────			∨ ↻	Search Local Dis
Name ^	Date modified	Type	Size	
hiberfil.sys	9/22/2018 11:06 AM	System file	3,307,624 KB	
pagefile.sys	9/20/2018 5:18 PM	System file	11,010,048 KB	
swapfile.sys	9/20/2018 5:18 PM	System file	262,144 KB	

Figure 7-41. *The location of Swapfile.sys, Hiberfil.sys, and Pagefile.sys*

Pagefile.sys

We've already defined the concept of virtual memory (*Pagefile.sys* in Windows OS) in Chapter 5. Forensic examiners should not omit the forensic value of virtual memory, as this file can hold important information shifted from RAM. For example, fragments of decrypted files can still reside there, and encryption keys or passwords (or a fragment of it) can also be found here.

The capacity of the physical memory increases with the continual advance of computing power (for example, it is common these days to buy a laptop with 16 GB of RAM memory). This effectively limits the need to swap any files to the virtual memory. All these issues result in low expectations of computer forensic investigators when investigating pagefile.sys.

> **Note!**   pagefile.sys is a hidden system file, it resides by default at
> `%SystemDrive%\pagefile.sys`; however, a user can change its default
> location to learn the exact location of pagefile.sys. If in doubt, check the following
> registry key:
>
> `HKEY_LOCAL_MACHINE\SYSTEM\CurrentControlSet\Control\Session`
> `Manager\Memory Management.`

Despite the limited possibility in modern computers of finding valuable data inside pagefile.sys, we can't discard its importance during an investigation. Most computer forensics suites can analyze pagefile.sys; consult tool documentation for related instructions.

Hiberfil.sys

This is a file used by Windows to support the hibernation feature, the approximate size of this file is about 3/4th of your RAM. The hibernation file in earlier versions of Windows (e.g., 7 and Vista) stored kernel session, device drivers, and application data while in modern versions of Windows (like 8 and 10) it stores only the kernel session and device drivers, making it notably less in size.

hiberfil.sys can store a wealth of information about the running machine. The following tools can investigate the hiberfil.sys file:

- Volatility, free and open source tool: `www.volatilityfoundation.org`

- Belkasoft Evidence Center (commercial application):
  `https://belkasoft.com`

Swapfile.sys

Used to store the idle and other nonactive objects ejected from the RAM memory, whenever a user tries to access an idle process again, its information will get shifted to the RAM memory again. In modern Windows versions (like 8 and 10) we can see that both Pagefile and Swapfile exist together on a system drive; we can consider that these two files form together what is known now as virtual memory in Windows OS. Swapfile has a fixed size in modern Windows versions (8, 10), which is 256 MB.

More information about the Swapfile can be found at the Microsoft Technet web site (`https://blogs.technet.microsoft.com/askperf/2012/10/28/windows-8-windows-server-2012-the-new-swap-file/`).

Windows Volume Shadow Copies Forensics

The Volume Shadow Copy Service (VSS)—available in all Windows versions beginning with Windows XP—is a service that coordinates the creation of a consistent snapshot of data at a specific point in time for each partition where it is activated. VSS helps Windows to recover if some of its files get corrupted; in such case, Windows will restore the good version of files from the previous backups (restore points). These restore points are taken at specific time intervals determined by Windows. The VSS feature is only supported on volumes formatted as NTFS and can be accessed using the system restore functionality.

Investigating Windows restore points snapshots can reveal a wealth of forensically useful information; the biggest gain from examining this feature is locating deleted files and folders that still reside in restore points after the original versions are deleted by the user.

Windows restore point snapshots also capture the registry hive files, opening the door to examining previous snapshots of the Windows registry as we did before. To extract Windows registry files from a particular Windows restore point, you can use a free portable tool from Nirsoft named RegistryChangesView (`www.nirsoft.net/utils/registry_changes_view.html`).

Note!   To configure VSS under Windows 10 (also applies to Windows 8 and 7), we can access it from Control Panel ➤ System ➤ System protection ➤ System Protection tab; then, select the drive you want to turn ON/OFF system protection and click the Configure… button (see Figure 7-42).

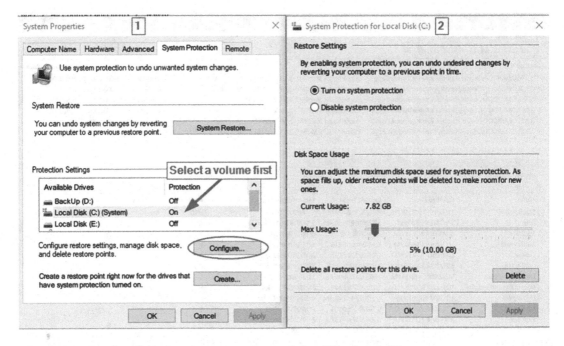

Figure 7-42. *Configuring restore points under Windows 10*

Investigating Windows restore points can be done manually using a built-in command-line utility called VSSadmin, which comes with Windows Vista, 7,8, and 10. However, we will not cover this method here, as it is already described in detail in the author's blog (www.darknessgate.com/security-tutorials/date-hiding/volume-shadow-copy-data-hiding) and there are other excellent free tools that can do the same task of analyzing Windows restore point files. The following are two popular tools for analyzing Windows restore point file contents:

ShadowCopyView

ShadowCopyView (www.nirsoft.net/utils/shadow_copy_view.html) lists all restore points of your hard drive created by the 'Volume Shadow Copy' service of Windows. It supports Windows 10, 8, 7, and Vista.

To use this tool, just execute it on the target machine; it will automatically detect and list all available restore points on the target machine in addition to relevant information for each snapshot (like the name, explorer path, volume path, created time, snapshot ID, and others). Detected snapshot files will appear in the upper pane; select any snapshot and the lower pane will display its contents (see Figure 7-43).

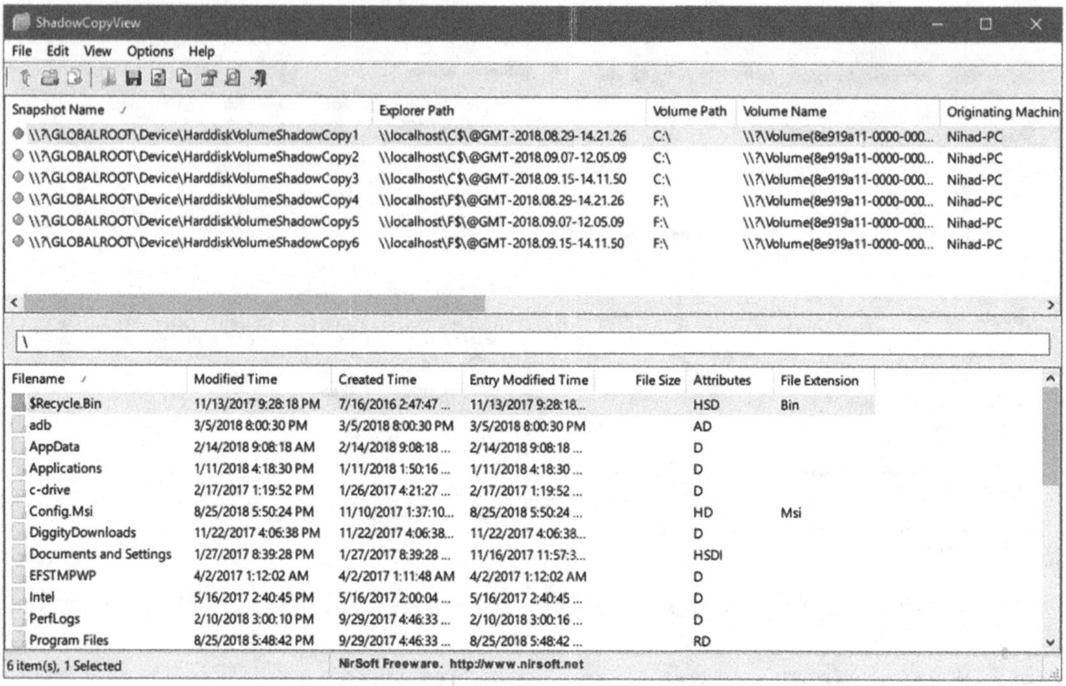

Figure 7-43. *Using ShadowCopyView to list/view existing restore points in Windows*

To extract files/folders from any snapshot, select it first from the upper pane, then select the file/folder you want to extract from the lower pane, right-click over the target file, select "Copy Selected Files To...", choose the destination folder, and then press "Do it!" (see Figure 7-44).

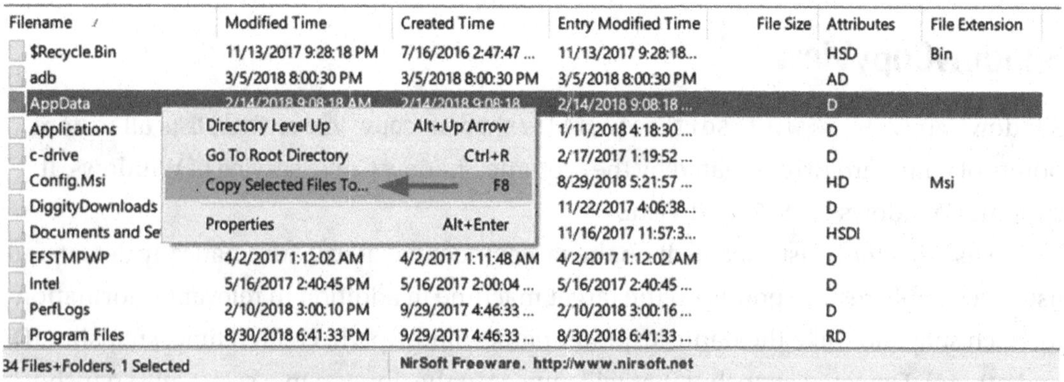

Figure 7-44. *Extract/copy files from selected snapshot using the ShadowCopyView tool*

Shadow Explorer

ShadowExplorer (www.shadowexplorer.com) is another free utility for investigating old Windows restore points easily. To use this tool, select the volume (partition) that has a system restore activated for it and then select the point that you want to browse. Right-click the file or folder you want to recover and select "Export..." to save it in your desired location (see Figure 7-45).

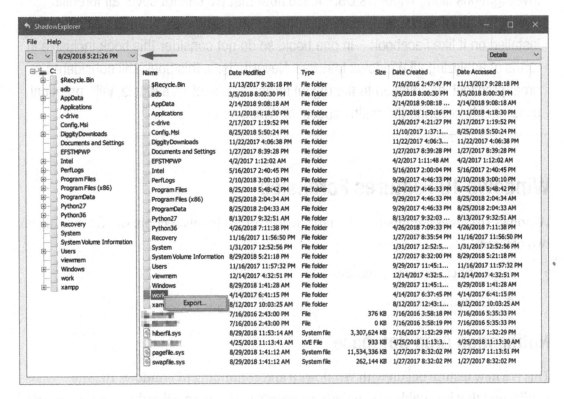

Figure 7-45. *Using ShadowExplorer to browse old restore point contents*

Windows 10 Forensics

Windows 10 introduces new features and applications to its users like Edge browser, Windows 10 apps, Cortana (Microsoft's voice-controlled digital assistant), and many more. The most important one was the introduction of Universal Application Platform (UAP), which enables the same application to run on different device types like laptops, desktops, IoT devices, tablets, smartphones, and so on.

We already covered how to implement various digital forensics investigation techniques covering different Windows versions, with a special focus on Windows 10. In this section, we will cover how to conduct digital forensics' analysis covering two common features of Windows 10.

Note!   The scope of this book is to teach you how to conduct digital forensic investigations using Windows OS. Please note that we cannot cover all forensic aspects of all Windows features—and other popular third-party apps that could be installed on it like Facebook—in one book, so do not consider this book inclusive in terms of analyzing all Windows features. Nevertheless, this book still considered a great practical introduction to the digital forensic subject as a whole, with practical experiments covering the main aspects of Windows OS.

Windows 10 Features Forensics

Windows 10 comes equipped with many new features. In this section, we will investigate two of them:

1. Notification area database

2. Cortana forensics

Notification Area Database

This is a new feature begun with Windows 8 and continuing to Windows 10. Any application that is capable of generating a systray notification will subsequently record this notification in a centralized database. The notification area database can be found at

`\Users\<UserName>\AppData\Local\Microsoft\Windows\Notifications` under the name `wpndatabase.db`

Note!   Images displayed on the Start menu tiles or appearing within notification are stored at `\Users\<UserName>\AppData\Local\Microsoft\Windows\Notifications\wpnidm`

The notification database holds various notification types seen by Windows users on the bottom right corner of the screen, such as pop-up messages from various parts of the OS (e.g., backup and restore), e-mail alerts, and messages related to specific apps like Torrent downloads, among other things. The forensic value of Windows notification is that it can reveal previous user activities on the target machine.

The notification area database is of type SQLite (**.db** extension). To analyze this database's contents, follow these steps:

- Go to `http://sqlitebrowser.org` and download DB Browser for SQLite; select the version appropriate for your OS version.

- Launch the program, go to File menu ➤ Open Database...; browse to `\Users\<UserName>\AppData\Local\Microsoft\Windows\Notifications`; and select *wpndatabase.db*.

- In Figure 7-46, we can see the database schema of the Windows notification area (wpndatabase.db). In the Notification table, we can find the following attributes:

  - "HandlerId", which tells which program has created the notification (retrieve program name from table "NotificationHandler").

  - "Payload" contains notification contents (see Figure 7-47).

  - "ArrivalTime"; date/time when notification received.

  - "ExpiryTime"; date/time when notification will be deleted from the database.

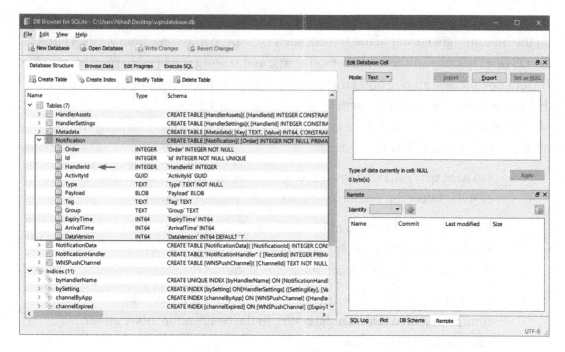

Figure 7-46. *Browse Windows notification area database using DB Browser*

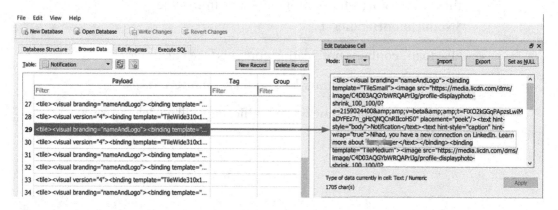

Figure 7-47. *Notification content shows a pop-up notification by LinkedIn (adding a new connection on LinkedIn)*

The values of "ArrivalTime" and "ExpiryTime" are stored in decimal format; to convert them into a readable format, we need first to convert the number into Hex, then use the DCode tool (as used previously; available at www.digital-detective.net/dcode) to convert the number into a readable date/time (see Figure 7-48).

Figure 7-48. *Convert date/time attributes from decimal values into a readable format using the DCode tool*

Cortana Forensics

Cortana is a voice-activated personal assistant (similar to Siri developed by Apple Inc. for its iOS). Cortana is a relatively new feature first introduced in Windows phone version 8.1; later, with the release of Windows 10, it has ported into Windows desktop as well. Its main task is to provide a personalized experience for Windows 10 users by offering suggestions when conducting searches in addition to remembering events, sending e-mails on the user's behalf (when configured properly), searching the Web, checking weather forecasts, and many more useful things. Cortana works through cumulative learning. Hence, when the user communicates with it more (through the PC microphone or by typing), it will understand the user's personal habits and attitudes more, leading to more accurate results in future interactions.

From a digital forensics perspective, Cortana can provide a wealth of information about a user's previous activities on the target machine in addition to web searches and geolocation data (latitude/longitude of the triggered location-based reminders). Bear in mind that despite the important information that can be retrieved from the Cortana feature, we cannot always expect to have it enabled on all Windows machines, as this feature has a reputation of being a privacy invader for Windows users and many of them have already deactivated this feature due to privacy concerns.

Cortana keeps some information related to its work on two extensible storage engine (ESE) databases that can be found at the following locations:

\Users\<UserName>\AppData\Local\Packages\Microsoft.Windows.Cortana_xxxx\
AppData\Indexed D**IndexedDB.edb**
\Users\<UserName>\AppData\Local\Packages\Microsoft.Windows.Cortana_xxxx\
LocalState\ESEDatabase_CortanaCoreInstance**CortanaCoreDb.dat**

Note!   If you cannot find the second database named "CortanaCoreDb.dat," this
means the Cortana feature is disabled on the examined machine.

The "CortanaCoreDb.dat" holds forensically valuable information related to user
geolocation data in addition to reminders set by a user and where and when these
remainders have triggered. Please note that Cortana can record extensive private
information about its users; however, it seems that Microsoft has shifted many user
interactions with Cortana onto Microsoft cloud servers.

Another location where some Cortana-related artifacts can be found on the local
machine is \Users\<UserName>\AppData\Local\Packages\Microsoft.Windows.
Cortana_xxxx\LocalState\LocalRecorder\Speech (see Figure 7-49).

Local Disk (C:) › Users › user › AppData › Local › Packages › Microsoft.Windows.Cortana_cw5n1h2txyewy › LocalState › LocalRecorder › Speech						
Name	#	Size	Date created	Title	Contributing artists	Album
SavedAudio			10/1/2018 2:09 PM			
SpeechAudioFile_0.wav		163 KB	10/1/2018 2:09 PM			
SpeechAudioFile_1.wav		112 KB	10/1/2018 2:11 PM			
SpeechAudioFile_2.wav		95 KB	10/1/2018 2:12 PM			
SpeechAudioFile_3.wav		94 KB	10/1/2018 2:31 PM			
SpeechAudioFile_4.wav		68 KB	10/1/2018 2:32 PM			
SpeechAudioFile_5.wav		89 KB	10/1/2018 2:33 PM			
SpeechAudioFile_6.wav		120 KB	10/1/2018 2:33 PM			
SpeechAudioFile_7.wav		110 KB	10/1/2018 2:33 PM			

Figure 7-49.   *The location where Cortana stores voice command recordings*

This folder stores voice command (WAV audio files) recordings issued by a user to
Cortana to perform a task.

Please note that not all computer forensic suites support decoding the Cortana
database; always consult the manual or tool features before buying it. For instance,
EnCase has a script to decode Cortana search terms of user-specified *IndexedDB.edb* files.

Note!   ESEDatabaseView from Nirsoft (`www.nirsoft.net/utils/ese_database_view.html`) is a tool for displaying data and available tables inside the ESE database.

Chapter Summary

Windows records huge amounts of information about its users; this information, which is also known as artifacts in the computer forensics domain, can be scattered across the system in different locations. For example, few people know that the artifacts of all applications that have been launched and all USB thumb drives that have attached to a particular Windows machine since its installation will remain stored in multiple locations in Windows. The same thing happens with deleted items: the recycle bin will hold information about each deleted file in addition to the account responsible for deleting it. Even if the data has been deleted on purpose or simply overwritten, copies of the deleted, formatted, modified, damaged, or lost files and folders can still be located on various places in the target system.

This chapter has been about Windows forensics only; we tried to cover the main areas where forensics artifacts can be found. In the next chapter, we will continue our examination work and see how web browsers and e-mails can be investigated for forensic evidence.

CHAPTER 8

Web Browser and E-mail Forensics

Investigating web browsers and e-mail messages for forensics artifacts

Internet applications already installed on Windows can give important information about user actions performed previously on his/her computer. For instance, a web browser is the only way to access the Internet, and criminals are using it to commit crimes related to the Internet or to target other users online. Internet users use web browsers to socialize, purchase online items, or to send e-mails and browse the web contents, among other things. This fact makes web browsers the preferred target for malicious actors to steal confidential information like account credentials.

Note! The main sources of malware/spyware/adware are e-mails in addition to social networking web sites, and all these resources are usually accessed using web browsers.

Analyzing web browser artifacts is a major part of any computer forensic investigation, as it can effectively in many cases determine the source of compromise or the user's previous activities. For example, if we investigate web browsers and see that the suspect was downloading or searching online for information on steganography and encryption tools, this will give a clear sign that this user may employ such techniques to conceal secret data.

In this chapter, we will describe how to investigate different web browsers for interesting leads that can help us to solve the case at hand. E-mail also plays an integral role in today's digital age communications; understanding how to analyze e-mail messages to find clues will also get covered in a dedicated section.

247

© Nihad A. Hassan 2019
N. A. Hassan, *Digital Forensics Basics*, https://doi.org/10.1007/978-1-4842-3838-7_8

Web Browser Forensics

As of September 2018, the web browser market share was mainly divided between Google Chrome (67.88%), Mozilla Firefox (10.94%) and Internet Browser (6.45%) from Microsoft.[1] The focus of the first section will be on using various digital forensic techniques to analyze artifacts from these three major web browsers.

Note!   To keep the privacy of the end users, different web browsers introduce special configuration known as Private Browsing (Firefox) or Incognito Mode (Google Chrome), which allows a user to browse the web without storing local data that can reveal a user's previous web activity on his/her machine. When this mode is activated, information like browsing history, cookies, form and search bar entries, download list history, entered passwords, and offline web contents will get deleted upon closing the browser. Tracking protection will also get activated as a part of this configuration, preventing web sites from tracking user browsing history across multiple sites.

The focus of this book is on Windows systems, so we will begin with the Windows default web browser, Internet Explorer (IE), and its new successor, Microsoft Edge.

IE

IE comes preinstalled with all versions of Windows. Its main registry key is located at `HKEY_CURRENT_USER\Software\Microsoft\Internet Explorer`. You will notice that under this key there are many keys; however, we are mainly concerned with the following ones.

- **HKEY_CURRENT_USER\Software\Microsoft\Internet Explorer\Main** This key stores IE configuration settings like the home page, search bar, default search engine, and so on.

---

[1]Statcounter, "Desktop Browser Market Share Worldwide (Sept 2017–Sept 2018)," July 10, 2018. `http://gs.statcounter.com/browser-market-share/desktop/worldwide`

- **HKEY_CURRENT_USER\Software\Microsoft\Internet Explorer\ TypedURLs** The TypedURLs key maintains a list of the URLs the user types in the address bar in IE (see Figure 8-1).

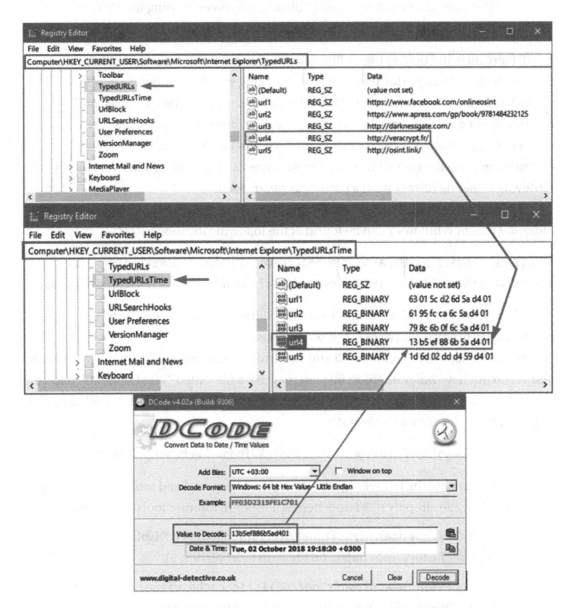

Figure 8-1. *Windows showing previous URLs and their associated access dates/ times entered by a particular user of IE*

- **HKEY_CURRENT_USER\Software\Microsoft\Internet Explorer\ TypedURLsTime** Reveals the browsing time (visit time) when a particular URL (from the previous key [TypedURLs]) was accessed. The date/time value is stored in binary, so convert it using the DCode tool, as we have done many times before (see Figure 8-1).

IE (version 9 and below) uses a file called *index.dat*; this is a database file used to improve the overall performance of IE by indexing various contents (e.g., store all the URLs you have visited using IE in addition to search queries, cookies, and recently opened files) in one place to offer a more customized experience for the user. For example, when a user wants to access a previously visited web page, IE can autocomplete the web address as the user types it in the browser address bar by retrieving browsing history from a particular *index.dat* file.

The location of *index.dat* files is different for each version of Windows; for instance, *index.dat* files in Windows 7 can be found at the following locations:

```
\Users\<UserName>\AppData\Roaming\Microsoft\Windows\Cookies\index.dat
\Users\<UserName>\AppData\Roaming\Microsoft\Windows\Cookies\Low\index.dat
```

Other locations of *index.dat* files in various Windows versions can be found at www.milincorporated.com/a2_index.dat.html.

Newer versions of IE (versions 10 and 11), which come preinstalled with Windows 8 and 10, do not have *index.dat* files; instead they use a file called "WebCacheV01.dat" to store all user browsing information (the information that was previously handled by the *index.dat* file). This file can be found at

```
\Users\<UserName>\AppData\Local\Microsoft\Windows\WebCache\WebCacheV01.dat
```

We can automate the IE investigation task by using specialized tools. Nirsoft offers many tools that can simplify this issue; here is a list of IE forensic tools from Nirsoft:

1. IEHistoryView (www.nirsoft.net/utils/iehv.html): Displays browser history from *index.dat* files (up to IE version 9).

2. IECacheView (www.nirsoft.net/utils/ie_cache_viewer. html): Displays all cache folder contents of IE (supports IE versions 6.0-11.0).

3. IECookiesView (www.nirsoft.net/utils/iecookies.html): Display all cookies saved by IE.

4. IE PassView (www.nirsoft.net/utils/internet_explorer_
    password.html): Display all passwords stored by IE. This tool
    supports a modern version of IE like 10 and 11 in addition to
    Microsoft Edge.

Microsoft Edge Web Browser

Microsoft Edge (code name Spartan) is the replacement of the IE browser and the default
browser for Windows 10. This is a lightweight web browser that integrates with the
Cortana feature available in Windows 10, allowing a user to complete many tasks (e.g.,
open web pages, conduct online searches) using voice commands only.

From a forensics perspective, we can expect more users to use Microsoft Edge instead
of IE, so knowing where this browser stores its data is essential for our forensics work.

Note!   IE version 11 comes preinstalled side by side with Edge on Windows 10.

Edge browser storage relies on an ESE database to store its configuration settings; the
database is located at

\Users\<UserName>\AppData\Local\Packages\Microsoft.MicrosoftEdge_xxxx\AC\
MicrosoftEdge\User\Default\DataStore\Data\nouser1\xxxx-xxx\DBStore\spartan.edb

We can use the ESEDatabaseView from Nirsoft (www.nirsoft.net/utils/ese_
database_view.html) to display data within the *Spartan.edb* database (see Figure 8-2).

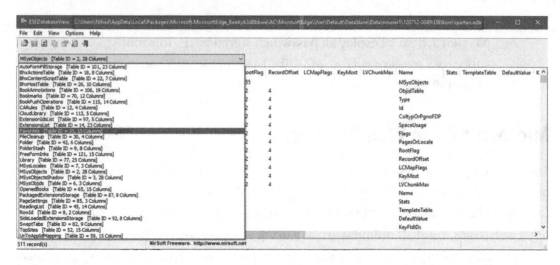

Figure 8-2. *Display database scheme of Spartan.edb using ESDatabaseView from Nirsoft; image display saved web favorites in the "Favorites" container*

Microsoft Edge cache content is stored at

\Users\<UserName>\AppData\Local\Packages\Microsoft.MicrosoftEdge_*****\
AC\#!001\MicrosoftEdge\Cache

Microsoft Edge stores its browsing history in the same location (same database file) where IE version 10 and 11 store their data!

\Users\<UserName>\AppData\Local\Microsoft\Windows\WebCache\WebCacheV01.dat

The last browsing session of Microsoft Edge is stored at

\Users\<UserName>\AppData\Local\Packages\Microsoft.MicrosoftEdge_****\AC\
MicrosoftEdge\User\Default\Recovery\Active

Further analysis of Edge artifacts can reveal valuable forensics information; as we already saw, the valuable information is located in the Edge databases named **spartan. edb** and **WebCacheV01.dat** and in various locations inside its main folder, located at:\
Users\<UserName>\AppData\Local\Packages\Microsoft.MicrosoftEdge_*****\

Firefox

Firefox is a free, open source web browser developed by Mozilla; it is considered among the most used web browsers in the world. Firefox does not use the Windows registry in the same way as the IE browser; Firefox stores its web history, download history, and bookmarks in a central database file named *places.sqlite*. This file exists within your Firefox profile. You can access your profile by pressing the Windows key and typing the following:

```
%APPDATA%\Mozilla\Firefox\Profiles\
```

In the search box, your Firefox profile will appear in the search result as a folder; click to access it.

Note!   You can also access the Firefox profile folder by pressing Windows button + R, and then typing the following in the Run window: %APPDATA%.

Now click OK. A Windows Explorer window will appear. Go to Mozilla ➤ Firefox ➤ Profiles.

What we care about in our forensic search are the files surrounded with squares, as shown in Figure 8-3. We'll describe each one briefly and suggest tools to automate our search:

1. **places.sqlite**: Holds bookmarks, visited web sites, and download history.

   The following tools can be used to retrieve information from the **places.sqlite** database file:

   - DB Browser for SQLite (http://sqlitebrowser.org). We can browse target sqlite database tables and their content using this tool as we did previously.

   - *MZHistoryView* (www.nirsoft.net/utils/mozilla_history_view.html). Displays list of previously visited web sites from the **places.sqlite** database.

2. **cookies.sqlite**: Stores cookies planted by web sites you already visited (cookies are usually used to save login usernames and passwords of previously visited web sites and/or to store web site preferences where applicable).

   The following tools can be used to retrieve information from **cookies.sqlite** database file:

   - MZCookiesView (www.nirsoft.net/utils/mzcv.html). Displays all cookies stored in a Firefox cookie file; you can also export results into a text, XML, or HTML file.

   - DB Browser for SQLite.

3. **formhistory.sqlite**: Stores your search keywords used in Firefox search bar and your searches entered into web forms.

4. **key4.db** and **logins.json**: Here is where Firefox saves your passwords. (Older versions of Firefox use the name **key3.db** for the key database file; beginning from Firefox version 58, the name changed to **Key4.db** while the **logins.json** file name—which stores passwords in encrypted format—remain as it is.)

   You can use PasswordFox (www.nirsoft.net/utils/passwordfox.html) to display all usernames and passwords stored by Firefox. When executing this tool on the target machine, it will display the passwords for the current Firefox profile; if you want to view passwords of another profile, go to File menu ➤ Select Folders and select your target profile folder (see Figure 8-4).

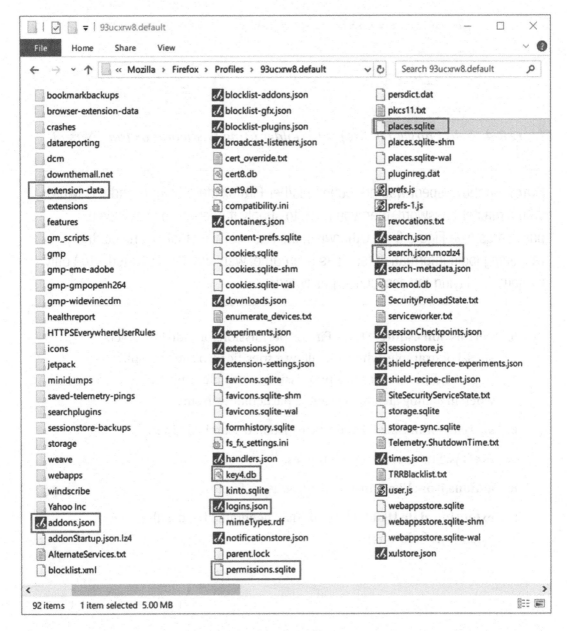

Figure 8-3. *Firefox profile folder contents*

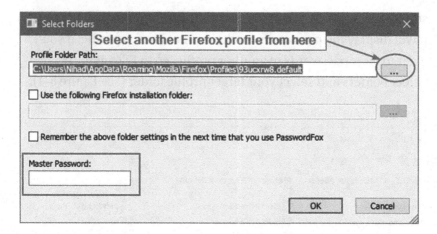

Figure 8-4. *Select target Firefox profile folder using PasswordFox from Nirsoft*

Note!   If the suspect was protecting his/her Firefox stored logins and passwords with a master password, then you need to supply it in order to view saved passwords (see Figure 8-4). Otherwise, the PasswordFox tool will reveal the remaining login information (such as username, web site, date created, etc.) only without displaying the associated passwords.

---

5. **permissions.sqlite**: Stores Firefox permission for individual web sites. For example, when you allow a specific web site to display pop-ups, Firefox saves this permission in this file. The same is true when installing an add-on from a particular web site.

6. **search.json.mozlz4**: Holds user-installed search engines.

7. **prefs.js**: Stores Firefox preferences.

8. **addons.json**: Views installed add-ons on Firefox.

9. **extension-data [Folder]**: Holds data generated by installed extensions (add-ons).

Google Chrome

This is the fastest and most used web browser on desktop computers worldwide today; most digital forensics examiners will likely come across this browser in one of their investigations.

Google Chrome is based on Chromium, which is an open source browser project developed by Google. The Chromium project has not seen the light as a standalone browser, so we can consider Google Chrome as the public version of this project. Many third-party web browsers are based on the Chromium project, like Vivaldi (https://vivaldi.com), Yandex browser (https://browser.yandex.com), Cent browser (www.centbrowser.com), and Opera browser (www.opera.com), to name a few.

Most web browsers that are based on the Chromium project are going to store data in a similar way; this fact allows examiners to use the same investigative techniques used with Google Chrome to investigate these browsers, making investigating Google Chrome act as a standard template for most Chromium-based web browsers.

Similar to other web browsers, Chrome (developed by Google Inc.) stores its configuration settings and user private information in SQLite databases; these databases are files without extensions, so do not get confused on how to open them when using SQLite browser. Just navigate to target the Google Chrome profile folder and make sure that the option "All files (*)" is selected as appears in Figure 8-5; then select the file you want to examine.

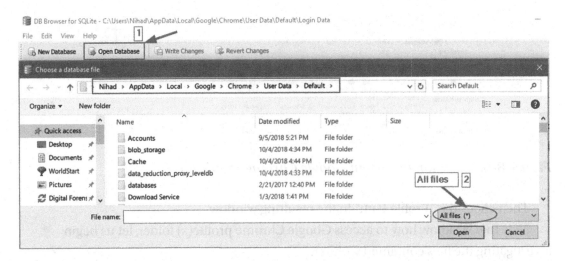

Figure 8-5. *Open Google Chrome SQLite database files using DB Browser for SQLite*

The Google Chrome profile is where Google Chrome stores its configuration settings, apps, bookmarks, and extensions. Google Chrome can have more than one profile; however, there is also a default profile that can be found at

`\Users\<UserName>\AppData\Local\Google\Chrome\User Data\Default`

If there is more than one profile in Google Chrome, each profile will have its own folder where browser settings and user (profile owner) private data (e.g., passwords, browsing history, bookmarks, etc.) is stored. Google Chrome does not name any additional profile according to its username; instead, it uses a generic name (e.g., Profile 1, Profile 2, and so on). The location of additional Chrome profiles can be found here:

`\Users\<UserName>\AppData\Local\Google\Chrome\User Data\Profile x`

(x could be any positive integer number beginning from 1).

To know the folder location of any Google Chrome profile (see Figure 8-6), just open a Chrome window that shows profile name/image in the top corner of the browser window, type the following in the browser address bar, and finally press the Enter button:

`chrome://version`

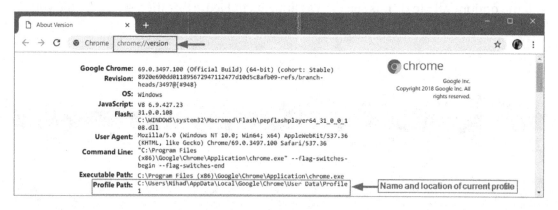

Figure 8-6. *Location of current Google Chrome profile folder*

Then check the "Profile Path" in the resulting window.

Now that we know how to access Google Chrome profile(s) folder, let us begin investigating the files contained within it.

Note!   We are using Google Chrome Version 69 (official build; 64 bit) and the default profile folder located at \Users\<UserName>\AppData\Local\Google\ Chrome\User Data\Default during our coming experiments.

History

Google Chrome store user browsing history, downloads, keywords, and search terms in the "History" database file are located under the Chrome user's profile. This file can be examined using DB Browser for SQLite (see Figure 8-7). Note that there are 12 tables in this file and 11 indices.

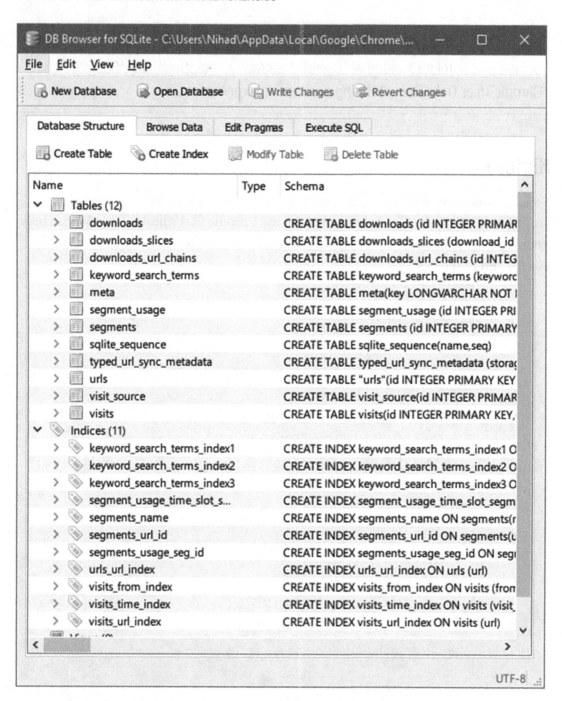

Figure 8-7. *Database schema of Google Chrome "History" file*

To know when a particular file has been downloaded in addition to much information related to download history, go to the "Downloads" table under the "Browse Data" tab (see Figure 8-8). The DB Browser for SQLite displays time information using Google Chrome values stamps (also known as the Webkit format, which points to the number of microseconds passed since 00:00:00 UTC of Jan 1, 1601). To convert it into a readable form, use the DCode tool.

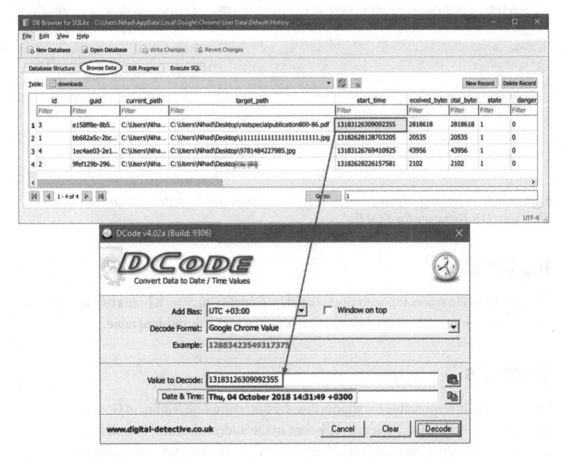

Figure 8-8. *Reveal the start date/time of a particular download found in the "Downloads" table of the Google Chrome "History" file*

Nirsoft offers a tool to reveal Chrome history; it is called ChromeHistoryView (`www.nirsoft.net/utils/chrome_history_view.html`). This tool reads the "History" file of the Google Chrome web browser.

Cookies

Google Chrome stores cookies information in the "Cookies" file located under the Chrome user's profile; we can view "Cookies" file contents using DB Browser for SQLite, as we did with the "History" file before, to show detailed information about saved Chrome cookies (see Figure 8-9).

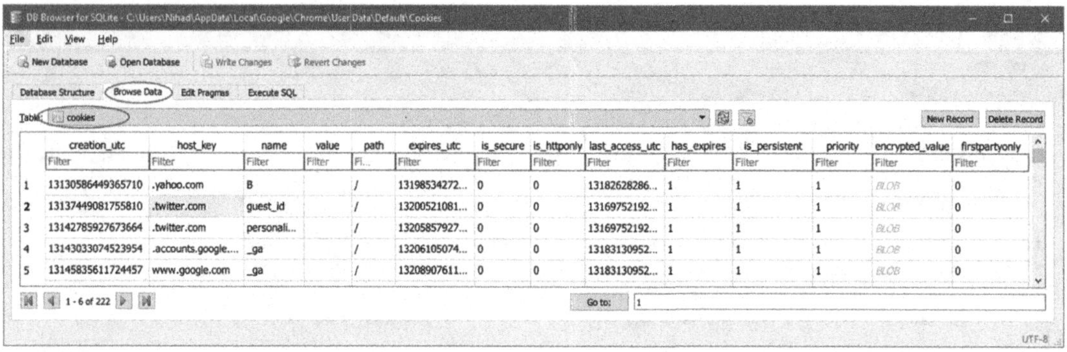

Figure 8-9. *Viewing saved cookies information in the Google Chrome "Cookies" file using DB Browser for SQLite*

Top Sites

This database file stores top web sites visited by Google Chrome. It holds two tables, *meta* and *thumbnails*, and the information is stored in the thumbnail table.

Shortcuts

This database is responsible for supporting the autocomplete feature of Google Chrome when typing (e.g., a search keyword in the address bar and in web forms). It contains two tables: *meta* and *omni_box_shortcuts*. The second table holds the autocomplete text and URLs.

Login Data

This database file holds three tables: login, meta, and stats. The "login" table holds usernames and passwords (sometimes encrypted), in addition to other related attributes, for various web sites.

A portable tool by Nirsoft can reveal all usernames and passwords (in clear text) stored by the Google Chrome Web browser. It's called ChromePass (see Figure 8-10) and can be downloaded from www.nirsoft.net/utils/chromepass.html.

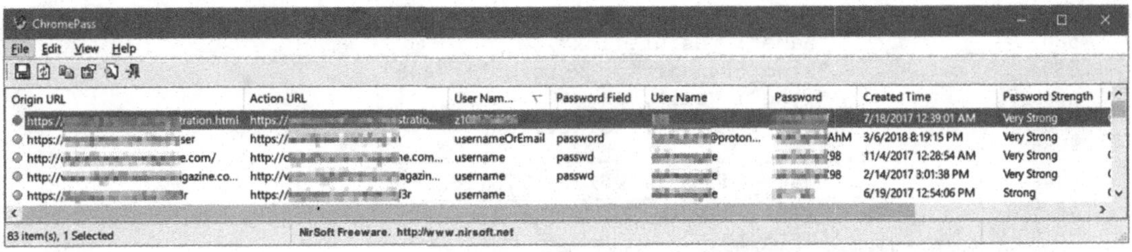

Figure 8-10. *ChromePass by Nirsoft reveals all passwords stored by Google Chrome browser*

Web Data

This function stores the login credentials of users (without passwords, as Chrome moved the login passwords to another file "Login Data" in newer Google Chrome versions), so when a user fills in a login form next time, searches keywords, and so on, Google Chrome will offer its autocomplete suggestions while typing.

Bookmarks

A browser bookmark (also known as a "favorite") is a URL that points to a web site address stored by a user for later retrieval. The "Bookmarks database" file in Google Chrome holds a user's current bookmarks. To view the contents of this file, we can open it using Windows Notepad. To check the date/time when a particular bookmark was added to Chrome, we need to convert the associated "date_added" value into a readable format; we can use the DCode tool as we did many times before (see Figure 8-11).

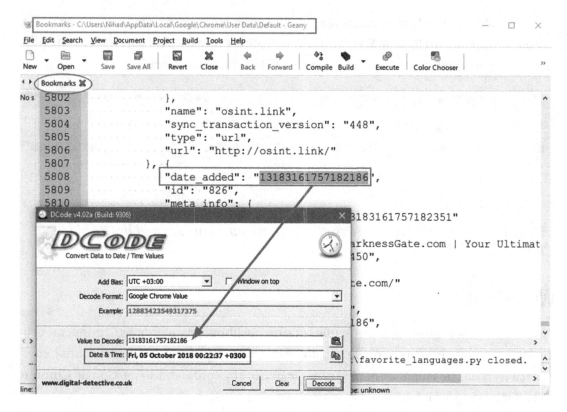

Figure 8-11. Analyzing Google Chrome "Bookmarks" database file using a free text editor, Geany (www.geany.org)

Bookmarks.bak

This database file holds recent backups of the Chrome bookmarks; please note that this file will get overwritten periodically, each time Google Chrome launches. The forensic value of this file is that if a suspect deletes a particular bookmark(s) before closing his/her Chrome browser, we can find the deleted bookmark(s) here in this file (we should not launch Google Chrome till we have a copy of this file in a safe location to avoid overwriting it as we have already described).

Cache Folder

This folder holds frequently accessed static contents like images and parts of HTML files, so the next time a user visits the same web site, the browser loads it faster because it loads parts of contents from a local cache folder instead of downloading it again from the origin server housing the web site.

We can automate the extraction process of Google Chrome cache by using a tool from Nirsoft called ChromeCacheView (`www.nirsoft.net/utils/chrome_cache_view.html`). This tool reads the contents of the cache folder (see Figure 8-12) of the Google Chrome web browser, which is located in

`\Users\<UserName>\AppData\Local\Google\Chrome\User Data\default\Cache.`

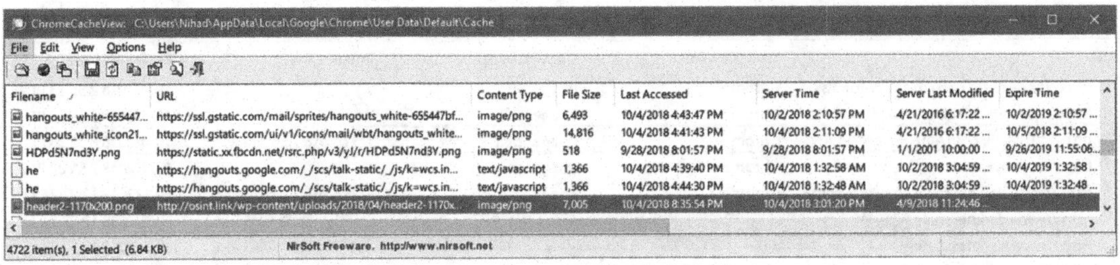

Figure 8-12. *Using ChromeCacheView to view Google Chrome cache folder contents*

As we saw, Google Chrome stores quite a lot of personal information about its user. Investigating all these artifacts can help examiners to draw a complete timeline of a user's activities online in addition to understanding his/her intentions or interests by analyzing browsing history.

To conclude the last section of web browser forensics, we are going to give additional tools that can prove useful for digital examiners when investigating the three most widely used web browsers mentioned in this section.

Other Web Browser Investigation Tools

There are other general tools for investigating web browser artifacts, mainly from Nirsoft. Here is the list:

1. WebCacheImageInfo (`www.nirsoft.net/utils/web_cache_image_info.html`): Search and list all JPEG images with EXIF metadata information stored inside the cache folder of the following web browsers: IE, Firefox, and Google Chrome. As we have already discussed in Chapter 2, EXIF holds important information about JPG images like the camera model used to take the photo, and the date and time when that image was created.

2. ImageCacheViewer (`www.nirsoft.net/utils/image_cache_viewer.html`): Scan cache folder in any of the three major browsers (IE, Firefox, and Google Chrome) and list all images found inside (see Figure 8-13).

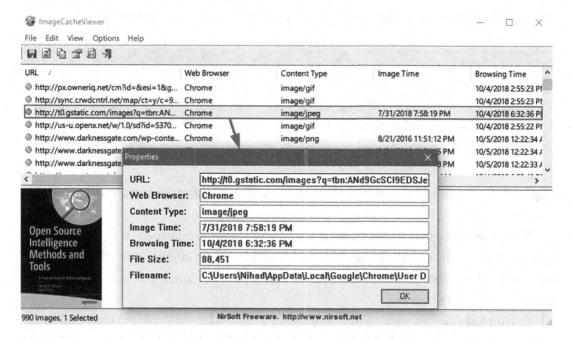

Figure 8-13. *Using the ImageCacheViewer tool to display all cached images stored in three major web browsers (IE, Firefox, and Chrome)*

3. BrowserAddonsView (`www.nirsoft.net/utils/web_browser_addons_view.html`): Display all add-ons/extensions installed on all major web browsers (Chrome, Firefox, and IE). For Firefox and Chrome, if there is more than one profile for each browser, the tool can show add-ons for all profiles.

4. MyLastSearch (`www.nirsoft.net/utils/my_last_search.html`): Scan web history in all major browsers (Chrome, Firefox, and IE), cache folder, and retrieve all search queries made previously. This tool is important to know what a suspect was searching for at any date/time and what search engine he used to conduct this search.

5.   WebBrowserPassView (`www.nirsoft.net/utils/web_browser_password.html`): A general password recovery tool that reveals passwords stored in IE (Version 4.0-11.0), Mozilla Firefox (all versions), Google Chrome, Safari, and Opera.

6.   Web Historian (`www.webhistorian.org`): This is a great tool (browser extension for Google Chrome) to visualize web browsing history stored within Google Chrome; it shows graphical circles of the number of days a web site was visited (based on the time order of your web site visits) and keyword search terms, in addition to showing the most active browsing hours of a day and days of the week.

In this section, we shed light on how to perform a manual forensic analysis—in a variety of places and using a variety of utilities—of major web browser artifacts. Please keep in mind that commercial forensics suites have the ability to analyze and extract information contained in various web browsers automatically. As we always repeat, consult a computer forensic tool's features list for the ability to investigate different web browsers' data before buying it.

E-mail Forensics

E-mails have become the primary means of communications in today's digital age; for instance, it is rare to see a person who owns a computer, smartphone, or tablet without having an active e-mail account. A study conducted by The Radicati Group[2] estimated that there are 3.8 billion e-mail users (March 2018), and this number is estimated to exceed 4.1 billion in 2021. This is a huge number already and yet is continuing to increase steadily as more people around the world enter the digital era.

Basically, there are two standard methods to send/receive e-mails: the first one is using an application to send and receive e-mails (e.g., e-mail clients like Mozilla Thunderbird), and the second is using a web interface browser to access your e-mail account (e.g., Gmail, Yahoo, Outlook).

---

[2]Lifewire, "The Number of Emails Sent per Day in 2018 (and 20+ Other Email Facts)," July 10, 2018. `www.lifewire.com/how-many-emails-are-sent-every-day-1171210`

From a digital forensics viewpoint, we are concerned about finding and recovering e-mails from a suspect forensic image file/device, analyzing the e-mail header, extracting useful information from it like IP address and date/time when a particular e-mail was sent, and finally tracing e-mail back to its origin (the sender).

E-mail can be mainly abused through

- Sending spam e-mails

- Using it to commit a crime, e.g., e-mail harassment

- Invading other user's privacy by stealing their e-mail login credentials

Before we begin our discussion on how to track e-mails, let us give some important prerequisite information regarding how e-mail communications work.

Steps in E-mail Communications

To demonstrate how e-mail delivery works (see Figure 8-14), let us give this simple example:

1. Susan composes an e-mail (susan@apress.com) using her computer for Nihad (nihad@darknessgate.com); the message needs to be sent to her sending SMTP server (smtp.apress.org) using the SMTP protocol.

2. The sending server performs a lookup to find the mail exchange record of the receiving server (darknessgate.com) through DNS protocol on DNS mx.darknessgate.com for the domain darknessgate.com.

3. The DNS server responds and gives the mail exchange server mx.darknessgate.com for the domain darknessgate.com.

4. Now, the sending server will establish an SMTP connection with the receiving server and send the e-mail to Nihad's mailbox on the receiving server.

5. The receiving server will receive the incoming e-mail and store it in Nihad's mailbox.

6. Nihad can either download the e-mail message from his mailbox
    on the receiving sever into his e-mail client (e.g., Mozilla
    Thunderbird) on local machine using POP3 or IMAP protocols or
    he can use webmail (through a web browser) to read the e-mail
    directly on the receiving server.

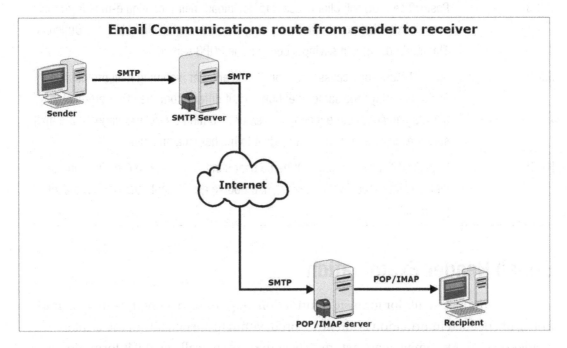

Figure 8-14. *How e-mail communication works. Source: www.darknessgate.com*

List of E-mail Protocols

In the previous section, we've mentioned many names of e-mail protocols that facilitate
e-mail delivery. Table 8-1 lists the main protocols used in e-mail communication and the
role of each one.

Table 8-1. *Common E-mail Protocols*

Protocol Name	Role
SMTP	Simple Mail Transfer Protocol: Used to transfer e-mail messages from client to server and between servers.
POP3	Post Office Protocol: Clients use it to download their incoming e-mail from their e-mailbox to their local machine (using a proper e-mail client like MS Outlook or Thunderbird) without saving a copy on the POP3 server.
IMAP	Internet Message Access Protocol: This is another incoming mail protocol (like POP3) and plays the same role; however, it differs from the POP3 protocol in allowing a user to store a copy of his/her incoming e-mail message on the mail server even after a user downloads it to his/her local machine.
HTTP	HyperText Transfer Protocol: When a user sends and receive e-mails using the webmail interface (Web browser), like Google and Yahoo!, the HTTP protocol will be used.

E-mail Header Examination

When examining e-mails for forensic information, (e.g., to see where the e-mail come from), the needed information is already stored within it, specifically in the e-mail header section. An E-mail header stores a wealth of forensically useful information about an e-mail under investigation, like the path it took over the Internet to arrive, stop points/delays made during e-mail delivery, and the IP address of the machine that sent this e-mail, in addition to the client (e.g., e-mail program) who sent this e-mail and the type of OS used (in some cases).

Please note that most of the information (including the technical information) in the e-mail header can be forged! Tech-savvy criminals can conceal the origin of their e-mails and even make it similar to an original e-mail that they are trying to reproduce (e.g., phishing e-mails); however, the role of a forensic examiner is to gather the information in the e-mail header and examine it thoroughly, as it can lead to something useful for solving the case at hand.

Reveal Full E-mail Header Information

Before we begin examining the e-mail header, let us give some examples of how to view e-mail headers using popular webmail services (Gmail and Microsoft Outlook mail) and e-mail clients (Thunderbird and MS Outlook).

View Full Gmail Headers

To display Gmail headers, follow these steps:

1. Access the target Gmail account using your preferred browser

2. Open the e-mail whose header you want to view

3. Next to Reply, click the down arrow (see Figure 8-15)

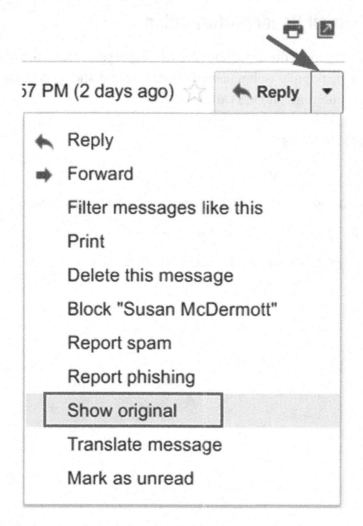

Figure 8-15. *Show Gmail e-mail message header*

    4.   Click "Show original"

View E-mail Header Using Outlook Mail

To display Outlook web mail header, follow these steps:

    1.   Access Outlook mail account using your preferred browser

    2.   Open the e-mail whose header you want to view

3. Next to Reply, click the down arrow in the top right-hand corner of the e-mail

4. Click "View message source" (see Figure 8-16)

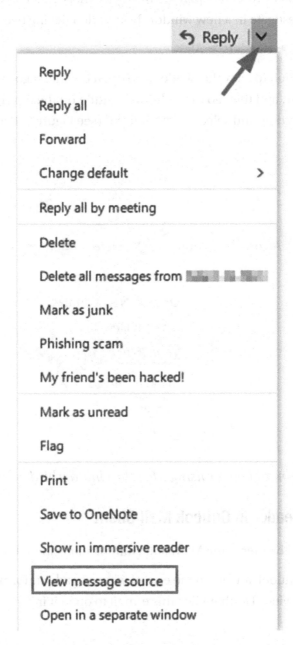

Figure 8-16. *View message source using Outlook Mail*

View Full E-mail Headers in Mozilla Thunderbird

To display e-mail headers using the Mozilla Thunderbird e-mail client, follow these steps:

1. Open Thunderbird, then open the message whose header you want to investigate in a new window by double-clicking over it.

2. Got to View ➤ Headers ➤ All.

3. Another option to view the header is to open the message in a new window, and then go to the "More" button on the top right message window and select "View Source" (see Figure 8-17).

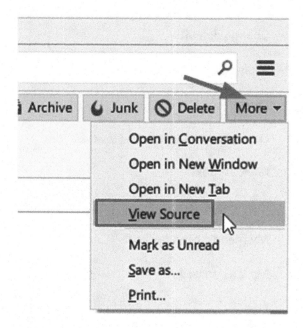

Figure 8-17. *View e-mail header using Mozilla Thunderbird e-mail client*

View Full E-mail Header in Outlook Mail Client

To display a full e-mail header using Microsoft Outlook mail client, follow these steps:

1. Open MS Outlook and go to the e-mail whose header information you want to view. Double-click this e-mail to open it in a new window.

2. Click File ➤ Properties; the header info is located in the "Internet headers" box (see Figure 8-18).

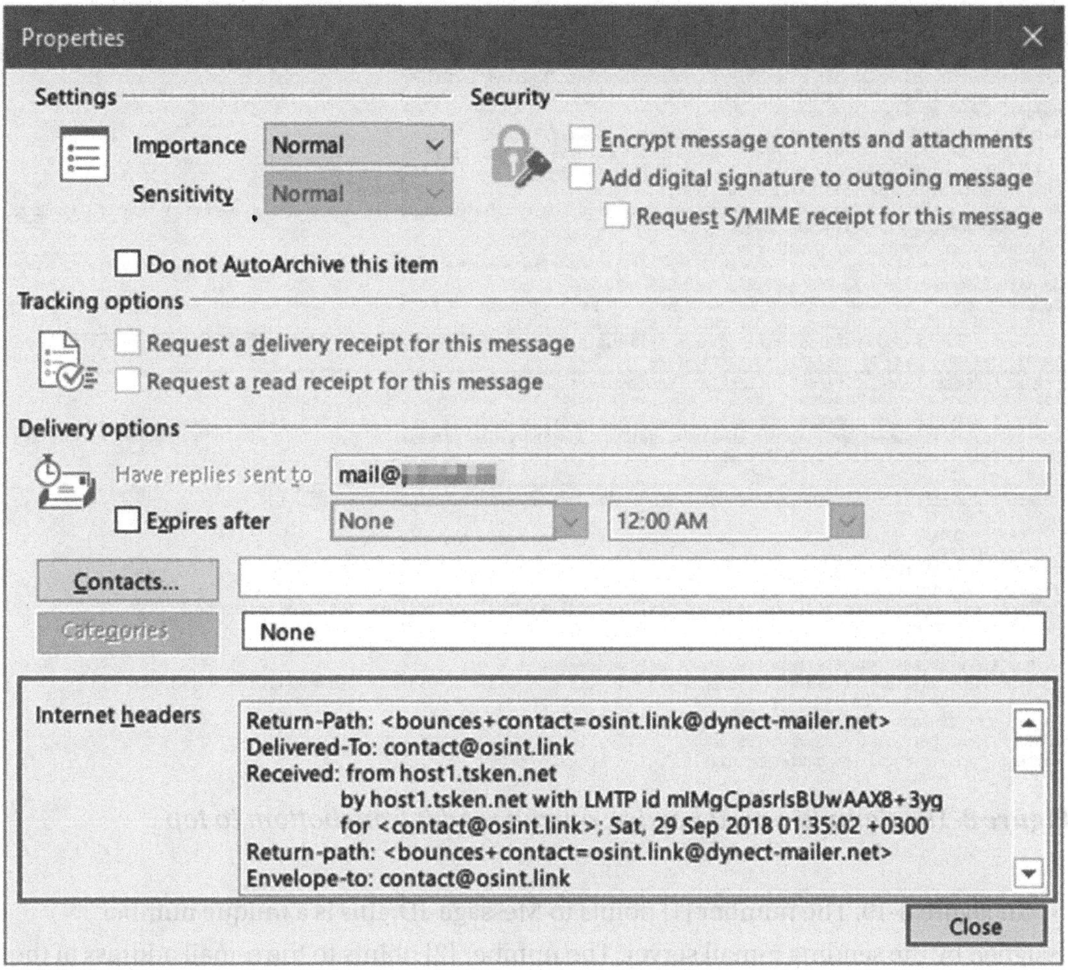

Properties ×

Settings

Importance | Normal ▾

Sensitivity | Normal ▾

Security

☐ Encrypt message contents and attachments

☐ Add digital signature to outgoing message

☐ Request S/MIME receipt for this message

☐ Do not AutoArchive this item

Tracking options

☐ Request a delivery receipt for this message

☐ Request a read receipt for this message

Delivery options

Have replies sent to | mail@▮▮▮▮▮▮

☐ Expires after | None ▾ | 12:00 AM ▾

Contacts... |

Categories | None

Internet headers |
```
Return-Path: <bounces+contact=osint.link@dynect-mailer.net>
Delivered-To: contact@osint.link
Received: from host1.tsken.net
        by host1.tsken.net with LMTP id mIMgCpasrIsBUwAAX8+3yg
        for <contact@osint.link>; Sat, 29 Sep 2018 01:35:02 +0300
Return-path: <bounces+contact=osint.link@dynect-mailer.net>
Envelope-to: contact@osint.link
```

Close

Figure 8-18. Viewing e-mail header info using MS Outlook e-mail client

Analyzing E-mail Headers

Now that we know how to reveal an e-mail header, we can begin analyzing it. **Keep in mind that the preferred method to read an e-mail header is from bottom to top.**

Figure 8-19 is a sample e-mail header from a message received using Gmail service.

```
Delivered-To: nihadhas@gmail.com 5
Received: by 10.55.9.10 with SMTP id 10csp902375qkj; 4
        Wed, 21 Dec 2016 09:53:25 -0800 (PST)
X-Received: by 10.237.35.181 with SMTP id j50mr6381006qtc.138.1482342801748;
        Wed, 21 Dec 2016 09:53:21 -0800 (PST)
Return-Path: <RitaFernando@apress.com>
Received: from mx2.springer.com (mx2.springer.com. [63.116.214.22])
        by mx.google.com with ESMTP id g48si15552934qta.95.2016.12.21.09.53.19
        for <nihadhas@gmail.com>;
        Wed, 21 Dec 2016 09:53:21 -0800 (PST)
Received-SPF: softfail (google.com: domain of transitioning ritafernando@apress.com does not designate 63.116.214.22 as
permitted sender) client-ip=63.116.214.22;
Authentication-Results: mx.google.com;
        spf=softfail (google.com: domain of transitioning ritafernando@apress.com does not designate 63.116.214.22 as
permitted sender) smtp.mailfrom=RitaFernando@apress.com
Received: from SENLDOGO0755.springer-sbm.com (senldogo0755.springer-sbm.com [10.9.1.240]) by mx2.springer.com (Postfix)
with ESMTP id BC918738C2; Wed, 21 Dec 2016 18:52:25 +0100 (CET)
Received: from SENLDOGO0428.springer-sbm.com ([10.9.1.67]) by SENLDOGO0755.springer-sbm.com ([::1]) with mapi id 3
14.03.0235.001; Wed, 21 Dec 2016 18:52:24 +0100
From: "Fernando, Rita, Springer US" <RitaFernando@apress.com> 2
To: Nihad Hassan <nihadhas@gmail.com>,
Subject: Hassan          : Apress template, guides, and SharePoint access
Thread-Topic:             : Apress template, guides, and SharePoint access
Thread-Index: AdJbsf+Kk7I3dnYEQ6S39bHGOjnGGg==
Date: Wed, 21 Dec 2016 17:52:22 +0000
Message-ID: <52CE62302A05B744BD03B51850021BD30165C2DEF9@senldogo0428.springer-sbm.com> 1
Accept-Language: en-US
Content-Language: en-US
X-MS-Has-Attach: yes
X-MS-TNEF-Correlator:
x-originating-ip: [10.9.1.250]
Content-Type: multipart/mixed; boundary="_009_52CE62302A05B744BD03B51850021BD30165C2DEF9senldogo0428s_"
MIME-Version: 1.0

--_009_52CE62302A05B744BD03B51850021BD30165C2DEF9senldogo0428s_
Content-Type: multipart/alternative; boundary="_000_52CE62302A05B744BD03B51850021BD30165C2DEF9senldogo0428s_"

--_000_52CE62302A05B744BD03B51850021BD30165C2DEF9senldogo0428s_
Content-Type: text/plain; charset="us-ascii"
Content-Transfer-Encoding: quoted-printable
```

Figure 8-19. *Sample e-mail header; always read it from bottom to top*

In Figure 8-19, The number [1] points to Message-ID; this is a unique number assigned by the sending e-mail server. The number [2] points to the e-mail address of the sender (this can also be false, as anyone can adjust the sender's "e-mail address" from his/her end). Number [3] points to the originating IP address (IP address of the sender); keep in mind that this IP address can be forged or spoofed. Expect to see more than one "Received" line. However, always read the e-mail header from bottom to top; this makes the first "Received" line highly probably point to the sender itself. Number [4] is the recipient IP address. Number [5] is the e-mail address of the recipient.

Lines starting with "X" in the e-mail header are comments written by the sending software (e.g., e-mail clients), by the SMTP servers, and even by the antivirus/spam servers found along the path the e-mail traveled.

E-MAIL HEADERS

When an e-mail travels through the Internet, each mail server the e-mail passes through will add a piece of information to the header, so the preceding e-mail header screen capture can contain more information like e-mail client and OS used to send the message. See Figure 8-20 for a partial e-mail header sent from Mozilla Thunderbird e-mail client using a Windows 10 machine.

```
Date: Sun, 7 Oct 2018 00:22:02 +0300
User-Agent: Mozilla/5.0 (Windows NT 10.0; WOW64; rv:45.0) Gecko/20100101
  Thunderbird/45.8.0
```

Figure 8-20. An e-mail header can reveal additional information about the message like an e-mail client's name and version and the OS used to compose and send the message

Analyzing e-mail headers manually can be a daunting task for beginners, but many tools and online services are available to extract useful information from e-mail headers automatically. Let us begin with a simple online tool developed by Google named "Message header" (https://toolbox.googleapps.com/apps/messageheader).

To use this tool:

1. Copy the target e-mail header as we did previously.

2. Paste the contents into the box "Paste email header here".

3. Finally, click "Analyze the header above".

The tool will analyze the supplied message header and show (in addition to who sent the message) the names of all attachments and the path the message took to reach from sender to receiver (see Figure 8-21) in addition to any delay that may have happened during delivery.

#	Delay	From		To		Protocol	Time received
0	1 sec	senldogo5224.springernature.com	→		senldogo5224.springernature.com	mapi	11/2/2018, 10:03:44 PM GMT+2
1		senldogo5224.springernature.com	→		senldogo5220.springernature.com		11/2/2018, 10:03:44 PM GMT+2
2	4 hours	senldogo5220.springernature.com	→		hermes2-dordint.springernature.com		11/3/2018, 1:39:46 AM GMT+2
3	-4 hours	hermes2-dord.springernature.com.	→	[Google]	mx.google.com	ESMTPS	11/2/2018, 10:03:44 PM GMT+2
4			→	[Google]	2002:a50:d88e::	SMTP	11/2/2018, 10:03:44 PM GMT+2
5			→	[Google]	2002:a0c:8343:0:0:0:0:0	SMTP	11/2/2018, 10:03:44 PM GMT+2

Figure 8-21. *Message route from sender to receiver revealed by the Message header online tool (`https://toolbox.googleapps.com/apps/messageheader/`)*

There are various tools to analyze e-mail headers. The following are some popular one:

E-mail Header Analyzer (`https://mxtoolbox.com/EmailHeaders.aspx`)

This is an online tool for parsing e-mail headers, making them human readable. To use this tool, just go to the web site and paste the target e-mail header info. The result will show—among other info—the path this e-mail took over the Internet in addition to any delays that may have happened.

eMailTrackerPro (`www.emailtrackerpro.com`)

This is a commercial tool (it offers a 15-day fully functional trial version) for tracking e-mails using e-mail headers. To use this tool to track a particular e-mail header, do the following:

1. Go to the tool web site, and download and install the tool as you do with any Windows app.

2. Launch the program and click the "Trace Headers" button in the main tool window (see Figure 8-22).

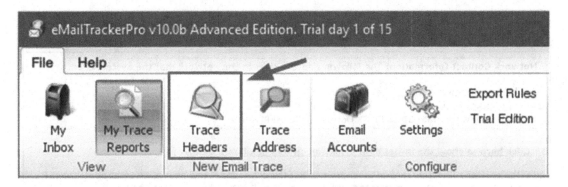

Figure 8-22. *Using eMailTrackerPro to track e-mail headers*

3.   A new window appears, in which you can paste the target e-mail
     header and press the "Trace" button to begin tracing.

4.   When tracing finish, click the "My Trace Reports" button in the
     main program window to show a detailed tracing report (see
     Figure 8-23).

Computer 195.128.10.15 has been found. It is almost certainly located in **Netherlands** as it has an exact match in the eMailTrackerPro database. 1

Network Contact Information: The following details refer to the network that the system is on.

✉ hostmaster@springer.com 2
☎ +31786576555
🖳 Van Godewijckstraat 30 3311 GX Dordrecht NETHERLANDS

▣ **Click here to show the in-depth information on this email** *(more info)*

- The sender's IP in this case is taken from a 'Received' header stamp from a different server to the one the sender first communicated with because the IP in that line was not usable. The closest traceable IP to the sender was - 195.128.10.15

- The sender of this email appeared to have the address susanmcdermott@apress.com. This 3 information is easily faked so should not be treated as conclusive.

▣ **Click here to show the route map** *(more info)*
▣ **Click here to hide information on each hop along the route** *(more info)*

The table below identifies the Internet route taken to reach the destination requested.

4
This is valuable data when tracking the end location because it helps qualify the actual final position. In some instances the final location has been derived from the network registration details, which is often the head office location for the Internet Service Provider (ISP). The ISP location is often local to the destination traced, but sometimes also located elsewhere, particularly in the case of large national ISPs. The physical (authoritative) locations of systems in last 2 or 3 hops of the route provide helpful location information as they are often in the vicinity of the destination being traced. Authoritative locations are shown in **bold**, locations derived from registration details appear in *italic*.

Address of Hop	Name of Hop	Location
10.8.8.1		(Private)
109.201.133.254		*Rosendaal, Gelderland, Netherlands*
185.107.116.22		*Australia*
193.239.117.149	surfnet.telecity2.nl-ix.net	*Netherlands*
145.145.176.2	ae1.500.jnr01.asd001a.surf.net	*Netherlands*
145.145.24.150	springer-wkap-router.customer.surf.net	*Netherlands*
-	(unnamed)	
195.128.10.15	hermes1-dord.springernature.com	**Netherlands**

Figure 8-23. *Report generated by eMailTrackerPro for tracing an e-mail address using its header*

From Figure 8-23 we note the following:

1. Sender originating IP address: keep in mind that this address can be internal (private IP address) or simply a fake/spoofed IP address.

2. Information about the network responsible for sending this e-mail.

3. Sender e-mail address.

4. Internet route that the target e-mail follows to reach its final destination.

Determining a Sender's Geographic Location

As we have seen, the sender's IP address can be extracted from the e-mail header (go to the line that begins with "Received: from" beginning from the bottom header); then we can use this IP address to determine the geographical location of the sender. There are already many online services that can be used to map IP addresses to geographical locations like Wolfram Alpha (www.wolframalpha.com) or Ipfingerprints (www.ipfingerprints.com) (see Figure 8-24).

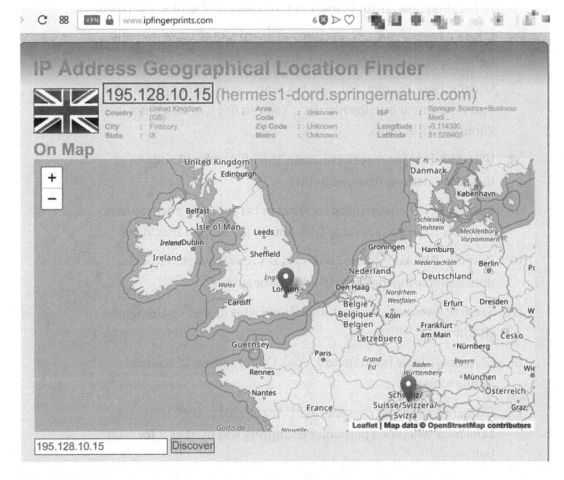

Figure 8-24. *Mapping IP address to geographical location using* www.ipfingerprints.com

To find more information about any IP address or domain name, check these free services:

1. IPverse (`http://ipverse.net`): This shows the IPv4 and IPv6 address block lists by country code.

2. IP2Location (`www.ip2location.com/demo.aspx`): This is a free IP location service.

3. DB-IP (`https://db-ip.com`): This shows the IP geolocation and network intelligence.

4. IPINTEL (`https://ipintel.io`): This shows the IP address on a map and shows the ISP.

5. IP Location (`www.iplocation.net`): This shows IP geolocation data.

6. UTrace (`http://en.utrace.de`): Locate IP address and domain names.

7. Onyphe (`www.onyphe.io`): This is a search engine for open source and cyberthreat intelligence data. You can use it to find more info about any IP address.

8. IP to ASN (`https://iptoasn.com`): This shows the IP address to the ASN database; updated hourly.

9. Reverse DNS Lookup (`https://hackertarget.com/reverse-dns-lookup`): This shows reverse DNS entries for a target IP address.

10. Reverse IP lookup (`https://dnslytics.com/reverse-ip`): Find domains sharing the same IP address or subnet.

11. Same IP (`www.sameip.org`): This shows sites hosted on the same IP address.

12. IP Address Tools (`www.ipvoid.com`): Offers various IP address online tools.

13. ExoneraTor (`https://exonerator.torproject.org`): Here you can check whether a particular IP address was used as a Tor relay before.

Determine Sender Geographic Location Using Sender's Time Zone

In some cases, the sender IP address can be missed or not included in the message header. This is true when the sender uses a webmail service like Gmail to send e-mails. In this case, we can determine the sender's location by checking the sender's computer time zone information. To learn this piece of information, we can use `https://toolbox.googleapps.com/apps/messageheader/` (already used) and check the "Created at:" field (see Figure 8-25).

| MessageId | 4341d222a118██ ███ ██ █ █ █ ███ ██ @senIdogo5210.springernature.com |
| Created at: | 10/4/2018, 11:57:13 PM GMT+3 (Delivered after 1 sec) |

Figure 8-25. *Revealing sender local time zone*

Investigating E-mail Clients

Many users rely on e-mail clients to send/receive e-mails; for instance, the most two popular e-mail programs are MS Outlook and Mozilla Thunderbird.

Autopsy has a default ingest module to investigate e-mail messages (Thunderbird and Outlook e-mail clients) found within the supplied data source (e.g., forensic image or e-mail client folder when performing analysis of logical files).

Thunderbird is a free, open source e-mail client by Mozilla; it stores its e-mails and attachments using the MBOX extension. Thunderbird files can be found at

`\Users\<UserName>\AppData\Roaming\Thunderbird\Profiles.`

The following steps will guide you on how to use Autopsy for investigating e-mail messages stored by the Thunderbird e-mail client:

1. We already covered how to create a new case using Autopsy; in this experiment, we will create a case as we did previously. However, we will change the data source to include only the Thunderbird profile folder instead of a whole hard drive image as we did previously.

2. We will not demonstrate all steps of creating a new case from the beginning, so begin the wizard, and when you reach the "Add Data Source" window, select "Logical Files" (see Figure 8-26) and then click "Next" to continue.

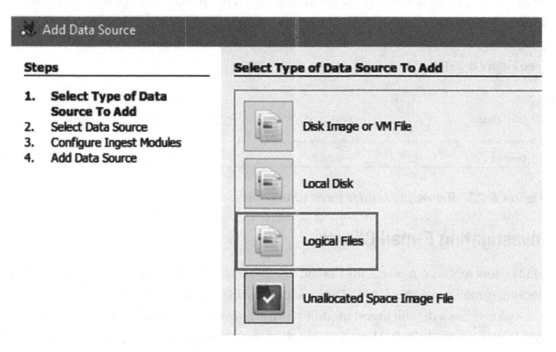

Figure 8-26. *Select "Logical Files" as a data source*

3. Now, click the "Add" button to select the Thunderbird profile folder; make sure the option "Local files and folders" is selected (see Figure 8-27). Click "Next" to continue.

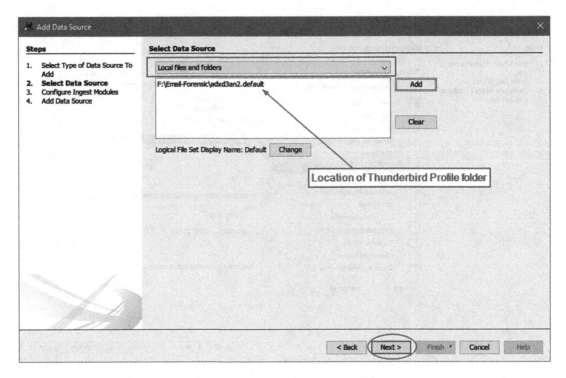

Figure 8-27. *Select Thunderbird profile folder as a data source*

4. Now, you need to configure the ingest modules; for instance, we are concerned with e-mail forensics only, so we will select two ingest modules only: Email Parse and Keyword Search (see Figure 8-28). Click "Next" to continue.

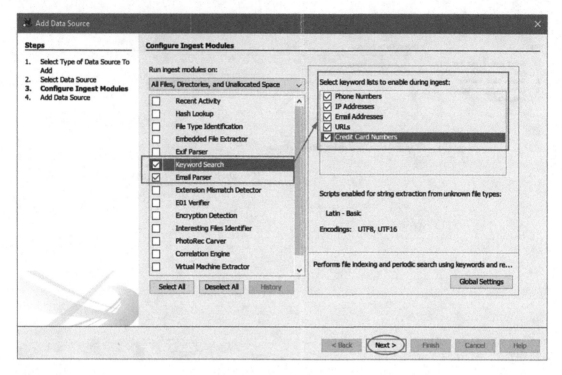

Figure 8-28. *Configure ingest modules window; select only two modules to parse e-mails and search within returned results*

5. The final window in the wizard appears, announcing that the data source has been added successfully. Click "Finish" to continue.

Now, Autopsy will begin analyzing files; this takes some time to finish. When Autopsy finishes processing the supplied data source, we can see collected e-mail messages in the "Data Explorer" pane on the left side of the window under the "Email messages" section (see Figure 8-29).

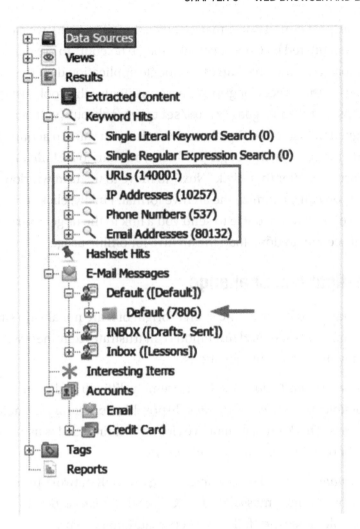

Figure 8-29. The results of parsing the Thunderbird profile folder

Webmail Forensics

Sometimes, we may need to investigate a case where e-mails are stored in the cloud (e.g., Gmail, Yahoo!, Outlook Mail). The first step needed to conduct such an examination is to acquire the data (hence, e-mail messages) from the cloud for analysis. The following options are available:

1. Most webmail providers give their users POP3/IMAP access to their stored e-mail. We can use an e-mail client like Thunderbird to synchronize a target e-mail account for offline analysis—of course, we need to have access to this account first.

287

2. If the suspect e-mail is in Gmail (Google e-mail service), we can use a tool offered by Google called "Google takeout" to create/download an offline backup of all Google application data that belongs to the target Google user account. To use this tool, just go to `https://takeout.google.com/settings/takeout` (you need to be signed in first to the Google account that you want to acquire) and then select which Google products you want to include in your archive. After that, click "Next" to move to the next window where you can customize the archive format. Finally, click "Create Achieve" and wait Google to send you a link to the target user Gmail account to download the archive for offline usage.

E-mail Investigations Challenge

Investigating e-mails and knowing the source/origin of it are not always straightforward tasks; the following challenges and limitations can frustrate examiners when dealing with cases that involve e-mail investigations.

1. *Disposable e-mail addresses*: It is extremely difficult and even impossible in many cases to track disposable (temporary) e-mail addresses. This kind of e-mail lives for a short time and is usually used for one time (or one contact) only.

2. *Anonymous e-mails*: For example, using the TOR network to send anonymous e-mail messages. Tracking such e-mails is nearly impossible, since they follow strict precautionary steps.

3. *Shared e-mail accounts*: Here, a suspect creates an e-mail account using a free service like Yahoo! or Gmail, then shares the access to this account with his/her partner. The parties do not exchange e-mails: a suspect has just to write an e-mail (e.g., instructions for criminal activity) and then leave it in the draft folder. His/her partner will access this account, read the instructions, and then delete the draft message.

4. *Different jurisdictions*: We have already covered this in Chapter 1; cloud e-mail providers may store your e-mails in servers located in countries other than the one in which you currently reside. For example, consider a suspect involved in a criminal activity in the United States who has an e-mail account with an e-mail provider in Switzerland; can law enforcement in the United States force the Swiss provider to release suspect data?

Chapter Summary

In this chapter, we have thoroughly covered how to investigate the most used web browsers—Google Chrome, Firefox, and IE/Edge—for forensic artifacts. The dependence in this chapter was on manual analysis, in addition to using some simple, free tools that can aid investigators in their forensics work.

Currently, most cybercrimes involve using the Internet in one way or another to commit or facilitate a criminal activity. This leaves digital traces on both the client machine (e.g., browsing history, previous searches, download history, and login credentials to social media accounts) and the web server such as communication logs (e.g., IP address and timestamp information).

In the next chapter, we will reverse the situation and show you how criminals can use various techniques to frustrate computer forensic examiners' efforts and prevent them from doing their jobs in capturing and analyzing digital evidence.

CHAPTER 9

Antiforensics Techniques

How to mislead digital forensics investigations

As we mentioned before, digital forensics, also known as cyber or computer forensics, is a branch of forensic science that uses scientific knowledge, methodology, and rigor to aid the solving of crimes and incidents by collecting, analyzing, and presenting digital evidence to use in remedial action or a court of law. The primary goal of digital forensics is to perform a structured investigation of digital evidence and prepare this evidence for presentation in a court of law. Digital forensic investigators use different forensic tools to collect, preserve, and interpret digital evidence. Based on their findings, they will draw conclusions and present these conclusions to those who will act on them.

Antiforensics science, on the other hand, is the set of techniques used to fight against forensics analysis. It tries to stop and mislead investigations by making acquiring and analyzing digital evidence difficult or even impossible. Antiforensics techniques aim to destroy or conceal digital evidence, thus frustrating forensic investigators and increasing the time needed to perform the initial analysis. The best definition of antiforensics techniques comes from Dr. Marc Rogers of Purdue University, who defined them as follows:

> *Attempts to negatively affect the existence, amount and/or quality of evidence from a crime scene, or make the analysis and examination of evidence difficult or impossible to conduct.*[1]

In this chapter, we are going to describe the nature of digital antiforensics techniques and explain how these techniques may be used to mislead the forensic investigation process, thereby making it very difficult to carry out a digital investigation or even gather enough evidence to debate during a trial.

---

[1]Rogers, D. M. (2005). Antiforensics presentation given to Lockheed Martin. San Diego.

© Nihad A. Hassan 2019
N. A. Hassan, *Digital Forensics Basics*, https://doi.org/10.1007/978-1-4842-3838-7_9

Users of Antiforensics Techniques

Antiforensics techniques can be used by different actors for different purposes; in addition to its use by criminal and terrorist groups, antiforensics is used for good by any entity (organization or individual) wishing to maintain its online privacy and/or destroy its private data securely, such as the following:

- Military professionals

- Law enforcement

- Politicians and diplomats

- Security researchers

- Journalists and whistleblowers

- Business corporations

- Casual Internet users seeking privacy

From a digital forensics perspective, it's necessary for digital forensics examiners to know about such techniques and how they work, so they have a better understanding of what they should do if they encounter it during their investigations.

Classification of Antiforensics Techniques

Antiforensics has become a broad field, and its techniques cover many computer security angles. The following is a list of the main digital antiforensics techniques that any forensic examiner may face during his/her digital investigation:

1. Data hiding techniques (known as steganography)

2. Data destruction techniques (antirecovery)

3. Encryption techniques

4. Cryptographic anonymity techniques

5. Direct attacks against computer forensics tools

Digital Steganography

Steganography is the science of concealing a secret message within an ordinary honest file, thus maintaining its secrecy during delivery. Steganographic techniques have been used since ancient times; they have been used to convey secret messages during battles and to deliver secret espionage information from spies.

Old steganographic techniques were mainly dependent on physical objects (e.g., paper, eggs, invisible ink, and even human skin) as the medium to conceal the secret message, However, with the advance of computing technology and Internet communications, modern techniques become largely based on exploiting digital files (whether images, videos, audio, or even a file system like Windows NTFS) and IPs to convey secret messages between communicating parties.

In practice, any digital file type can be used to conceal a secret message within it; most digital steganographic techniques will not alter the appearance of the overt file—used as a carrier—so that it cannot be dedicated by an outside observer (see Figure 9-1).

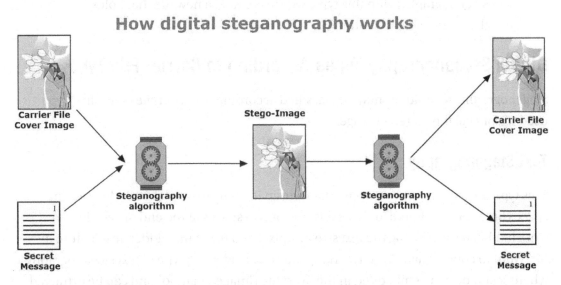

Figure 9-1. *How digital steganography works*

Digital Steganography Techniques

There are mainly three ways by which you can embed a secret message in a digital file:

1. **Injunction:** Using this method, we embedded a secret message in a trivial, nonreadable location of the overt file. An example of this technique is embedding a secret message after the end-of-file marker (EOF). Hiding with this method will not have an effect on overt file quality or appearance.

2. **Substitution:** Using this method, we are replacing insignificant bits that belong to the overt file with the one that belongs to the secret message. This method is more secure than the previous one, as the overt file size will not get increased because we are just replacing bits without adding anything new.

3. **Generation:** This is the most secure method to achieve digital steganography; with this type, we are creating a new file that holds the secret message within it.

Digital Steganography Types According to Carrier File Type

Steganographic techniques may be classified according to carrier file (overt file) type used to conceal the secret message.

Text Steganography

This type uses text to conceal secret data within it. Some examples include inserting spaces between words and/or inserting one or two spaces at the end of each line to store hidden bits, reducing the text size to 1 pixel and using the hidden text feature in MS Word to conceal data. Watermarking is also considered a type of text steganography where secret data are embedded in the overt file (image or audio) and can be extracted only by the owner using a secret key.

The main disadvantage of this type is the small amounts of secret data that can be embedded in text compared with other digital file types.

A simple way to achieve text steganography is by changing a text's spelling while preserving its visual appearance. This method is used in some countries to fool surveillance systems used by their governments to filter/block Internet traffic; by changing the spelling of important words, we can avoid getting caught by the monitoring machines.

Spider Army (`http://txtn.us`) is an online service that provides free tools for transforming Unicode text into another string that looks visually similar to the original text; See Table 9-1 for illustration.

Table 9-1. *Changing Spelling to Fool Surveillance Systems and to Conceal Data in Plain Sight*

Original Text	Misspelled Text Variation		
Attack	Aтrack	Aтtack	AttacK
Train	Trαɪn	Train	Train
London	London	Loϖdon	Londoϖ
Plane	PIaɲe	Pļane	PIaɲe

Note!   A secret message can be concealed within Twitter tweets in plain sight. `http://holloway.co.nz/steg/` is a web site that offers such a service.

Other areas to consider when investigating for hidden data is searching in MS Office files (the modern versions beginning from version 2007, as these versions are based on the XML- file structure called OOXML [Office Open XML]). The OOXML structure opens various possibilities to embed different types of digital files (text, image, audio, and video files) inside the MS Office file structure.

Image Steganography

This is the most used file type to conceal secret messages. As we all know, in today's digital age, it is common for people to exchange and post images online (e.g., to social media sites); the large volume of exchanged digital images daily make this file type less suspicious to outside observers. In image steganography, a user embeds a secret message within an image file using a specific steganographic algorithm; the result, called a stego-image, is then sent to the receiver, who will use a similar algorithm to extract the secret message from the overt file.

Let us demonstrate an experiment on how a suspect can employ image steganography to conceal secret information using a simple tool called Steghide.

To camouflage data using this tool, follow these steps:

1. Download the tool from http://steghide.sourceforge.net/
index.php; in my case I downloaded the Windows version and
unzipped the contents of the zip file into my working directory,
which is **c:\work.**

2. Since this is a command-line tool, launch a command prompt and
navigate (using the **CD** command) to where you have extracted
the tool; type the command shown in Figure 9-2.

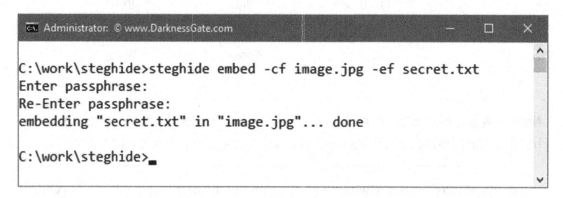

Figure 9-2. *Using Steghide tool to conceal a secret text file in an image file*

From Figure 9-2, this command will embed the text file named "secret.txt" in the
overt file image.jpg. Please note that when you type the passphrase after executing the
command, it will not appear on the screen, so do not worry about this issue.

Check Figure 9-3 for a comparison between the two images; on the right is the
original, and the left has a hidden message (text file) inside it. We note that the visual
appearance of the image after the hidden data is inserted remains the same.

Figure 9-3. *On the left is the image with the hidden message (hence, a secret text file) embedded inside it. On the right is the original image. No difference appears visually between both images.*

Data concealed in digital images have some limitations. For instance, for many implementations of an image's steganographic algorithms, if you update the image (resize it, change the format, edit it, or crop it), the secret message within it will get destroyed, so you should always work with a copy of acquired digital evidence—as we have insisted before many times—to avoid destroying the evidence accidentally.

Audio-Video Steganography

In a nutshell, audio steganography conceals secret data in digital audio files. The most popular audio steganography tool is MP3stego, which conceals secret data in the most used audio file format, MP3. You can find it at `www.petitcolas.net/steganography/mp3stego`.

Techniques used to conceal secret data in images and audio files can be utilized to conceal secret data in video files. Video files are composed of a series of audio and image files, thus allowing for a huge capacity of secret data without affecting the quality of the original file (overt file).

Network Steganography

Experiments show that we can exploit networking protocols like the TCP/IP suite to embed secret messages. The design features of many networking protocols allow for this possibility. An example of a program to conceal data within networking protocols (TCP/IP header) is called covert_tcp; you can find it at `http://firstmonday.org/ojs/index.php/fm/article/view/528/449`.

Digital Steganography Tools

A suspect can use a plethora of free and easy-to-use tools to conceal secret information within different types of digital files. Table 9-2 lists the most popular digital steganography tools.

Table 9-2. *Popular Digital Steganography Tools*

Program	Supported Overt Files	Support Encryption	URL
Crypture	Bmp	YES	`http://sourceforge.net/projects/crypture/`
OpenStego	Different media files	YES	`www.openstego.com/`
Gifshuffle	GIF	YES	`www.darkside.com.au/gifshuffle/`
wbStego4open	Bmp , text files, HTML, pdf	YES	`http://wbstego.wbailer.com`
SilentEye	JPEG , BMP , WAVE	YES	`https://sourceforge.net/projects/silenteye`
Steghide UI	Different media files	YES	`http://sourceforge.net/projects/steghideui/`
Camouflage	Different media files	YES	`http://camouflage.unfiction.com/`
DeepSound	Audio files	YES	`http://download.cnet.com/DeepSound/3000-2092_4-75758214.html`

Data Destruction and Antirecovery Techniques

Offenders use data destruction techniques to make their incriminating data impossible to recover even after using specialized tools for data recovery. There are three ways in which a user can destroy his/her data stored on digital devices:

- Physical destruction: In this type, digital storage media (like hard drives, memory sticks, magnetic tapes, CDs, DVDs and Blu-ray discs, credit cards) are destroyed physically to avoid recovery. The equipment used in this case is called "hard drive shredders" or "destroyers."

- Degaussing technique: This technique works by exposing the magnetic storage devices such as HDD or the magnetic tape to the powerful magnetic field of a degausser to eliminate magnetically stored data. This method is valid only to destroy data stored on magnetic devices, and cannot destroy data stored on SSD and USB thumb drives.

- Logical destruction (sanitizing): This is the most commonly used technique to destroy data. It uses a wiping tool to destroy data without affecting the hardware that holds this data. Please note that although this technique offers a high level of secure erasure, it still cannot guarantee 100% removal of data from some type of storage media (especially the magnetic storage media like HDD and tapes), as some hardware-based techniques can recover data even after it is wiped with disk sanitization tools.

Different wiping algorithms have been developed to securely erase data on hard drives. Table 9-3 shows the most popular ones.

Table 9-3. *Algorithms Used to Wipe Data on Hard Drives*

Erasing Technique	Security Level	Overwriting Passes
RCMP TSSIT OPS-II	High	7
HMG Infosec Standard 5	High	3
DoD 5220.22-M	High	3
Bruce Schneier's Algorithm	High	7
German Standard BSI/VSITR	High	7

Different programs exist to wipe data securely, and the majority support more than one wiping algorithm/standard. Table 9-4 lists the most popular ones (free tools only).

Table 9-4. *Tools Used to Securely Wipe Your Hard Drive Data*

Program name	URL
DBAN	`https://dban.org`
Secure Erase	`https://cmrr.ucsd.edu/resources/secure-erase.html`
Eraser	`www.heidi.ie/eraser/`
CCleaner	`www.piriform.com/ccleaner`
SDelete	`https://technet.microsoft.com/en-us/sysinternals/sdelete.aspx`

SSD manufacturers offer utilities to erase data securely from their devices. Table 9-5 gives direct links to some of them.

Table 9-5. *Specific Manufacturer Tools Used to Securely Wipe SSD Drives*

Tool Name	URL
Intel SSD Toolbox	`https://downloadcenter.intel.com/download/26574?v=t`
Corsair SSD Toolbox	`www.corsair.com/en-eu/support/downloads`
Samsung Magician	`www.samsung.com/semiconductor/minisite/ssd/download/tools.html`
SanDisk SSD	`https://kb.sandisk.com/app/answers/detail/a_id/16678/~/secure-erase-and-sanitize`
Kingston SSD Manager	`www.kingston.com/us/support/technical/ssdmanager`
Micron's Storage Executive software	`www.micron.com/products/solid-state-storage/storage-executive-software`

Note!   The existence of wiping tools on a suspect machine (even the leftover of such tools existing on the registry or other places like the Prefetch folder) will raise suspicions that the examined PC contained incriminating data or was used to destroy such data on attached storage devices.

Please note that using wiping tools will also leave clear clues about their usage on a hard drive; for instance, wiping tools usually work by repeating a predefined pattern many times over the unallocated space on the hard drive, and this can be easily seen when investigating the target hard drive on the bit level using any Hex editor.

Employing data destruction techniques in the correct way will make recovering data from suspect digital devices impossible.

Files' Metadata Manipulation

Metadata timestamps in digital files play an important role in computer forensic investigations, because they help investigators to limit their search within a specific timeframe that is related to the case in hand (e.g., before or after an incident took place). For instance, a suspect can change the four main timestamp attribute values of any digital file under a Windows NTFS file system. These values are as follows:

- File created: This is the time when the file was "created" on the hard drive.

- File accessed: This is the date/time when the file was last accessed. When a user opens or moves the file from one location to another, the access time will get changed. When scanning files, antivirus programs can change their access times.

- File modified: This is when the data within a file was modified.

- MTF last written: This attribute does not appear in Windows Explorer (when right-clicking the file and selecting Properties); it can be seen by some computer forensic tools like EnCase and AccessData FTK.

BulkFileChanger (www.nirsoft.net/utils/bulk_file_changer.html) is a
portable tool from Nirsoft; this tool can modify the main date attributes of any NTFS
file like the created/modified/accessed date in addition to other file attributes (like
Read Only, Hidden, System). To change the time attribute using this tool, just execute
the tool, select the file whose attributes you want to change, select the file from the
list, and then click the "Clock" icon on the program toolbar menu to change attribute
values (see Figure 9-4).

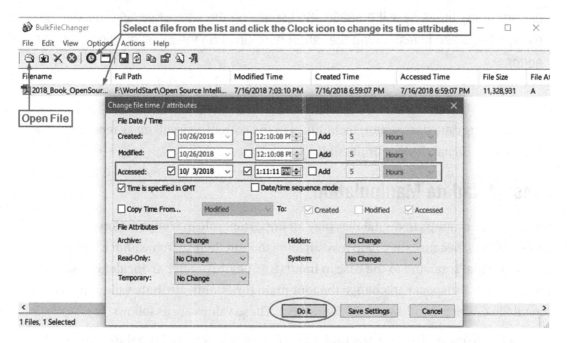

Figure 9-4.   *Using BulkFileChanger tool to change file's date/time attributes*

Figure 9-5 shows you a comparison of the date attributes of the same file, before and
after implementing the modifications.

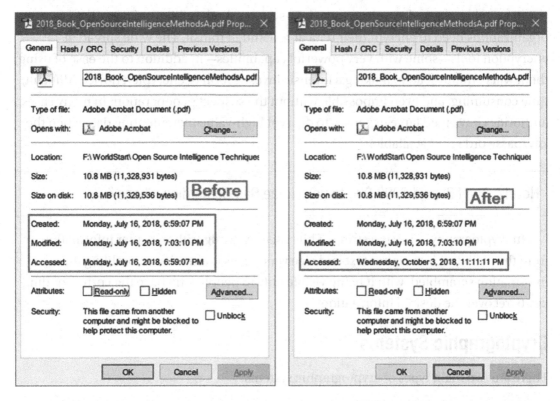

Figure 9-5. *Comparison of date/time attribute values after changing them using the BulkFileChanger tool*

Changing the date/time stamp of files is still an effective method to fight against computer forensics; however, bear in mind that if a professional examiner suspects that a specific file attribute has been changed in this way, s/he can perform deep analysis of this file's hidden timestamp attributes located in the MFT. This will clearly uncover that the time attributes of the subject file have been changed manually.

Encryption Techniques

While the aim of steganography is to hide secret data, making it hard to notice, encryption techniques perform a similar job through scrambling the data. Encryption is the practice of concealing information by obscuration, thus making it unreadable for unintended recipients.

Encryption plays a key role in today's IT systems: both public and private organizations need to encrypt their data at rest and in transit. The wide spread of encryption tools—some with very powerful capabilities—in addition to the ease of using them will certainly lead to making a forensic investigation of encrypted devices difficult, time consuming, and even impossible without the suspect's cooperation. In many cases, authorities have paid large expenses to decrypt high-value incrementing data when the key/password is not available.

Note!   The FBI paid $900,000 to unlock the San Bernardino iPhone.[2]

In cryptography, a key is a string of bits used by an algorithm to alter information from the plain text into cipher text and vice versa. This is aimed at scrambling this information scrambled, with it being visible only to people who have the corresponding key to recover the desired information.

Cryptographic Systems

There are two main types of cryptographic systems:

- Symmetrical encryption: Also known as secret key cryptography (SKC), in this type, both the sender and the receiver use the same key to encrypt and decrypt the data. Having the key fall into the wrong hands will compromise the entire system.

- Asymmetrical encryption: Also known as public key cryptography (PKC), this cryptographic type uses two different keys for encryption and decryption. The two keys are mathematically linked. However, no one can derive the decryption key (private key) from the encryption key (public key).

FDE

FDE uses a cryptographic method (either a symmetric key or an asymmetric key) to encrypt each bit of data that exists on the target drive. This form of encryption is becoming increasingly required by enterprises and individuals willing to protect their

---

[2]Engadget, "Senator Confirms FBI Paid $900,000 to Unlock San Bernardino iPhone," October 26, 2018. www.engadget.com/2017/05/08/fbi-paid-900000-to-unlock-san-bernardino-iphone/?guccounter=1

private data, especially when using mobile devices like tablets, laptops, and external drives. FDE is now supported by major vendors (Android, Windows, and Apple) for both desktop and mobile devices and can be applied easily with minimal effort.

FDE has become integrated into many operating systems (e.g., BitLocker encryption for Windows and FileVault available in Mac OS X 10.3 and later) to protect private user data; this poses real challenges to computer forensic examiners who will become unable to access suspect private data without knowing the key (password) for decrypting it.

Windows BitLocker

BitLocker drive encryption is a data protection feature offered by newer editions of Windows beginning with Vista. By using BitLocker, a user can encrypt the entire disk drive, including the Windows partition and removable USB drives (using BitLocker To Go), securely.

BitLocker uses the AES encryption algorithm with a 128-bit key size by default; however, you can strengthen the encryption by changing the key length to 256 bits for enhanced security.

BitLocker can be found in the following Windows editions:

- Windows 10 Pro, Enterprise, and Education editions

- Window 8 and 8.1 Enterprise and Pro editions

- Windows Server 2008 R2, all editions

- Windows 7 Enterprise and Ultimate editions

- Windows Vista Enterprise and Ultimate editions

BitLocker requires a computer with a Trusted Platform Module (TPM). TPM is a small microchip found on the computer motherboard. Most modern Windows-certified devices come equipped with this chip. The main role of the TPM with regard to BitLocker encryption is to store BitLocker encryption keys. It also offers a security mechanism to detect any attempt to change the host OS software or hardware by attackers to decrypt your encrypted drive (e.g., planting a keylogger on the bootloader of the OS). However, if your PC does not contain a TPM chip, you can continue to use BitLocker on your Windows device and unlock the encrypted drive using either a password or a key file stored on a thumb drive.

Decrypting a machine with BitLocker enabled is nearly impossible, so it is very advisable if you come across a running machine with BitLocker enabled to capture its RAM memory immediately and then capture the entire hard drive before powering the machine OFF, as this could be your only chance to get evidence from that computer.

EFS

Encrypting file system (EFS) is a feature of the Windows NTFS file system; it allows a user to enable encryption on a per file or folder basis. EFS can also be used to encrypt the entire volume. Using it is simple: right-click over the file/folder/volume you want to enable encryption for, and then select Properties ➤ General tab. Click the "Advanced..." button, and a new window will appear; check the option "Encrypt contents to secure data" (see Figure 9-6).

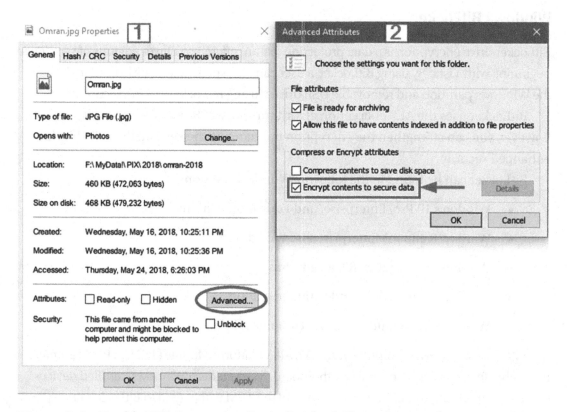

Figure 9-6. *Enable EFS encryption for individual file under Windows NTFS file system*

EFS uses a combination of symmetrical and asymmetrical encryption algorithms to encrypt data. To secure encrypted data without entering a password from the user, EFS uses the currently logged-on Windows account (username and password) as a part of the encryption private key.

Disk Encryption Using Open Source Tools

There are various encryption tools already available; some of them are free while others are commercial. The most popular open source encryption program (used for file and disk encryption) is the legendary program TrueCrypt. TrueCrypt development ended suddenly in 2014; however, the popularity of TrueCrypt and its advanced encryption capabilities has encouraged some developers to create other forks for this project. The following are the main projects based on this tool:

- VeraCrypt (`www.veracrypt.fr/en/Home.html`): This is based on TrueCrypt 7.1a. It is a free open source encryption disk supported on Windows, Mac OSX, and Linux. VeraCrypt allows the creation of a hidden volume (this resides within a virtual encrypted disk) and hidden operating system partition in addition to its ability to encrypt the entire hard drive and portable storage devices like USB sticks and external HDD.

- CipherShed (`www.ciphershed.org`): This is another fork based on TrueCrypt. It maintains backward compatibility with the previous TrueCrypt container format.

Cracking the encryption of many open source cryptographic programs is impossible if an offender refuses to disclose the encryption key; many legal cases have already been stopped due to the inaccessibility of the encrypted files.

Password Cracking

It is almost certain that all digital forensics examiners will come across encrypted files/volumes during their investigative work. When there is no way to acquire the needed key to decrypt subject data, using password cracking tools becomes the last hope to acquire something useful out of suspect encrypted data. The following are the most popular password cracking software:

1. Cain and Abel (`www.oxid.it/ca_um`): A popular tool for cracking encrypted passwords—using brute force, dictionary, and cryptanalysis attack techniques—and sniffing passwords out of network traffic.

2. Ophcrack (http://ophcrack.sourceforge.net): This is a free password cracker that utilizes rainbow tables to crack Windows passwords.

3. RainbowCrack (http://project-rainbowcrack.com/table.htm): This speeds cracking password hashes from Windows XP, 2000, Vista and 7.

4. John the Ripper (www.openwall.com/john): A password cracker for Unix, Windows, DOS, and OpenVMS.

Cryptographic Anonymity Techniques

Digital anonymity works by hiding any traces between the sender and message receiver when communicating through open networks like the Internet. It uses a combination of encryption algorithms to encrypt messages and cryptographic anonymity software to hide your identity during the transmission.

Anonymous networks like the TOR network help users to maintain their online privacy when going online through concealing their true IP address from outside observers, including the ISP. The most famous anonymous network is the TOR network. To access the TOR network, you need to use the TOR Browser, which can be downloaded from www.torproject.org/projects/torbrowser.html.en.

Tracking users through the TOR networks is almost impossible when the user follows strict precautionary security measures. Other anonymous networks include I2P (https://geti2p.net/en) and Freenet (https://freenetproject.org).

WEB BROWSERS' PRIVATE MODES DO NOT RECORD USERS' ONLINE ACTIVITIES

Employing antiforensics techniques does not need to be that hard, as some applications used every day—such as web browsers—can be configured in one click to forget a user's previous activities automatically. For instance, many web browsers have introduced a special configuration known as Private Browsing (Firefox) or Incognito Mode (Google Chrome). Firefox Private Browsing will automatically erase all browsing history, form and search bar entries, download lists, passwords, cookies and cached web content, offline web content, and user data from a user's machine upon closing the browser; the private mode will also block ads with hidden trackers making following a user across different websites very difficult. You can

---

open a new private Firefox window by going to the right corner of the main Firefox window and clicking New Private Window. Alternatively, you can press the Ctrl+Shift+P button combination to open a new private browsing window.

Google Chrome has a similar feature called Incognito Mode that can be accessed from the Chrome menu on the right top corner (new Incognito window; see Figure 9-7).

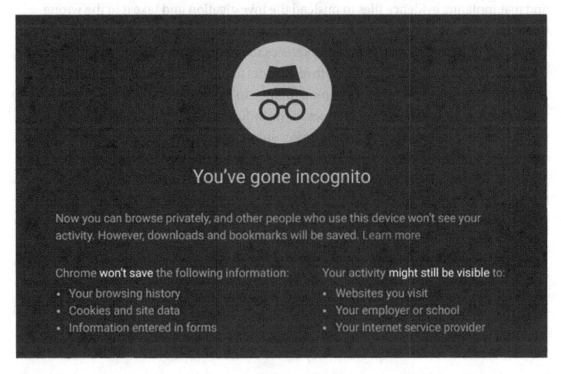

Figure 9-7. *Google Chrome Incognito Mode window launched*

Direct Attacks Against Computer Forensics Tools

Some tech-savvy criminals employ modern techniques to attack forensic tools used to acquire or analyze digital evidence. Such attacks include program packers, anti–reverse engineering techniques, and attacking the integrity of digital evidence acquired during the investigation. If successful, such attacks can hinder the credibility of the acquired evidence during legal trial.

Chapter Summary

This chapter was the reverse of the previous one. Antiforensics techniques are concerned with making digital forensics investigations very difficult to conduct and time consuming; they focus on frustrating digital forensics examiners through destroying digital evidence, hiding incriminating information so examiners cannot notice it, and manipulating evidence files to mislead the investigation and take it in the wrong direction.

As computing advances, more antiforensics tools will be developed. This will impose real challenges for computer forensic investigators to have their skills up to date. The branch of cyberforensics requires its practitioners to continue their education and stay updated with the latest tools/techniques in the industry. Antiforensics capabilities should be integrated into computer forensics suites to automatically discover technical measures implemented by offenders to conceal their incriminating activities.

In the next chapter, we are going to cover a sophisticated topic that has gained extensive coverage lately: the use of OSINT to aid law enforcement officers during their search to solve criminal cases.

CHAPTER 10

Gathering Evidence from OSINT Sources

What is OSINT and how is it used in the digital forensics context?

In today's digital age, it is rare to meet a person with an Internet connection who doesn't also own one or more accounts on different social media sites. People tend to post considerable amounts of personal details on their social media profiles: this includes personal photos, social interactions, and any kind of personal information you can imagine.

From a digital forensics perspective, investigating the person of interest's interactions with social media sites and with the Internet in general can give a wealth of personal information about him/her. For instance, the word "social" in social media means "public"; law enforcement can gather a huge amount of information about anything you can imagine by just examining the public information available on social media platforms such as Facebook and Twitter. For example, investigating a person's profile on Facebook can reveal quite private information about him/her, such as work and home addresses, friend list, family members, and preferred places to spend vacation; even when a subject person is sleeping or outdoors can be learned by examining his/her social profiles and online interactions.

One of the most important aspects of any criminal investigation is the ability of law enforcement to acquire timely and accurate intelligence about the case or incident at hand. OSINT refers to all the information that is publicly available. Before the Internet revolution, OSINT was mainly collected from traditional media sources like TV, radio, newspapers, magazines, books, and other types of traditional publications; however, with the widespread usage of the Internet, the main source of OSINT intelligence comes from online sources (sometimes referred as cyber-OSINT).

© Nihad A. Hassan 2019
N. A. Hassan, *Digital Forensics Basics*, https://doi.org/10.1007/978-1-4842-3838-7_10

The "OS" in OSINT means "open source." Please note that I'm not referring here to the open source software initiative (`https://opensource.org`); instead, by "open source" I mean any publicly available source that is free and legally accessed by the public without breaking any copyright, patent, or privacy law.

Goals of OSINT Collection

OSINT can be used by different actors in different scenarios; for instance, maybe you will think after reading this short introduction about OSINT that it is mainly associated with cybersecurity and cyberwar., Although this is somewhat true, there are other entities that use OSINT daily in other contexts as a part of their regular work. In this section, I will mention the main users of OSINT and what motivate each one to search for OSINT resources.

1. **Government**: Governments gather and analyze OSINT sources for different purposes such as national security, counterterrorism, cybertracking of terrorists, and predicting political and economic changes on a global level, in addition to using it to better understand local peoples' opinions about internal and external governmental policies.

2. **Law enforcement**: In the law enforcement arena, OSINT has become the eyes of the police in many cases. As more people are using the Internet in their daily life, most criminals have shifted their illegal work online. Police use OSINT to protect citizens from different types of crime; they can achieve this by monitoring social media sites (also known as social media intelligence), tracking suspects through e-mails, geolocation data, and other indicators available online. Police can gather valuable information about criminals using the free online sources alone.

3. **Security services**: According to the CIA, OSINT has surpassed classified information in many intelligence areas like terrorism, monitoring foreign countries' military capabilities, counterintelligence, and countering the illegal drug and arms trade. OSINT is less risky and more cost effective to gather than other intelligence sources like spy satellite images, spying electronic stations, and agents.

4. **Business organizations**: OSINT has become a necessity in today's digital age for business corporations. Acquiring OSINT is useful in the following areas: predicting market changes at the global level (e.g., collecting different indicators online to predict future oil prices), gathering intelligence about a foreign market before accessing it, tailoring marketing activities according to habits prevalent in local communities, monitoring competitors' business activities, investigating data leakage, and creating and maintaining a threat intelligence strategy.

5. **Criminals and Black Hat Hackers**: These people exploit OSINT sources to gather intelligence about their victims; this knowledge can be used later to target those victims with customized social entering attacks. Black Hat hackers use technical reconnaissance acquired from domain name information, e-mail server addresses, and e-mail naming criteria of a subject entity to gather intelligence about target IT infrastructure (e.g., type of OS and network topology in addition to any vulnerabilities discovered) before launching attacks against it.

6. **Casual Internet users seeking privacy**: These people can use OSINT sources to observe their online exposure level; by using OSINT search techniques and tools, an Internet user can learn about personal data leaked about him/her and try to delete it from online repositories.

OSINF Categories

According to the *NATO Open Source Intelligence Handbook* V1.2 (2001), there are four categories of open information and intelligence:

1. **Open source data (OSD)**: This is raw data coming from primary sources such as satellite images, telephone call metadata, scientific datasets, surveys, draft manuscripts, and radio and TV broadcasts. This information is isolated; hence, it has little intelligence value in its current state.

2. **Open source information (OSINF):** This is data that has undergone some filtering (categorization) according to the requester's need. Books, articles, research papers, and dissertations on a specific subject are examples. OSINF is also referred to as secondary sources. What distinguishes OSINF from other types of public information is that you need to have a permit, make a request, or pay for the material/information you want to obtain.

3. **OSINT:** This is the information that has been determined to be of intelligence value and disseminated according to a specific intelligence need. OSINT has undergone some processing and filtering to become readily available to use in any intelligence endeavor.

4. **Validated OSINT (OSINT-V):** This kind of information has higher certainty; hence, it is accurate to a large degree as it has been validated using another non-OSINT source. Combining information from TV news with intelligence captured from a spying satellite is an example of OSINT-V.

As we noted, OSD and OSINF form the main sources (primary and secondary) of information that OSINT uses to drive its results.

PUBLIC SOURCES

There is a type of public source that deserves special mention. Gray literature is a part of OSINF: it is produced by the world publishing system (mainly produced by researchers and practitioners in the field) and is available to the public through specific channels (mostly, you need to pay for it) and sometimes cannot be obtained through traditional routes.

Gray literature includes the following and more: academic papers, working papers, patents, bulletins, unpublished work, business documents, white papers, research reports, marketing reports, technical documentation, doctoral theses/dissertations, fact sheets, symposia, trade publications, government reports and documents not published commercially, translations, newsletters, and market surveys, in addition to books and journals. Some of these resources can be obtained from traditional bookstores, subscription agents, and online merchants like Amazon.com, while others can be obtained using specialized services such as Factiva (http://new.dowjones.com/products/factiva).

The WorldCat portal at www.worldcat.org/advancedsearch allows researchers to search within the largest network of local and global libraries that cover all of the world's spoken languages.

OSINT Benefits

No one can underestimate the key role that OSINT plays in the different intelligence arenas, especially for improving data collection capabilities of security services and law enforcement departments.

1. **Less risky**: Acquiring intelligence from OSINT sources is less risky and less suspicious compared with other forms of intelligence like using security agents to collect information about a specific entity.

2. **Cost effective**: Gathering OSINT will mainly require a computer and an Internet connection; of course, there are some OSINT-gathering activities that trigger expenses like gray literature and acquiring satellite images from commercial satellite providers. However, OSINT gathering is still very cost effective compared with traditional intelligence activities.

3. **Ease of accessibility**: As we have already seen, many OSINT-gathering activities will be conducted online; the nature of online contents makes it available from any point on earth and at any time in addition to being always up to date!

4. **Legal accessibility**: OSINT resources are gathered from public sources only without breaching any copyright or patent laws. Remember, some restrictions apply when collecting gray literature materials.

5. **Financial fraud investigation**: OSINT can reveal important information about entities involved in tax evasion crimes. For example, monitoring a celebrity's Facebook profile can reveal important financial information about the subject person (e.g., going on costly vacations and posting photos while wearing expensive jewelry and/or driving expensive cars). Investigating

social media intelligence will offer valuable information for any government inspector who could be chasing a subject entity for undeclared income.

6. **Countering counterfeiting online**: OSINT techniques can be used to locate illegal online sites that sell false products (especially, false pharmaceutical and natural health products) and direct law enforcement officials to close it or to warn others about it.

Challenges of OSINT

OSINT is a great intelligence-gathering methodology; however, as with other methodologies, it has some limitations. In this section, we will mention the main challenges that can face any investigator when conducting OSINT gathering.

- **Vast volume of data**: Gathering OSINT will produce a tremendous volume of data; although there are automated tools to filter this data, this will still pose a problem for the OSINT gatherer.

- **Trustworthiness of the source**: OSINT sources need to be verified before using it in an intelligence and criminal investigation context. For example, an offender may try to mislead the investigation by spreading wrong information on social media sites.

- **Human efforts**: The tremendous volume of collected OSINT will certainly need more people to analyze it; even though an automated machine/tool is used to filter obtained data, any piece of information should be verified by a human before using it as evidence during a legal trial.

- **Legal and ethical concerns**: OSINT gathering may raise problems or conflicts when used in some scenarios. For example, let's say an investigator has used OSINT sources to find the username and password of a subject's social networking account by using online repositories that publish data stolen from breached web sites; if the investigator uses this info to justify an honest case, how should the legal system handle such an issue?

The OSINT Cycle

There are different approaches (methodologies) to conducting OSINT gathering; however, there is a standard model that is shared between different intelligence methodologies. To collect and process information, this model uses the following phases:

1. Collection

2. Processing

3. Analysis

4. Production

5. Classification

6. Dissemination

In the context of OSINT gathering, we are concerned with only four stages (see Figure 10-1), which are as follows:

1. **Collection**: In the first phase, we identify the information that should be collected and prioritize our gathering efforts to acquire only the information needed for the case at hand. The obtained information/material—whether physical, like paper, books, and journals, or digital—should be retained safely, so we can return to it later during the investigation.

2. **Processing**: In the processing phase, the obtained data from the first phase is reviewed to identify their intelligence value. For example, if we collect materials in foreign languages (e.g., Arabic or German) in the first phase, we need to translate it into the English language so it becomes usable.

3. **Exploitation**: Also known as analysis, in this phase, collected data should be investigated thoroughly to extract useful intelligence from it.

4. **Production**: The final output is delivered to the requesting person/entity.

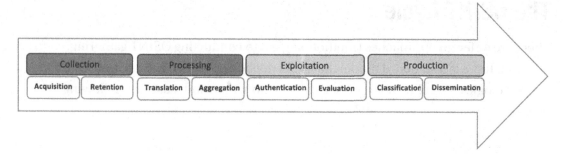

Figure 10-1. *The standard OSINT operations cycle*

OSINT Gathering and the Need for Privacy

While conducting OSINT research online, a researcher will leave traces behind him/her; for instance, nearly, anything we do online is recorded somewhere! From a digital forensic perspective, OSINT search is usually undertaken to track/collect information about a criminal entity or a suspect. Consider an example where an investigator conducts an OSINT search about the illegal arms trade in Eastern Europe. What if the people the investigator was searching for discover this search? Many organized criminal organizations hire experienced IT experts—who use techniques similar to those of law enforcement—to gather intelligence online about anything that threatens their illegal activities.

OSINT-gathering activities should be conducted secretly to avoid revealing the searcher's identity, as this can have dangerous—and even legal—consequences on him/her. An online investigator should know clearly about the different types of cyberrisks and how to avoid them; s/he should know how to anonymize online communications using anonymous networks like the TOR network. Privately exchanging online information with peers in other locations is essential for successful OSINT-gathering activity. VPN, steganographic, and encryption techniques can prove useful in such situations.

An Internet user can be tracked online using different methods other than his/her IP address; an OSINT researcher should be familiar with such tracking techniques (e.g., digital fingerprints, cookies) and must know how to check his/her computer's digital fingerprint (to know the amount of private information exposed to the public) before gathering OSINT.

> **Note!**   We cannot teach you how to become 100% anonymous in just a few
> lines! To understand all concepts in depth and learn how different actors can
> invade your privacy, you should read our book *Digital Privacy and Security Using
> Windows* (Apress, 2018), which is considered a definitive guide to online privacy
> and anonymity.

OSINT and the Darknet

Investigators cannot limit their search for OSINT resources to the surface—ordinary—
Web only; indeed, most Internet resources are buried in the deep layers of the Internet
where conventional search engines like Google and Yahoo! cannot go easily. Let us first
differentiate between Internet layers, so we have a better understanding of what we
mean by the terms surface web and deep layers of the Internet.

Internet Layers

The Internet is composed of the following three layers:

1. Surface web

2. Deep web

3. Dark web

Surface Web

This is the segment of the Web that can be accessed using typical web browsers using the
standard HTTP/HTTPS web protocol. Contents on the surface web can be indexed by
typical search engines, like Google, Bing, and Yahoo!, so acquiring information from this
layer of the Web is relatively easy. The surface web portion constitutes about 4% of the
entire information available on the Web.

Deep Web

This layer is also accessible to Internet users using typical web browsers over HTTP/ HTTPS protocols; however, conventional search engines cannot index its contents easily, making deep web contents hidden from casual Internet users. Deep web resources are usually buried within web databases that require a user to enter a search term(s) (query the database) in order to retrieve the needed information. A web site that requires some form of registration is also considered a part of the deep web. For example, Springer Link (`https://link.springer.com`) resources—which include scientific documents, journals, books, series, protocols, and reference works—are considered a part of the deep web, because a user needs to register (have an account) in order to access these resources. Most Internet resources are located in the deep web portion; many studies estimate that the deep web size is approximately 500 times that of the surface web.

Darknet

Located underneath the surface and deep web, darknet—or the dark web—contains all the resources that have been designed to be purposefully hidden and/or anonymous. No one can accurately state the size of the darknet; however, it might form about 1% or less of the entire content of the Web. What differentiates the darknet from the surface and deep web is that darknet cannot be accessed using regular web browsers and typical search engines cannot index its contents. Accessing darknet requires specialized software such as TOR (short for The Onion Router), which allows access to the TOR darknet. There are different types of Darknet networks. The most common ones are:

- TOR network (`www.torproject.org/index.html.en`)

- I2P network (`https://geti2p.net/en/`)

- Freenet (`https://freenetproject.org/index.html`)

OSINT investigators commonly use darknet networks—especially the TOR network—to navigate the surface web anonymously, so that their surfing activities and real identities are not monitored/identified by outside observers. Using the TOR Browser (`www.torproject.org/projects/torbrowser.html.en`) (see Figure 10-2) to surf the surface web is famous among OSINT practitioners.

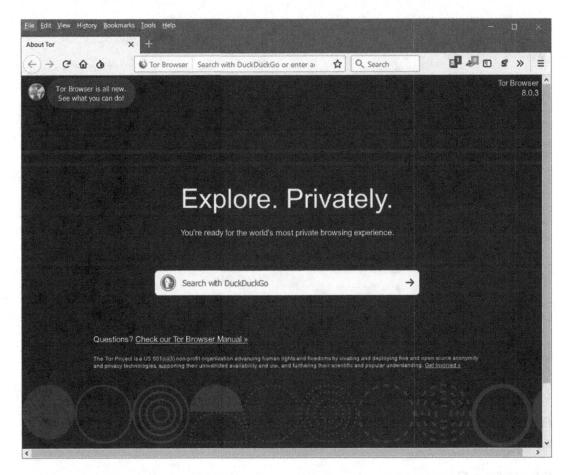

Figure 10-2. *Using the TOR browser to surf the surface web anonymously AND to access the TOR darknet*

Online Resources

Everything mentioned so far about OSINT types, users, and suggested methodologies needs to be supplemented with technical implementation, so investigators can know how to practically utilize OSINT resources in their investigations.

Technical implementation of OSINT includes all tools, techniques, and methods to acquire intelligence, mainly from online resources. Listing all these resources and techniques would require a book all on its own; however, if you prefer to get down to business immediately, I recommended checking the author's dedicated OSINT portal (see Figure 10-3) at `www.OSINT.link`. This web site lists hundreds of online services and tools that help OSINT gatherers to collect and analyze information; most of these resources/tools are free.

Figure 10-3. List of OSINT resources available on `www.OSINT.link` *(web site updated continually)*

Chapter Summary

In this chapter, we introduce the term OSINT, define its types, main users, and legal implications, and learn how it can be used in different scenarios by different parties to acquire valuable intelligence.

OSINT-gathering activities should be conducted privately to avoid revealing researcher identity and intention. Using the TOR Browser is common among cyber OSINT gatherers.

In the next chapter (the final one), we will conclude our book by talking about how to write an investigative report to summarize our investigation's findings.

CHAPTER 11

Digital Forensics Report

Presenting the findings of your investigation

Creating a report is the final phase of any investigation, where an investigator presents his/her findings during the digital forensics examination to the entity which was impacted by the cyberattack, or to the court if it is a public investigation.

Report elements and style will depend on the investigator's expertise and writing style, the type of crime/incident, and the level of IT knowledge of the person(s) who will read this report. For instance, investigating civil cases may not require including extensive technical details as opposed to public investigations (a jury in a criminal or civil proceeding), which requires as much detail as possible to strengthen the examiner's allegation.

Creating an effective digital forensics report requires the digital forensic examiner/ analyst to use simple language with easy-to-understand technical terms; presenting examples and figures is great to demonstrate how a particular technology works. Remember, your report should be understood by different user segments with varying IT skills; this is necessary to have your report understood by top management (in corporate disputes) and judges/juries (in public investigations).

Creating a timeline of events is excellent for understand what happened in succession; many computer forensic suites create such timelines automatically and allow an examiner to put tags and notes where needed along this timeline.

Report Main Elements

The following are suggested components of any digital forensics report:

- Investigator Information: Brief information about the examiner(s) who handled the case and what was his/her role was in the investigation.

© Nihad A. Hassan 2019
N. A. Hassan, *Digital Forensics Basics*, https://doi.org/10.1007/978-1-4842-3838-7_11

- Case Description: Brief description of the case/incident (e.g., investigating Arthur's USB thumb drive for possible violations of company IT usage policy) and what was required from the examiner in this regard.

- Investigation: This is the longest part of the report; the investigator should explain the forensic acquisition process, indicate what tools and techniques were used to analyze digital artifacts, and give some details about the technical procedures undertaken by the examiner(s) to extract data relevant to the case in hand. He/she also needs to submit a copy of chain of custody forms and describe the methodology applied to handle and retrieve digital evidence.

- Summary of Findings: This is the conclusion of the report; it presents the investigator's opinion about the innocence or guilt of the accused party, and it may also include a note to expand the investigation to other areas if needed.

- Explanation of Terms: Like unallocated disk space, device configuration overlay, slack space. These terms should be described in simple language with examples so a nontechnical audience can understand it.

Note!   The version of the forensic software used during examination should be documented in the final investigative report.

The digital evidence is usually submitted along with the report using CD/DVD (i.e., write-once media). The original evidence media should be reserved and not used for demonstration purposes, as using it to present the digital evidence may destroy or alter the original evidence.

Autogenerated Report

Most computer forensic suites can generate their own report automatically; the generated report can include the tags or notes the examiner has added during the analysis phase in addition to discovered artifacts like the names of undeleted and hidden files/folders discovered during the investigation.

To generate an investigative forensics report using Autopsy, do the following:

1. Go to the Tools menu ➤ Generate Report.

2. The Generate Report wizard appears; the first window allows you to select Report type (see Figure 11-1); select the "Report Module" and click "Next" to continue.

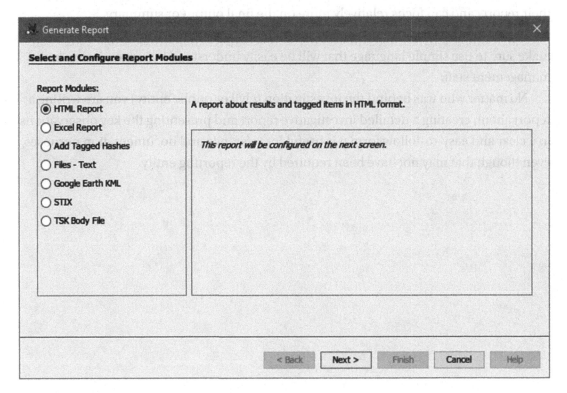

Figure 11-1. *Generate report using Autopsy*

3. The next window allows you to configure the artifacts that you need to appear in the report. You have two options: All Results and Tagged Results. Upon selecting any choice, you will be presented with a window that asks you which artifact types you would like included in your report.

4. Finally, click "Finish" and you are done!

The report generated by the computer forensic tool should be supplemented by another one written manually (e.g., using MS Word file) to present any additional information about the subject case that has not been included by the reporting tool.

Chapter Summary

Reporting is a key issue in any type of investigation; public investigation that involves courts usually needs more technical details and comprehensive descriptions of the methodology used to acquire and analyze the digital evidence, while cases that involve internal investigation of civil cases like company policy violations require less detail in their reports and can focus relatively more on the final output or summary.

Digital forensics reports are usually submitted to nontechnical audiences, so make sure to use simple language that will be easily understood by judges, juries, and management staff.

No matter who was behind the investigation (civil or public entity) you are writing a report about, creating a detailed investigative report and presenting the key observations in a clear and easy-to-follow format is useful for reference and documentation purposes, even though that may not have been required by the reporting entity.

Index

A

AccessData Certified Examiner (ACE), 32

Acquiring volatile memory (live acquisition)

Belkasoft Live RAM Capturer, 120

capturing RAM (*see* Capturing RAM)

challenges

administrative privileges, 117

capturing tool footprint, 117–118

Windows Is Locked, 116

virtual memory, 115

Advanced forensic format (AFF), 112

Alternative data stream (ADS), 59

American Standard Code for Information Interchange (ASCII), 41

Antiforensics science, 291

Antiforensics techniques

antirecovery, 292

cryptographic anonymity, 292

defined, 291

direct attacks, 292

encryption, 292

steganography, 292

users, 292

Arsenal Image Mounter, 142–143

Asymmetrical encryption, 304

Audio-video steganography, 297

AutomaticDestinations-ms, 221–222

Autopsy, 80, 325

Autopsy wizard

analysis process, 154

case information, 147

data source, 148–149

features, 145

forensic image, 150, 153

hash database

autopsy analysis, 159

features, 158

hash ingest module, 158

hash lookup module, 160–161

hash set dialog, 158–159

MD5 hashing, 157

NSRL hashset file, 159–160

ingest modules, 151–152, 155

installation, 145–146

optional case information, 148

recovery, 157

run ingest modules, 156

version, 151

B

Belkasoft live RAM capturer, 80, 120

Binary to decimal conversion, 37

BitLocker

AES encryption algorithm, 305

TPM, 305

Windows, 305

Bit-stream disk-to-disk, 126

327

Printed in the United States
By Bookmasters